Praise for *IMC—The Next Generation*

"Where the first book on IMC validated the concepts, this new work evolves the core principles into a blueprint for customer-focused businesses. It delivers a practical, step-by-step framework for future-proofing forward-thinking organizations. There's something valuable for managers in every chapter."

**—John R. Pearce, partner,
Simon Richards Group**

"Schultzian IMC makes provocative progress in marketing strategy. . . . Every chapter is a revelation."

**—Yasuhiko Kobayashi, Ph.D.,
professor of IMC, Aoyama Gakuin University, Tokyo**

"*IMC—The Next Generation* will be welcomed by managers throughout the world. Its blend of new thinking, practical guidelines, and insightful examples will help all of us think about IMC in a new way, showing us a process for how IMC works, how to determine the value of customers, and how to measure the financial contribution of IMC. This is the most important book about an important business area."

**—Charles H. Patti, Ph.D., professor,
Head School of Advertising, Marketing, and Public Relations,
Queensland University of Technology**

IMC
THE NEXT GENERATION

Five Steps for Delivering Value and
Measuring Returns Using
Marketing Communication

Don Schultz • Heidi Schultz

Boston, Massachusetts   Burr Ridge, Illinois
Dubuque, Iowa   Madison, Wisconsin   New York, New York
San Francisco, California   St. Louis, Missouri

The *McGraw·Hill* Companies

Library of Congress Cataloging-in-Publication Data

Schultz, Don E.
    IMC—the next generation : five steps for delivering value and measuring returns using marketing communication/ by Don E. Schultz, Heidi F. Schultz.
        p.   cm.
    Includes index.
    ISBN 0-07-141662-5 (hardcover : alk. paper)
    1. Marketing.   2. Business communication.   3. Brand name products.   4. Customer services.   I. Schultz, Heidi F.   II. Title.

HF5415.S3595   2003
658.8—dc21   2003003687

7 8 9 BKM BKM   0 9 8 7 6

ISBN 0-07-141662-5

McGraw-Hill books are available at special quantity discounts to use as premiums and sales promotions, or for use in corporate training programs. For more information, please write to the Director of Special Sales, Professional Publishing, McGraw-Hill, Two Penn Plaza, New York, NY 10121-2298. Or contact your local bookstore.

CONTENTS

Part VII BUILDING SHARE VALUE INTO THE FUTURE

PREFACE

Back in the late 1980s and early 1990s, we developed the concept of integrated marketing communications (IMC) and published what has since become the seminal work on this still-emerging topic, *Integrated Marketing Communications: Putting It Together and Making It Work* by Don E. Schultz, Stanley I. Tannenbaum, and Robert F. Lauterborn. Today, while the book remains a popular and useful work for marketing communications (marcom) specialists as well as top management, anyone reading it will clearly see that times have changed. George Herbert Walker Bush occupied the White House. Russian president Mikhail Gorbachov won the Nobel Peace Prize. China was just beginning to open its borders and its economy to the outside world. Asia was booming, driven by the Tiger economies. The Internet and mobile telephony were still the domain of computer geeks and a few academics, and not many of the rest of us even had E-mail addresses. No one had yet heard of dot.com companies.

The field of marketing communications also bore little resemblance to today's environment. Advertising—particularly television advertising—was still the dominant form of commercial communication. While David Aaker was on the verge of popularizing the branding phenomenon, most marketers still thought in terms of products, not brands. Most firms, too, were just beginning to realize that globalization of communication, finance, and transportation could tie the world together in ways that had never been previously imagined. Consolidation and concentration in manufacturing and distribution were just beginning to surface. And Wal-Mart was just starting its march to become the biggest retailer in the world.

Against this background, integration was a new concept and one that businesspeople had difficulty understanding. Organizations were strictly divided into individual business functions or units, all separate, independent, and managed from the top down. There was little talk of cross-functional teams, and the concept of the "flat" organization— without the usual management hierarchy—was little seen outside of Japan.

The explosion of technology in the 1990s changed all that, radically altering the ways businesses and communication operated. It was into this tumultuous environment that IMC emerged.

When Don Schultz, Stan Tannenbaum, and Bob Lauterborn—along with colleagues at Northwestern University—began to take integration seriously, many thought they had taken a wrong step. Some business practitioners, for instance, could not see beyond the functional systems around which their organizations were built. Others, notably advertising agencies, saw integration of marcom activities as a threat to their single-minded specialization. Others thought the reliance of integration on data, databases, and analysis would destroy marcom "creativity." Still others recognized the benefits of integration but believed the process was too difficult to implement within their own organizations. Despite the naysayers, integration hit its mark with a few forward-thinking pioneers who began to develop and implement IMC methodologies within their organizations, their agencies, their media systems, and, most of all, their classrooms and seminar halls.

Today, few people involved in any form of marketing or marketing communication would say that integration is a bad thing. While there are still significant challenges to its implementation, the concept has achieved acceptance in businesses of all types. We talk of business systems, of integrated processes, of aligned and focused business teams, and of cross-functional work groups. And while the concept of integrated marketing communication has evolved more rapidly in some organizations than in others, it continues to take a stronger hold in companies around the world.

So, since IMC has already gained in acceptance—in part because of the publication of the first book and its translation into at least twelve major languages—why is there a need to revisit the subject? The reasons are many and complex, representing the growth to maturity of what was, less than fifteen years ago, a revolutionary concept.

In this book, we begin by reviewing the research, teaching, and practice that have taken place since the first book was published. Five major changes are immediately apparent.

A Move to Brands and Branding

Over the years, it has become clear that customers relate to brands, not to the various forms of marketing or marketing communication. Thus, branding becomes the basis for much of our discussion of integration. In today's business environment, disintegration can destroy a brand, whereas coordinated and aligned communication—such as that practiced at companies like Dell, FedEx, and Starbucks—not only builds brands, but does so faster, more easily, and at less cost than traditional communication approaches.

A Five-Step Implementation Process

The first IMC book offered a conceptual framework but conceded that implementation of truly integrated communication remained a formidable challenge. The main reason was the constraints imposed by technology in the early 1990s. Today, phenomenal advances in communication technology provide a new platform for integration. In this book, our five-step process offers a disciplined and focused methodology through which to implement integrated communication programs for all types of firms. It presents marcom managers with the first viable model for developing communication since the timeworn marketing concepts of the Four Ps and the hierarchy of effects model.

A Focus on Individuals, Not Market Segments

The concept of one-to-one communication has had great play during the past decade. Yet while the idea of communicating with customers at the individual level has intuitive appeal, its practical implementation has proven to be nearly impossible. In this book, we take the best of the one-to-one approach and combine it with a model that aggregates individuals into like-behaving groups in order to communicate with them effectively and efficiently. In short, IMC now blends the best of the old with the best of the new in a formalized process that is easy to understand and implement.

A Move Toward Measurement and Accountability

The biggest change in marketing communication since the first book was written is the increased focus on measurement and accountability. Back then, we talked in terms of what could be done to integrate communications at the tactical level. As IMC has evolved, it has become clear that its initiatives are strategic, not tactical, in nature. They are closely linked to the short- and long-term goals of the entire organization, not just to product sales objectives. In this book, our approach to IMC is primarily strategic and value-driven. It is designed to answer the questions senior management and shareholders ask, namely: How much should we invest in marketing communication? What will we get back from that investment? Over what period of time will those returns occur?

Traditionally, practitioners have assumed that marketing communication is a "creative process," even an art form, and as such is neither measurable nor accountable in financial terms. We argue that this is simply not the case. Like any other asset the firm owns, its investment in customers and prospects through marketing communication must deliver identifiable and measurable financial returns, building value for the organization and its shareholders. Using our value-based IMC process, companies are able to measure those returns in both the short term and the long term, putting a clear and distinct value on their marcom investments.

A Global Approach

Since the publication of the first book, IMC has circled the globe. When the concept was first being developed, many thought IMC could be practiced only in established, data-rich, sophisticated economies. Such is not the case. The concepts can and have been adopted in markets as diverse as India and China, Chile and Mexico, Japan and the Philippines. In short, as the cases and examples in this text show, IMC is one of the few approaches that really can be developed and implemented on a global basis.

As you read *IMC—The Next Generation*, it is important to keep these five areas of change that help define IMC clearly in mind, for you will find as you develop IMC programs in your own organization and watch the development of programs elsewhere that all five areas continue to change. You will see that integrated marketing communication is a dynamic, evolving concept that will help prepare you and your organization to succeed in the future business landscape.

ACKNOWLEDGMENTS

The list of people who have assisted in the development of integrated marketing communication (IMC) over the past decade is too long to recount. Our knowledge and understanding of the principles of IMC have matured through their challenges, contributions, advocacy, and practices. The colleagues and associates we acknowledge here have helped shape not only this book but all our writing, research, and thinking on the subject.

First, we wish to thank our colleagues in the Integrated Marketing Communications Department at Northwestern University. A special thanks goes to our students—past and present—in the Master's Degree Program. Since the formation of the department in 1990, more than one thousand students have matriculated. They have contributed much to our own learning through their questions and classroom discussions, while at the same time developing their own perspectives on IMC. To those students and the dedicated faculty, our thanks and appreciation.

Our deep appreciation goes to a special faculty member, the late Stanley Tannenbaum, coauthor of the first book in this field, *Integrated Marketing Communications*. Stan influenced our thinking more than any other person. Thanks also to Dick Christian, former Associate Dean and the spiritual leader of IMC in its early days. Faculty members Ted Spiegel and Martin Block helped hone the concepts. Clarke Caywood and Paul Wang assisted in the initial research and thinking. Later, Frank Mulhern, Tom Collinger, Pat Whalen, and Ed Malthouse helped instill IMC concepts in our students. And while not on the Medill IMC faculty, Bob Lauterborn (University of North Carolina at Chapel Hill), also a coauthor of the original book, has successfully carried the IMC banner around the world.

Our special thanks also to Tom Duncan and Sandy Moriarty (University of Colorado, Boulder), two early believers and advocates of the IMC approach. Christian Gronroos (Hanken School of Economics, Helsinki), Adrian Payne (Cranfield Institute of Management, UK), Peter Reed (Monash University), and Chuck Patti (Queensland University of Technology) have added to our store of knowledge and our development of IMC concepts through their associations and affiliations.

Perhaps the greatest academic support has come from Professor Philip Kitchen (Hull University, UK), who has collaborated on a number of IMC research studies and articles and has coauthored two books using the IMC approach.

In addition, we would like to thank Philip Kotler (Kellogg School of Management, Northwestern University), who has supported the concept of IMC in his writings, seminars, and teaching. Given his stature, one cannot have a better advocate.

We have benefited immensely from our associations with business leaders around the world. Many have contributed substantially to the development of IMC or have furnished concepts that we have adapted and incorporated into our work. Chief among them are Jack Wolf, Jeff Walters, Dana Hayman, and Scott Bailey (Targetbase Marketing, Dallas); Clive Humby and colleagues (dunnhumby llp, London); David Haigh and his team (Brand Finance, plc., London); Peter Simon and John Pearce (Simon Richards Group, Melbourne, Australia); Kaj Storbacka (CRM Group, Helsinki); John Wallis (Hyatt International); and the talented and dedicated staff of the American Productivity and Quality Center in Houston.

Finally, we extend our thanks to all those who contributed to this manuscript. April Love (IMC Class of 2000) did the initial data gathering that contributed to the final text. A special class in the IMC Master's Program went through the manuscript chapter by chapter, critiquing, commenting, challenging, and sharpening the concepts that are articulated here. Tracy Roth (IMC Class of 2002) added much with her research skills and development of examples and illustrations. Kate

Monte (Agora, Inc., Evanston, Illinois) did much to make sure the chapters were processed and reprocessed and then reprocessed again during the development days. And lastly, thanks to Anne Knudsen, our patient, dedicated editor, who brought clarity and focus to the manuscript. Her input was invaluable in helping us shape and polish the final product into what you see here.

None of the following would have been possible without this global team's support, suggestions, challenges, criticisms, and encouragement. It is the work of many. To all, our thanks and best wishes.

PART I

WHAT IS VALUE-BASED IMC?

CHAPTER 1

IMC: FROM COMMUNICATION TACTIC TO PROFIT-BUILDING STRATEGY

Integrated marketing communication (IMC)—a process through which companies accelerate returns by aligning communication objectives with corporate goals—has its roots in the boom times of the 1980s. Yet back then, few firms were interested in the idea of integrating any of their business functions. Companies were neatly divided into departments that operated as independent silos. Each one—whether it was responsible for particular products or services, geographic areas, logistics, or other activities—operated as a unique profit center. From the top down, a regimen of "command and control" kept all units operating by top-down direction. It was the rare exception for firms to think of integrating these separate functions. Fewer still felt there was any need to integrate their marketing or marketing communication (marcom). The problem? Business was good! And since businesses had enjoyed unprecedented growth when they were structured around specific functions and skills, most assumed that their prosperity had something to do with that organizational structure. All the signs indicated that businesses were structured appropriately—for many, profits were consistently rising, shareholder value was at an all-time high, and there were career opportunities for employees at all tiers of the organization. So, why change business structures when everything was ticking along like clockwork?

To answer this question, we must first look outside the limited perspective of the U.S. business organization. Early moves toward integrating business activities were made soon after the end of World War II—but not in the United States. Instead, Japan and Europe led the way. To compete in what was swiftly becoming a global economy, managers needed to find ways to work across boundaries and borders. Those boundaries were not just geographic and cultural, but internal, too. Like voices crying in the wilderness, proponents of integration gradually influenced—or at least came to the attention of—corporate America. Management thinkers like W. Edwards Deming and Joseph Juran, for example, argued for the use of total quality management (TQM) systems based on the Japanese model they had helped to develop.[1] Michael Hammer and James Champy advocated organizational reengineering, while C. K. Prahalad and Gary Hamel championed organizational focus.[2] Yet despite the successes of cross-functional teams overseas, U.S. companies, for the most part, held on to the structures that had served them so well in the past. Nowhere was this more evident than in the marketing function. After all, U.S. managers had "invented" marketing. And that function was solidly and unwaveringly organized around four independent marketing concepts—the Four Ps of product, price, place, and promotion.

A Shift Away from the Four Ps

First popularized by Jerome McCarthy in the late 1950s and proselytized by Philip Kotler and other marketing academicians, the Four Ps quickly became the theory base for almost all marketing education and practice.[3] It governed the manner in which businesses conducted their marketing activities. But notice there is no mention of customers or profits in the Four Ps model—a clear sign of its internal, "siloed" orientation. Using the Four Ps approach, managers managed things they knew and controlled—selection of products, setting of prices, organi-zation of distribution channels, and implementation of advertising and promotion programs. The theory was that if a company got each of the Four Ps right, business would grow and prosper. And the proof for this approach was right there in the growing marketplace. Or was it?

Well, it sure seemed to be. For more than forty years, companies spun out products and services as though there were an unlimited sup-ply of customers or prospects. Nowhere was this more evident than in the United States. With pricing, too, profit optimization was the name of the game. The mantra "Never leave any money on the table!" encouraged marketers to believe that new, higher-paying or faster-using customers were easy to get—customer retention was not terribly impor-tant. Further, marketers controlled distribution—as "channel captains" of manufacturer-driven programs, marketers assumed they would con-tinue to build their "value-adding chains" far into the future, govern-ing the way in which their products reached customers. And for a long time, this inwardly focused approach really seemed to work!

In the 1980s, the first major business database, developed at Harvard University, allowed companies to monitor their activities and perfor-mance relative to their competitors.[4] A new focus on "market share" as the key to future profits assumed that if the firm achieved a dominant—even monopolistic—share of the market, crowding out competitors and controlling customer choices, profits were sure to follow. And very often, that's what happened. The result was that organizations spent more time trying to outthink, outmaneuver, and outpromote compet-itors than they did trying to understand their customers and prospects. Mass media, mass distribution, and mass promotion were all themes of business management well into the 1990s. And some companies con-tinue to pursue these approaches even today.

But to get to mass, you had to have concentration, and this is where the silo system of organizational structure that had neatly accommo-dated the Four Ps model began to fall short. Achieving the economies of scale necessary to capture the lion's share of the mass market meant concentration of product and promotion. It was no longer enough to outspend, outpromote, or outdistribute. To gain a stronghold in mass markets, cost efficiency—rather than more spending—was critical at every stage of the supply chain, and this meant integration—not separation—of business functions. Among the first to realize this were retailers such as Wal-Mart, Home Depot, Toys 'R' Us, and Best Buy. These "category killers" found that by consolidating activities they could drive out smaller competitors and control more consumer dollars. Moreover, their size would allow them to influence and even dominate their upstream suppliers, the manufacturers. Almost overnight, the tables were turned. Retailers, until now merely distribution channel partners, suddenly became adversaries. And since manufacturers no longer controlled the distribution channel (place), the other components of the Four Ps model—product, price, and promotion—also began to slip from their grasp.

A Parallel Shift in Marketing Spending

As the Four Ps model began to show its flaws, similar factors were driving change in marketing communication, specifically advertising and promotion. Product proliferation, a plethora of new channels, and more competitive pricing all demanded new forms and types of marketing communication. In place of the so-called promotional mix of the early 1980s—which focused on the sales force, media advertising, and some forms of publicity—a new breed of communication strategies began to take shape. Sales promotion, direct marketing, and public relations activities all burgeoned as businesses sought ways to influence the behavior of customers and prospects in an increasingly cluttered marketplace.

Intent on keeping these interlopers in their place, old-line marketers—including advertising directors and general ad agencies—did what they could to maintain the status quo. New promotional techniques—including discounts, contests, and other incentives that increased volume only in the short term—were derisively referred to as "below the line" and were even thought to detract from the perceived value of the product or service. Traditional advertising was considered "above the line," since it contributed to so-called value-adding activities designed to build brand image in the long term. Yet as the new forms of promotion proved their worth—particularly in the form of measurable, incremental, fast-acting solutions to basic business problems—more and more marketing dollars were shifted to support them. Exhibit 1.1 illustrates the shift of funds from advertising to sales promotion during the twenty-year period from 1980 to 2000, which became a torrent of promotional dollars by the end of the 1990s.[5]

The world was changing fast, and once challenged, many of the old rules and methods of marketing were found wanting. Change was needed, but because of their prior successes, many organizations had become change-resistant. It was from this rapidly evolving marketplace of changing marketing and media alternatives that integrated marketing communication sprang into being in the mid- to late 1980s.

Demand for IMC

At its outset, integrated marketing communication was not a business model that marketers or advertisers demanded. Most were perfectly

Exhibit 1.1 Shift of Funds from Advertising to Promotion

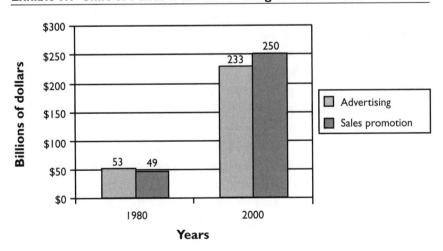

From Robert J. Coen, Universal McCann, *Insider's Report*. Used with permission from Universal McCann.

content with the functionally structured approaches already in place. Instead, the interest in IMC came initially from outside client marketing organizations and from the ad agencies that served those clients. And there was a real need on the part of agencies to move to integration: it was called greed.

Historically, a majority of the marketing organization's promotional funds, particularly among consumer products companies, were invested in traditional advertising media: newspapers, magazines, outdoor, radio, and increasingly, television. Ad agencies earned their money from commissions they received on these media purchases. As agencies noted the shift to "below-the-line" promotional investments by their clients, they immediately sought ways to protect their income streams. They could either convince clients to keep spending on media advertising or, better still, they could capture the funds marketers were directing into sales promotion, direct marketing, and so on by providing those services themselves. Either way, they thought, those funds would keep flowing through the agency's doors.

The first move by agencies was to offer their clients "one-stop shopping" for all their promotional needs. Ad agencies quickly sought to either develop new expertise in the areas of sales promotion, direct marketing, and public relations or to acquire companies that already had these capabilities. The pitch to client organizations was that since the agency now offered a full package of services, there was no need to shop around to spend those below-the-line dollars. Young & Rubicam's "whole egg" approach and Ogilvy and Mather's "orchestration" were both attempts to give these new, seemingly integrated agency models a creative—and competitive—cachet.

Integrated marketing communication was off to a shaky start. Born from a desire to protect the agency's bottom line rather than provide improved, coordinated communication programs for clients, it seemed destined to fail. Client organizations were the first to spot its flaws. They saw no reason why they should consolidate their marketing communication programs in a single agency and forfeit long-standing relationships with proven specialists. While the idea of "one sight, one sound" had great resonance at management levels and among external, integrated agencies, it did not generate much interest among functional managers who believed they had too much at stake to advocate a change in the status quo. In fact, an early study of the potential of IMC found that it could generate credibility as a business model only as a result of initiatives developed by client organizations, not by external ad agencies. And that meant either winning over those obstinate functional managers or changing the way organizations had been structured for decades.[6]

Drivers of IMC

Change did come, though not in the way most functional managers expected. Three shifts occurred in the mid-1980s to thrust IMC to the fore:

- The development and diffusion of digital technology across the entire spectrum of business operations
- The increasing emphasis on brands and branding as the major competitive differentiating tool
- The increasing focus on multinationalization and globalization as marketers spread across the traditional geographic boundaries

Today, there is one more key factor in support of IMC—the demand for value-based business approaches that generate cash flows and shareholder value. The demand for accountability in the form of six sigma, balanced scorecards, and the like is greater now than ever before. This concept of accountability and the measurement of financial returns on marketing communication activities are fundamental to the strategic, value-based approach to IMC illustrated throughout this book.

Technology

The desire to be customer focused—to understand and be able to respond to the needs of the customers one wishes to serve—has always been central to the marketing concept and a key objective of most marketing organizations. But it was not until the 1990s that computer technology made it possible for companies operating in mass markets to get close to their customers. The rapid development and diffusion of information technology in the form of data capture, storage, and manipulation made it possible for organizations to find out, for the first time, exactly what types of customers made up the mass market for their products. Organizations could also find out what motivated those customers to buy. Thus, while companies' activities had traditionally revolved around their products or services, they now had the opportunity to focus on customers and their wants and needs.

The rapid emergence of direct marketing during the 1990s is the most obvious early application of information technology to marketing. Indeed, direct marketing—with its focus on identification, contact, and measurement of returns from specific customers over time—was one of the key drivers in the development of IMC. Today, Internet marketers use technology-driven tools in much the same way. And even broad-scale marketing organizations such as retailers, banks, insurance firms, and auto dealers are making use of these same tools and techniques.

Branding

Since the 1950s, the marketplace has been one long series of new products, new technologies, and new innovations being sold to new groups of consumers and customers. "Innovate and grow" was the theme all through the 1960s, 1970s, and 1980s, even up to the early 1990s. From televisions to microwaves to computers to the Sony Walkman, companies brought innovation after innovation to the market. For the most part, each new product gave the originator a unique segment of the available consumer dollar.

Beginning in the mid-1980s, however, innovation became a competitive rather than just a market-leader tool. Emerging economies in Asia-Pacific and Latin America concentrated their resources not on innovation but on copying—and improving—existing products and technologies. The ability to duplicate innovations quickly became as important as the ability to innovate. A whole new breed of competitors emerged in the marketplace. Their modus operandi: find an innovative product, develop an enhancement, manufacture in an emerging country with low labor costs, underprice the market and capture what was available, and then look for the next innovation to duplicate.

The rise of generic or copycat brands crosses every category from technology-driven products to store brands and private labels. In the pharmaceutical industry, for example, generics represent a full tenth of the drug market. And while branded pharmaceuticals are projected to grow by 6 percent in coming years, generics are projected to enjoy double-digit growth.[7]

Even a simple trip to the grocery store will tell you that private labels are growing exponentially. According to a recent report by the Private Label Manufacturers Association, two out of five primary household shoppers buy store brands regularly or frequently in supermarkets. One-third of drugstore shoppers do the same. Other studies show that the sale of private labels is substantially outstripping that of overall sales for supermarkets, drugstores, and mass retailers. In fact, between 1998 and 2002, private label sales increased from $41.5 billion to $51.5 billion, an impressive rise of 24.3 percent.[8]

Clearly, the market still has room for copycats, and faster technology and lower costs have contributed to their success. Yet as the price-driven, multicompetitor marketplace developed, a new form of competition evolved: the brand. True, brands had been around for centuries, but they had been viewed primarily as product or service identifiers, not as powerful marketing and management tools. That was soon to change.

Marketing organizations were not the first to recognize the financial value of brands. In the mid-1980s, investment firms discovered that brands, because they commanded a base of loyal customers, were able to generate income flows into the future despite relatively modest investments. This often made the future value of a successful brand more important than its present income flow. Further, the future income flows the brand could create were often worth a great deal more than the tangible assets of the organization that produced the branded goods or services. As a result, the focus of much marketing activity changed from communicating what the organization made or did to the creation of brands that had the power to increase the future value of the firm. Intangible, rather than tangible, assets became the battle-ground for corporate raiders seeking to gain control over these future brand income flows. RJR-Nabisco, Rank-Hovis, and Rowntree are well-cited early examples of this transition.[9]

Globalization

The third factor that drove the emergence of IMC was the increasing globalization of the marketplace. While organizations such as Nestlé, Unilever, and Coca-Cola had marketed outside home borders for years, they were the exception rather than the rule. Driven by the emergence of new trading blocs such as the European Union, ASEAN (Association of Southeast Asian Nations), and MERCOSUR (Southern Common Marketplace) and the restructuring of Eastern Europe, brands began to cross national lines in ever-increasing numbers. In addition, firms began to stretch their wings through acquisition and consolidation. And with the rise of electronic communication systems, companies were able to operate in real time twenty-four hours a day, seven days a week, around the globe. Thus, the demise of borders and the growth of multinationals, always seeking new markets and new opportunities, created a completely altered global marketplace in the early twenty-first century.

With increased globalization came the need for organizations to change their communication strategies. It became critical to create a unified, consistent, and integrated brand strategy while remaining responsive to the unique needs of individual markets and cultures.

These three driving forces—technology, branding, and globalization—converged in the 1990s, pushing organizations toward integration of multiple business strategies, including marketing communication. In short order, integration—the alignment and coordination of marketing activities around the singular focus of the brand—became not just acceptable, but mandatory, in many organizations.

The primary holdouts to integration during this time were the large ad agencies and the holding companies that owned them. Ironically, the tables had turned and the very firms that had preached IMC were now reluctant to embrace it. The reason? Control. It had proven an all but impossible task for agencies to convincingly offer advertising, direct marketing, and public relations as a one-stop shopping package for the simple reason that this meant transfer of control from the client organization to the agency. Once organizations set out to integrate marketing communication under their own steam, IMC suddenly became a threat to the agencies that had once championed it.

IMC IN ACTION

While most large ad agencies failed to overcome the functional chasm that scuttled their attempts to integrate marketing communication for their clients, there are some early success stories. Most are from smaller or regional agencies, particularly those serving business-to-business and service organizations. The standouts include The Phelps Group (Santa Monica, California), Kilgannon McReynolds (Atlanta), Price McNabb (Charlotte, North Carolina), and Slack Barshinger (Chicago). All have practiced the underlying principles of integration coincidentally, some long before the emergence of IMC as a formal business model.

The Phelps Group believes that if a variety of tools is used to reach the consumer at different contact points, they can all work together to communicate consistent core product benefits and brand image. The distinguishing characteristic is the group's lack of functional departments for each discipline. Instead, the company works in what it calls "pyramids," composed of specialists and coaches who bring specific expertise to the various teams. For each project, discipline specialists meet initially to ensure that their objectives are well integrated into the plan before they begin the creative process. While this process requires an investment of time at the start of the project, it ensures that in the long run all marketing messages are coordinated, aligned, and—as a result—more effective.

Kilgannon McReynolds starts its process by looking among the client's customers and prospects for those segments that represent the greatest growth potential. According to founder Rena Kilgannon, "The agency itself has its own position, which is straight out of the IMC philosophy. The philosophy is built around 'Find. Keep. Grow.' This demonstrates the agency's commitment to help clients find new customers, keep old ones, and grow share among them."

Kilgannon McReynolds achieves this objective by reviewing all channels through which a customer or prospect could get information about a particular product or service. Next, the agency analyzes all messages being communicated in and through those channels. Additionally, the agency questions the current status of the product or service: What is going on? What is working? Why? What is not working? What still needs to be done?

Recently, Kilgannon McReynolds established its own advertising return-on-investment model. With this model, the agency can now tell a client that, for instance, its advertising was not effective, yet its public relations had a big impact on its success. Tools like these give the client the added value of an integrated perspective; rather than just focusing on separate elements of the marketing mix, the client gets a complete and—more importantly—integrated view of the business.

Agile, innovative agencies like The Phelps Group and Kilgannon McReynolds have proven that integration can work. Not only are they challenging the more traditional approaches used by larger national and international agencies, they are finding ways to demonstrate that IMC-based programs pay out for their clients.

New Challenges

By the end of the 1990s, IMC was on its way to becoming established as a legitimate marketing approach. While many organizations evolved to become the more fluid structures the new business environment demanded, only the most change-resistant argued in favor of keeping the old silo structure intact. Global, cross-functional teams replaced departmental structures, making way for the new marketing communications model that IMC represented.

One other factor pushed IMC to the fore: the explosion in Internet technology and E-commerce. The rapid emergence of electronic communication in which real-time buyer-seller interaction became possible gave rise to a sudden and more pressing need for integration. While IMC started as a means to coordinate and align *outbound* communication, quite suddenly it became a means to integrate all company-customer interactions, both outbound and *inbound*. The objective—to create meaningful and ongoing customer contact—remained the same, but IMC shifted from a focus on one-way, outbound communication to the creation of an interactive, two-way channel between the organization and its customers.

With this new, broader scope, IMC has progressed from a communication-only approach and is on its way to becoming a full-fledged business strategy. Unlike any other business model—including the highly touted customer relationship management approach—IMC uniquely integrates all the pieces of an organization around a single factor: the wants and needs of customers. Satisfying those wants and needs leads to the core business objective of creating value for shareholders. And that is the objective of this book: helping practitioners move from seeing IMC simply as a means of coordinating communication to viewing it as a core business strategy that is based on measurable communication inputs and outputs.

Moving On

In the early 1990s, when Don Schultz, Stan Tannenbaum, and Bob Lauterborn wrote *Integrated Marketing Communication: Putting It Together and Making It Work*, which has since become the seminal work on IMC, the goals were simple and quite clear. We wanted to help organizations bring together all the disparate tactics of external communication and put them together as one coherent whole for the benefit of the customer and prospect. With that, we believed, came some basic benefits for the organization as well. Yet the focus remained squarely on what the seller wanted to communicate or persuade the buyer to do or think or feel. The approach was mass market oriented in that communication revolved around what *the organization*, not necessarily the customer, felt was important. Our application of emerging technologies was crude by today's standards. Yet with all its limitations, IMC endured and proved—at least in concept—to be the precursor of several other business models, ranging from the "one-to-one" and mass customization approaches of Peppers and Rogers to the newest data-mining techniques of organizations such as Axiom, Harte-Hanks, and EDS to the customer relationship management initiatives of Siebel, SAP, and Epiphany.[10] For better or worse, it was accepted as a basic business tool and was put into practice by such organizations as Dow Chemical, CIGNA Insurance, Kraft, FedEx, IBM, Dell, and Hyatt International, to name just a few.

So, where does all this lead us in today's business environment, and what is the future value of IMC? Is mastering the coordination and alignment of outbound marketing communication programs all there is to it? The answer, as you've probably guessed, is no. Integrated marketing communication has come a long way since the days of functional silos, but it still has much further to go. The next logical step is for organizations to leverage IMC to meet the challenges and opportunities that globalization and the rapid pace of technology offer. As the marketplace becomes more cluttered and confusing than any of us ever imagined possible, the value of fully integrated marketing communication systems increases. In many cases, such systems will separate those companies that thrive and prosper from those that ultimately fail. For if a firm cannot master communication, if it cannot use communication to influence and bind customers to it, if it cannot turn its brand and brand relationships into a sustainable competitive advantage, and if it cannot find ways to use communication to build long-term brand loyalty, that firm will not survive.

The chapters that follow explain how IMC can play a vital, strategic role in the future of today's organizations. In the next chapter, we take a closer look at how IMC has evolved, with particular emphasis on best practices where results have been proven and benchmarked. Future chapters use this core knowledge and experience to explore how IMC can best be leveraged by organizations in the future. To work effectively, integration requires major changes within organizations, changes that straddle structure, focus, workplace behaviors, and compensation. It also requires new approaches to the financial aspects of marketing communication, that is, how much to invest and how to measure results. Remember as you read that IMC is far from being a static business model; it's a dynamic process that will prove critical in helping organizations compete in a radically changing business environment.

CHAPTER 2

WHAT WE KNOW ABOUT IMC

W hen innovative agencies and their clients began to practice integrated marketing communication (IMC) in the late 1980s, they took a leap of faith. At the time, there was no real evidence that the model would work. It was not until the early 1990s that formal studies on IMC and how best to implement it were carried out.[1] Since that time, IMC has been the topic of a flood of research and other writings aimed at both academics and marketing professionals.[2] As a result, a great deal is known today about IMC. Better still, existing research serves as a road map to help us identify aspects of the business model that are not yet fully understood.

To find out where we are going, we must first know where we have been. With this objective in mind, this chapter explores the development of IMC from three perspectives. First, we look at the results of a major benchmarking study that forms the basis for our recommended steps in developing a strategic IMC program for most types of organizations. Next, we examine the findings from a global study of advertising and marketing communication agencies to see how IMC is currently practiced in five English-speaking countries around the world. Third, we look at a recent study of how companies use technology to leverage customer information for the development of ongoing and rewarding customer relationships.

Best Practice Benchmarks in IMC

In 1997, the American Productivity and Quality Center (APQC) initiated the first systematic study to benchmark best practices in IMC.[3]
APQC is an American-based, nonprofit, membership organization that
conducts benchmarking studies across a wide variety of business processes. Researchers first identified those firms perceived to have developed "best practices" in the implementation of IMC, referred to in the
study as "partner firms." Using extensive organizational data as well as
intensive site visits, a team of researchers then analyzed an identified
range of activities at each firm, benchmarking them against other partner firms included in the study as well as against "sponsor firms" that
supported the study. Participating companies included Attorneys Title
Insurance Fund, CIGNA Insurance, Dow Chemical, FedEx, Fidelity
Investments, Hewlett-Packard, John Nuveen & Co., and USAA. The
sponsors included Arthur Andersen, Baptist Sunday School Board,
Bayer AG, Ernst & Young, GE Capital, GTE Services, Kaiser Perma-
nente, Mutual of Omaha, Nationwide Insurance, Prudential Insurance,
Public Service Electric and Gas Company, Texas Instruments, Texas
Utilities, and The Mutual Group. Note that the study was based on a
small number of nonrandom respondents. Its results, therefore, are
based on a qualitative assessment of overall findings rather than on statistical analysis of quantitative data.

Four Stages of Development

Since IMC was an emerging discipline at the time of the APQC study,
there was no universally accepted definition of what the term represented. To give all participants a common reference point, the following definition was developed at the outset and used throughout the
study:

> *Integrated marketing communication is a strategic business process used
> to plan, develop, execute, and evaluate coordinated, measurable, per-*

*suasive brand communication programs over time with consumers,
customers, prospects, and other targeted, relevant external and internal audiences.*[4]

Further, since there was no framework for IMC and only anecdotal
evidence of practical marketplace applications, the research team needed
a starting point against which to evaluate how each partner organization implemented different aspects of IMC. They created a basic model
that would capture the myriad marketing and communication activities
of a firm. The model, which is shown in Exhibit 2.1, assumed that firms
likely proceed through various stages of development and implementation, most likely driven by their organization-specific needs and
capabilities.

In general, the model suggested four stages of IMC development,
progressing from a highly practical, tactical orientation to one increasingly driven by an understanding of customers and their behaviors. As
an organization gains IMC experience, the focus becomes more strategic and encompasses an ever-widening circle of activities within that
organization. The research team observed how 'the model worked in
several of its benchmarked "best practice" companies. In the early stages
of IMC development, most companies addressed marketing communication activities with tactical "how-to" and "when-to" questions. Once
an IMC program was in place, they moved progressively to questions
about coordinating internal and external activities; using customer data
to drive priorities; and finally applying IMC principles to strategic issues
such as resource allocation, organizational alignment, and financial integration and accountability.

The best practices study amassed a substantial amount of information not previously known about the implementation of IMC. What
follows is a summary of those key findings that are still relevant in
today's—and tomorrow's—business environment. For clarity, the summary follows the same structure as Exhibit 2.1, identifying key insights
at each stage of IMC development within organizations. Note that in
many cases we have differentiated between performance at partner companies and sponsor firms to illustrate the varying levels of development.

Exhibit 2.1 The Four Evolutionary Stages of IMC

Stage 4: Financial and strategic integration

Emphasis on using the skills and data generated in the earlier stages to drive corporate strategic planning using customer information. Reform of financial information infrastructure to foster "closed-loop" planning capabilities to return-on-customer investment measures.

Stage 3: Application of information technology

Application of empirical customer data using IT to provide a basis to identify, value, and monitor the impact of integrated internal and external communication programs to key customer segments over time. Integration of various sources of customer data to obtain a richer and more complete view of customer/brand relationship.

Stage 2: Redefining scope of marketing communication

Marcom planners view communication as dynamic and ongoing and seek to incorporate customer insight at all points of contact. Scope of marcom activities broadens to encompass internal marketing to employees, suppliers, and other business partners and to align them with the existing external communication programs.

Stage 1: Tactical coordination

Focus on tactical coordination of diverse outbound marketing, communication elements, and achieving consistency and synergy between functional efforts. Emphasis typically on development of overall communication policies and practices and delivering "one sight, one sound" via marketing communication.

From "Integrated Marketing Communication: Best Practices Report," American Productivity and Quality Center (Houston: APQC, 1998). Used with permission from American Productivity and Quality Center.

Stage 1: Coordination of Tactical Communication Efforts

This is the entry point into IMC for most organizations. Commonly, an IMC initiative is driven by the desire to achieve better coordination, consistency, and synergy between the various tactical, external communication activities. At this stage, the organization is primarily focused on using IMC to achieve "one sight, one sound, one voice" in its outbound communication efforts. The goals are (1) to more effectively orchestrate the delivery of messages into the marketplace and (2) to apply the strengths of each communication discipline or technique so that the whole is greater than the sum of the parts and the optimal message impact is achieved.

> **Finding 1:** *Integration requires a high degree of interpersonal and cross-functional communication within the organization, across business units, and with outside suppliers. Integration cannot be driven by formal policies and procedures alone.*

Table 2.1 illustrates the various techniques both sponsors and partners use to achieve integration. Virtually all participating companies use some form of written policies, manuals, or procedural guidelines to achieve consistency and integration in their communication. While having such tools in place does not guarantee a successfully integrated outcome, it is considered by the best practice partners to be the minimum standard. However, best practice partners place much greater emphasis on the use of meetings and other forms of direct, personal communication in fostering IMC programs. They are more likely to use meetings productively and to communicate effectively with other areas of the organization, including research, sales, and customer service. A further organizational characteristic is the extent to which best practice partners expect their agencies and other marketing service suppliers to attend these cross-functional planning meetings.

> **Finding 2:** *Organizations are taking charge of the integration process themselves rather than looking to ad agencies or other suppliers.*

Table 2.1 Practices Used to Promote Integration

	Partners (n = 8)	Sponsors (n = 15)
Internal manual specifying policies, practices, and procedures for the tone, look, and personality of all communication efforts	88%	80%
Ultimate control and approval of all communication efforts centralized within the unit for which respondent is reporting	63%	53%
Regular cross-functional staff meetings to coordinate efforts among marketing communication specialists	100%	73%
Regular, interdepartmental meetings to coordinate efforts with other departments such as sales, research, customer service, and production	75%	40%
Written communication	88%	93%
Attendance of outside suppliers at cross-functional planning meetings	88%	40%

From "Integrated Marketing Communication: Best Practices Report," American Productivity and Quality Center (Houston: APQC, 1998). Used with permission from American Productivity and Quality Center.

Both best practice partner and sponsor firms strongly felt the integration of their marketing communication activities was a task the marketing group had to direct. Only 25 percent of partner firms reported that their ad agencies were responsible for overseeing integration and coordination of marketing communication programs. Most firms maintain control over the integration process themselves as a function of the marcom department, while orchestrating the work of multiple agencies, public relations firms, direct marketing providers, media experts, and so on. Note that this finding is supported by several other research studies (discussed later in this chapter).

Stage 2: Redefinition of the Scope of Marketing Communication

During this stage of development, IMC-focused firms shift their emphasis from simple tactical coordination to more extensive communication activities in the following three ways:

- Organizations begin to look at more than just the marketing communication efforts managed by the marcom department; they start to include all the possible information-bearing points of contact a customer may have with the firm.

- Organizations attempt to gather a broad and deep understanding of their customers and prospects, not just how they feel but what they do and why they do it.
- There is a concerted effort to identify, understand, and create cross-functional communication opportunities across customer contact points wherever they occur.

Finding 3: Organizations gather extensive information about their customers, using primary and secondary market research sources as well as actual customer behavioral data, and use that information in the planning, development, and evaluation of communication activities.

Both partners and sponsors capture and apply a variety of data on customers and prospects. Virtually all companies reported gathering and using data derived through market research, such as customer satisfaction data, primary attitudinal data and perceptual research, geographic and demographic data, and pre- and postcommunication research. Additionally, partner organizations were somewhat more likely to report extensive use of operationally derived data, such as transactional data, customer service reports, sales lead data, and so forth.

Perhaps just as important in the integration process is an understanding of how companies evaluate the usefulness of various types of data in planning communication programs. As shown in Exhibit 2.2, there are differences in how best practice partners and study sponsors look at the available data.

Finding 4: Best practice organizations create a variety of feedback channels to gather information about customers; they then use this customer feedback and share it throughout the company.

Research into feedback channels illustrates some of the major differences between the best practice partners and the sponsor organizations, especially in how widely information is disseminated and with

Exhibit 2.2 Data Sources Rated Above Average or Extremely Useful in Planning Marcom Programs

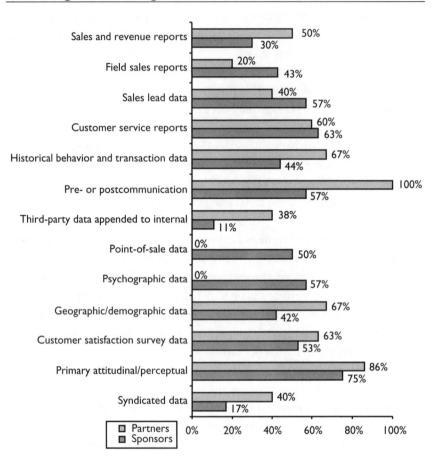

From "Integrated Marketing Communication: Best Practices Report," American Productivity and Quality Center (Houston: APQC, 1998). Used with permission from American Productivity and Quality Center.

whom customer and prospect information is shared internally. Best practice partners make much greater use of customer feedback data and share more of it within the same department and with other departments. Notably, best practice companies are far more likely to agree with such statements as the following:

• Market research data are broadly disseminated so employees have a better understanding of customer behaviors and attitudes.

- We regularly apply feedback from sales and customer service regarding the concerns/needs/wants of our customers to fashion more relevant messages.
- We use toll-free numbers, coupons, the Internet, and other interactive media to encourage feedback from customers.

Finding 5: One of the most difficult challenges of integration is aligning internal practices and processes with external communication programs.

At the second stage of IMC development, organizations expand their view of marketing communication to include more than outbound messages sent to customers. They recognize the need to establish an ongoing dialogue with customers and prospects. However, this also leads to recognition of the role that employees outside the marketing communication department play in sustaining that customer dialogue. Hence, there is a need to support these employees with internal practices and policies aligned with the promises that have been conveyed to customers through external communication.

However, even the best of the partner organizations ran into difficulties when it came to the question of effective internal alignment and getting employees to understand the firm's marketing mission. The APQC study revealed widespread agreement among participating companies that internal alignment presents a significant challenge on the way to integration. Additionally, it appears that few companies had experienced success in extending marketing communication to internal audiences. Thus, only about a quarter of participating firms could agree with the statement that "all employees—even those without regular customer contact—understand our marketing mission and their role in meeting customer needs."

The question of internal marketing and the alignment of internal processes and practices with external promises was just being recognized as a critical issue at the time this study was conducted. Thus, the few companies such as CIGNA Insurance, FedEx, and Hewlett-Packard who were already attempting to deal with this question were, in retrospect, pioneers in what would become an increasingly important aspect of IMC.

Stage 3: Application of Information Technology

At the third stage of IMC development, organizations use the power and potential of information technologies to improve their integration performance. The use of technology seems to occur in the following three ways:

- The use of one or more databases to capture, store, and manage information about customers and prospects, particularly information about their economic value to the firm
- The use of emerging technology to improve how and when messages are delivered to customers, prospects, and other targets
- The use of electronic communication to facilitate internal dissemination of information for and about customers and to keep the various business units informed about what is occurring in marketing and communication throughout the firm

Finding 6: *Leading best practice organizations maintain a greater number of data sources, and their marketing communication person-nel have greater access to the data for planning marketing communi-cation programs than do the sponsor organizations.*

As noted earlier, study participants typically capture and maintain substantial amounts of customer information. Unfortunately, in many cases, that data is not available to the marketing communication group. In general, however, best practice firms allow fuller and more timely access to such data when compared to that allowed by sponsor organizations.

Finding 7: *Best practice firms are more likely to use finance-based approaches to targeting and segmentation.*

Stage 3 involves the use of data to develop economic and behavioral views of customers. The study showed that best practice partners are more likely to use statistical techniques based on behavioral data; such techniques include profiling and scoring, customer retention calcula-tions, decile/quintile analysis, and the estimation of customer lifetime

Table 2.2 Respondents Who "Somewhat" or "Strongly" Agree with Statements About the Use of Customer Data in Marcom Planning

Statement	Partners (n = 8)	Sponsors (n = 15)
We regularly use customer data to assist in delivering communication messages.	88%	67%
We have formalized programs to identify and value the best, highest-spending customers and give priority to those relationships.	71%	20%
We can project a customer's long-term profitability to the organization.	50%	33%
We know the costs to acquire a new customer and/or retain an existing customer and use this data in developing communication budgets.	29%	13%

From "Integrated Marketing Communication: Best Practices Report," American Productivity and Quality Center (Houston: APQC, 1998). Used with permission from American Productivity and Quality Center.

value, all of which are used to provide a better understanding of the economics underlying the company-customer relationship. Some companies, notably FedEx, Fidelity Investments, and Dow Chemical, have become quite sophisticated in their analytical techniques and have developed an infrastructure of analysts, statisticians, and researchers to support the ongoing process of understanding customer economics.

Simply having extensive data on customers and prospects, however, does not ensure integration, nor does it necessarily lead to high-quality customer insights. Table 2.2 demonstrates the level of analysis conducted by participating firms on the customer data they held at the time of the study. Clearly, partner organizations not only have more data available, but they generally apply a greater level of analytical resources to understanding their data. Even so, at the time of the study, only a relatively small number systematically determined the costs of attracting a new customer or retaining an existing customer. This indicates that there was considerable room for improvement, even among the best practice leaders.

Stage 4: Financial and Strategic Integration

The highest level of integration occurs as organizations begin to operationalize the assets and skills developed during Stages 1 to 3. Once managers have come to grips with the basic issues of integration, they can then begin to incorporate this understanding through all parts of the organization. Typically, the focus is on issues of strategic importance to the firm, such as investments and returns on marketing communication programs. In short, at Stage 4, IMC is concerned much more with the issues facing senior management than those facing the marketing communication group. Having said that, it is apparent that marketing communication managers must develop more strategic views of what they do and how they invest the firm's finite resources. Two major issues emerge during Stage 4:

- The need to upgrade systems and processes to measure the effectiveness of communication activities
- The need to apply IMC tools and principles to the firm's overall strategic objectives

In our analysis, those companies that achieved Stage 4 represented the leading edge of IMC at the time the study was conducted. Most likely, those same companies are ahead of the game today, too. However, the study reveals that few organizations successfully addressed all the strategic issues that developing an advanced, value-oriented IMC approach entails. The last three key findings point out some of the issues yet to be resolved.

Finding 8: The role of the marketing communication department is perceived quite differently at partner companies than at sponsor organizations. Marcom departments at partner companies more often have bottom-line responsibilities and a more prominent role in strategic planning and new product introductions than do the same groups in sponsor firms.

The study found that while marcom departments at almost two-thirds of partner companies had bottom-line responsibility, that figure fell to less than one-fifth at sponsor organizations. Several best practice partners felt that their command of customer data and the related ability to measure the impact of marketing communication efforts had led to increased visibility of marcom, leading in turn to greater participation in strategic planning. At Fidelity Investments, for instance, marcom executives reported that the use of customer data and IMC planning meant they had become more deeply involved in the new product planning process.

Even so, only a minority of even the best practice firms had begun to carry out Stage 4 of integration in a serious and systematic way, at least at the time of the study. When participants were asked a series of questions regarding how IMC related to the financial and strategic direction of the firm—as shown in Exhibit 2.3—it was apparent that many firms (both partners and sponsors) were still tied to traditional views of their roles. Thus, while several firms felt that marcom was essential to strategic planning, few expanded the marcom role to encompass it.

Exhibit 2.3 Agreement with Statements Relating IMC to Financial and Strategic Planning Practices

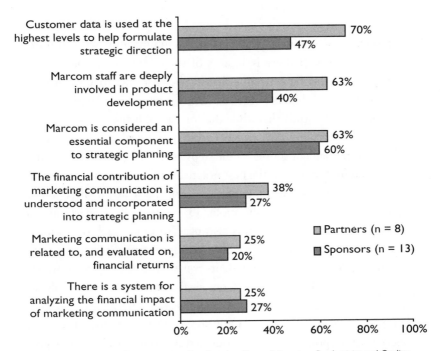

From "Integrated Marketing Communication: Best Practices Report," American Productivity and Quality Center (Houston: APQC, 1998). Used with permission from American Productivity and Quality Center.

Finding 9: Most organizations use a variety of tools to measure the effectiveness of marketing communication activities; however, relatively few incorporate financial measurement into the evaluation process.

Not surprisingly, there appeared to be no common agreement on what tools or techniques are most useful in determining returns on marketing communication investments. Participants listed ten measurement techniques, ranging from measurement of customer responses to rate of customer acquisition and retention to costs of customer acquisition to long-term financial performance. Only four (measurement of response, short-term financial measurement, pre- and postcommunication effects, and measurement of communication output and efficiency) were used by more than half the participating companies.

Finding 10: While organizations may claim to be customer focused, relatively few have fully grappled with the strategic and organizational implications of such a focus.

Marketing communication is all about communicating with customers and prospects. If there is an area of the organization that should practice the marketing concept—that is, "be customer focused or customer centric"—it should be the marketing communication group. Yet it is clear from the study that while the concept of being "customer centric" was gaining popularity in 1997 from a practical standpoint, most companies still had not addressed the steps necessary to make it a reality.

As noted in Exhibit 2.3, the best practice partner organizations were far more likely to use customer data to form the strategic direction of the company. However, only about 13 percent of all participants reported that customer data was also used to guide such operational areas as production planning, distribution, human resources, and accounting. Additionally, respondents were asked the extent to which they agreed with the statement "Compensation and promotion policies have been reviewed for alignment and consistency with corporate customer development objectives." Only about a third of partner firms and a mere fifth of sponsors felt they could agree "somewhat" or "strongly" with this statement, indicating that for many firms there was still a significant level of nonintegration between internal policies and what the organization attempts to convey to customers. Many organizations felt that this nonintegration was a critical barrier to the successful implementation of their IMC programs, one that they were actively developing plans to address and improve.

The Move Forward

Obviously, the 1997 study on the development of IMC contains a great deal more information than we are able to include here. These key findings, however, point to a number of issues that are explored more fully in the chapters that follow. When reviewing the results of the study, keep in mind that at the time it was conducted the full impact of the electronic communications explosion was only beginning to be felt. Note, too, that the study was limited to marketing organizations in the United States. It did not take into consideration changes that were occurring within ad agencies, nor did it look at developments overseas. The remainder of this chapter sets out to fill in the gaps by exploring the development of IMC from these two perspectives.

The Agency Role: A Global Perspective

Most marketing organizations believe that it is their responsibility to integrate their marketing communication programs rather than leave the job to an external supplier, as has been borne out by the APQC study as well as studies conducted by the American Association of Advertising Agencies (AAAA) and the Association of National Advertisers (ANA). However, it is equally clear that advertising agencies have major contributions to make. To understand their role in IMC, we turn our attention to a major global study conducted among advertising agencies in the late 1990s.[5]

Research Method and Participants

The research began as a series of exploratory studies among ad agencies in the United States and the United Kingdom; it was extended to include agencies in Australia, New Zealand, and India. The research was conducted through a self-administered questionnaire that was sent to advertising agency association members in each of the five countries. Eighty-nine questions covered a variety of topics, including personal and organizational demographics, drivers for IMC, and beliefs about IMC implementation, as well as the perceived barriers to successfully conducting IMC programs.[6]

Agencies of all sizes were represented in the study, with mean gross agency billings ranging from $28 million (NZD) in New Zealand to approximately $162 million (USD) in the United States. More important than total billing, however, was the amount of the clients' budgets placed through the agency devoted to IMC activities. The highs were recorded at 52 percent for the United States, 42 percent for the United Kingdom, 40 percent for New Zealand, 22 percent for Australia, and 15 percent for India.

Interaction Among Agencies

If the client managed the integration process, an obvious question was how well the various agencies could work together to develop and implement an IMC program. Responses showed that ad agency managers generally expected to offer clients a broad array of services beyond advertising. They also expected clients to allocate projects among a number of service providers. Further, ad agencies anticipated that as they developed IMC programs for their clients in the future, they would need to develop closer cooperation among various types of agencies, such as public relations, direct marketing, and sales promotion.

Agency Perceptions of IMC

Agency managers responding to the survey generally believed that client organizations drove the IMC initiative. Further, as might be expected, marketing and advertising management departments within client organizations were perceived to be the main drivers. This result may reflect the contact points agencies had with their clients. Interestingly, according to client companies included in the study, sales groups appeared quite prominently as IMC drivers. This may have been due to the move toward sales force automation, channel management, and other technology-driven customer-management programs.

Of particular interest, the agency study threw light on the perceptions of agency managers regarding how IMC programs might best be conducted. As Table 2.3 recaps, most ad agency managers in all countries surveyed believed an IMC approach greatly increased the impact and effect of the overall communication program. Further, they believed economies in time, effort, and perhaps even cost resulted from it. As might be expected, agency responses focused much more on the creative and communication aspects than on the business side of IMC.

Barriers to the Development of IMC

As the APQC benchmark study reflected, marketing organizations frequently encounter barriers when developing IMC programs. Agencies appear to experience the same challenges, as summarized in Table 2.4. Note that the statements with which agency executives agreed most strongly were primarily focused on internal agency capabilities, such as requiring staff to be more generalist, the need to develop new skills, and a lack of talent in integrated agencies across all marcom areas. Ranking much lower on the agreement scale were those items directly related to client difficulties, such as going against a client's corporate culture and constraints generated by the client's organizational structure. Thus, from this study, it appears that advertising agency executives believe the challenges of developing and implementing IMC programs are on their own turf rather than a result of client difficulties.

Leveraging of Customer Information: A Data Application Study

Having seen how agencies view IMC, let us turn our attention back to client organizations. Since customer information is key to initiating or

Table 2.3 Internal Beliefs and Considerations About Conducting IMC Programs

Abbreviated Statement	US	UK	NZ	AU	IN
Increased impact	9.4	9.0	9.1	8.5	9.1
Creative ideas more effective when IMC used	9.4	9.0	—	8.9	9.5
Greater communication efficiency	9.3	9.3	9.3	9.0	9.1
Increases importance of one brand personality, one voice	8.5	8.6	—	—	7.2
Helps eliminate misconceptions that can occur when several agencies are used	8.3	7.6	8.2	8.3	8.3
Greater client control over their communication budget	7.9	7.5	8.2	8.4	7.8
Provides clients with greater professional expertise	7.5	7.3	9.1	7.6	7.4
IMC necessitates fewer meetings	7.0	7.1	7.3	6.8	5.8
Enables client consolidation of responsibilities	6.9	7.0	—	6.6	6.9
Agency can provide faster solutions	6.9	6.2	6.9	6.9	6.9
Provides method for effective measurement	6.9	6.6	6.1	7.1	7.2
Reduces cost of marcom programs	6.8	6.9	6.8	6.3	7.6

Note: US = United States; UK = United Kingdom; NZ = New Zealand; AU = Australia; IN = India.

All figures are means based on a 10-point scale where 1 = strongly disagree and 10 = strongly agree.

From Philip J. Kitchen and Don E. Schultz, "A Multi-Country Comparison of the Drive for IMC," *Journal of Advertising Research* (January/February 1999). Used with permission from *Journal of Advertising Research*.

Table 2.4 Perceived Barriers to IMC Programs

Abbreviated Statement	US	UK	NZ	AU	IN
IMC programs at one agency help bring client's SBUs together	7.0	7.0	—	4.5	6.9
Requires staff to be more generalist	6.3	6.4	—	5.5	6.4
Integrated agencies do not have talent across all marcom areas	6.0	6.9	6.8	5.6	7.0
IMC means staff have to develop new skills	5.7	6.7	6.9	5.5	6.7
IMC gives a few individuals too much control	5.5	6.4	4.8	4.0	6.4
Clients decide the "what" and "how" of IMC programs	5.2	5.0	4.8	5.3	5.0
Client staff lacks expertise to undertake IMC programs	5.2	6.3	6.1	5.5	6.3
Client centralization difficulties	4.8	5.2	4.9	3.2	5.2
Client organizational structures constrain IMC	4.7	6.1	6.4	3.8	6.1
Goes against client's corporate culture	4.2	4.4	4.0	3.3	4.4
Overdependence on single suppliers	4.1	5.0	5.0	4.4	5.0
IMC implies additional staff to manage programs	3.7	4.2	3.9	4.8	4.2
IMC creates program modification difficulties	3.3	3.9	3.9	7.4	3.9
Provides advertising agencies with too much control	3.2	3.5	3.3	3.3	3.5
Increased cost	2.9	3.8	3.9	5.6	3.8

Note: US = United States; UK = United Kingdom; NZ = New Zealand; AU = Australia; IN = India.

From Philip J. Kitchen and Don E. Schultz, "A Multi-Country Comparison of the Drive for IMC," *Journal of Advertising Research* (January/February 1999). Used with permission from *Journal of Advertising Research*.

implementing IMC programs, we now look at a third study that investigates how organizations acquire, manage, and use customer information to develop effective customer-focused, integrated marketing programs. Like the best practices study discussed earlier in this chapter, this study from the spring of 2000 was conducted by APQC in cooperation with the Advertising Research Foundation (ARF).[7] The study used the same benchmarking methodology as the best practices study.

The new research was prompted by the first APQC study of best practices, in particular by one of the key organizational differences identified among best practice partners and sponsor firms. As noted in Exhibit 2.3, 70 percent of partner companies agreed with the statement that "customer data is used at the highest levels of the organization to drive strategic direction," compared with only 47 percent of sponsor firms. This difference prompted researchers to take a closer look at how best practice organizations go about gathering and integrating relevant, diverse customer data and how they apply it to guide decision making. The companies participating as best practice partners for the study were BellSouth, Dow Chemical, Eastman Chemical, FedEx, Marriott Hotels, Prudential Insurance, USAA, and US West. (Dow Chemical, FedEx, and USAA had participated in the first IMC study in 1997. They were invited to participate in the new study on leveraging customer information because they had represented the highest levels of achievement in applying customer information to IMC Stages 3 and 4 in the earlier effort.) Sponsoring organizations included British Telecom, Compaq Computer, Fidelity Investments, GTE Services, Intel Corporation, Joseph E. Seagrams, Lifeway Christian Resources, Miller Brewing, Pillsbury Company, and Southern Company. The primary aim of the study was to focus on activities and practices at Stages 3 and 4 of the IMC development process to discover how data was being leveraged to enable strategic decision making.

Exhibit 2.4 illustrates the general model used in the study. As shown, it consisted of three parts: (a) sources of customer data, (b) the database(s) in which the information was stored, and (c) application of the data to operational and strategic decision making.

Exhibit 2.4 Model for Leveraging Customer Data

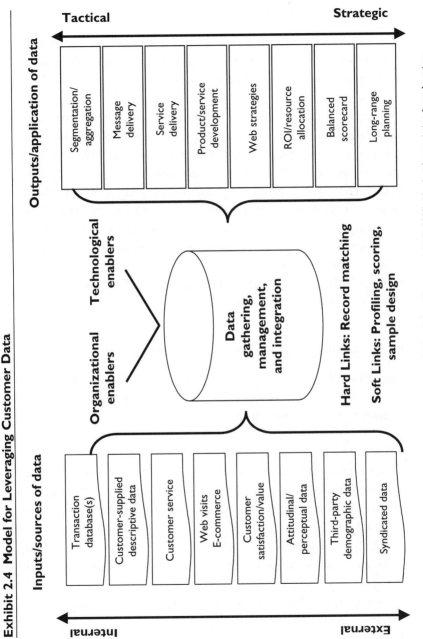

From "Leveraging Customer Information," American Productivity and Quality Center (Houston: APQC, 2000). Used with permission from American Productivity and Quality Center.

Sources of Customer Data

The sources of customer data captured by the participating firms proved to be widespread and varied, including demographic, transactional, attitudinal, and customer satisfaction, as well as syndicated data. As important as the data captured, however, was the company's perception of the value of that data. The study revealed that partners put a great deal more reliance on customer data and used it much more than did sponsor firms. Yet only half of partner firms and fewer sponsors said data was readily available for those who needed it. Recall, accessibility, and use of customer data by participating firms was also an issue confronting many of the firms participating in the study. From this, it appeared that organizations that did not feel data was sufficiently available to those who needed it faced both organizational and technological barriers. For instance, in some cases data may be "hoarded" by a particular business unit, or in others it may be difficult or time-prohibitive to access for technical reasons.

Data Gathering, Management, and Integration

Since this portion of the study dealt primarily with technology issues of how the data was handled, we summarize only a few points that are relevant to the development of an IMC program.

- Data integration needs organizational enablers—that is, steps the organization can take to facilitate the gathering, management, and integration of data—as well as technological enablers—that is, hardware, software, and systems that facilitate the combination of disparate data sets. Interestingly, best practice firms rely much more heavily on people and culture to understand customer data and gain insights than do sponsor firms, which tend to rely more on technological enablers of data integration to provide solutions. This is the same problem that seems to plague customer relationship management (CRM) initiatives around the world.
- Organizations used what are called "hard" and "soft" data links. Hard links primarily focus on data or record matching, while soft links

include profiling, scoring, sample design, and other methods to make inferences about large groups of customers.

- Less than half of the study firms were able to integrate their customer data to their satisfaction. Even among the best practice companies, half or less were able to link demographic data to basic customer identification or link demographic and behavioral data or customer satisfaction data to attitudinal data.

Application of Customer Data

The third part of the study dealt with the uses of customer data to which the organization had access. The statements in Table 2.2 show how participating organizations used the data they had available by referring to applications ranging from the tactical tools used by marketing and communication managers to the more strategic tools used primarily by senior management.

Four data uses appeared to be key:

- To reach customers more effectively
- To become a learning organization, that is, to continuously improve contacts and relationships with customers and prospects
- To support the operations area of the firm, that is, to provide valuable information and background to managers in all areas
- To improve the allocation of finite resources against customers who are perceived to be the most valuable to the organization

Table 2.5 lists the perceptions of partner and sponsor firms in terms of their self-assessment regarding how they apply customer data in their organizations. The evolution of IMC since the first study and the increasingly sophisticated use of customer data is apparent in this chart. Whereas in the first study only a limited number of leading best practice organizations reported that customer data were widely used across all operational areas within their organizations, such application had become the norm in best practice firms by 2000. Additionally, a significant percentage of best practice companies reported that the use of cus-

Table 2.5 Self-Assessment on Application of Integrated Customer Data to Decision Making

	Partners (n = 8)	Sponsors (n = 10)
We have a strategic initiative to further integrate customer data.	100%	80%
Customer data is used by nonmarketing areas to guide planning and improve operational performance.	100%	50%
Application of customer information has helped improve customer retention/loyalty.	100%	40%
Use of information provides a competitive advantage.	88%	40%
We have used data to maximize resource allocation.	75%	60%
We have trained staff to use customer data effectively.	63%	30%

From "Leveraging Customer Information," American Productivity and Quality Center (Houston: APQC, 2000). Used with permission from American Productivity and Quality Center.

tomer information had helped them gain a competitive advantage and maximize the allocation of their resources.

Additional findings from the study are discussed in Chapter 4, which addresses step 1 of the IMC process.

Moving On

In this chapter, we have presented a model of how IMC has typically evolved within the organizations that began adopting it in the early and mid-1990s. We have shown how the view of advertising agencies has, at least at times, differed from that of marketing organizations. And finally, we have revisited some of the leading practitioners in IMC to see how they have incorporated advanced approaches to customer data and data integration into their IMC programs. With this review of what we already know about the development of IMC skills and practices, we are now ready to move to the implementation of a strategic, value-oriented IMC approach to marketing.

CHAPTER 3

GUIDING PRINCIPLES OF VALUE-BASED IMC

As demonstrated by the best practice benchmarking study discussed in Chapter 2, most firms typically go through four stages of evolution on their way to reaching a totally integrated marcom program. The process places new demands on both the organization and marcom managers. In later chapters, we explore how exemplary firms have successfully made the transition from one stage to the next. This chapter lays the groundwork for the integration process by identifying and illustrating the basic elements that must be developed before the firm can proceed beyond the rudimentary stage of coordinating the traditional functional elements of marketing communication.

Before we begin, let's look again at where we are going. In the previous chapter, IMC was defined as "a strategic business process used to plan, develop, execute, and evaluate coordinated, measurable, persuasive brand communication programs over time with consumers, customers, prospects, and other targeted, relevant external and internal audiences." This definition has four key elements. First, it clearly elevates marcom from its traditional role as a tactical activity to a strategic management tool in which finite corporate resources can be invested and returns calculated. In short, IMC is promoted from marketing tactic to business strategy.

Second, this definition expands the scope of marketing communication. Rather than being confined to communication specialists who develop primarily external communication to targeted customers, consumers, and prospects, the new IMC involves the whole organization. It spans the entire spectrum of brand, customer, product, and service contacts the firm has with all stakeholders at all levels.

Third, as defined here, IMC requires ongoing measurement and evaluation. Stewardship and evidence of return on the IMC investment are integral to the process and must be built into all communication plans.

Fourth, the fact that IMC achieves desired results "over time" separates it from traditional communication programs. Unlike the "campaign" approach that represented communication efforts in the past, IMC is an ongoing process that boosts performance in the long term as well as the short term. While individual promotion activities or events may have an immediate impact, IMC requires evaluating these activities not only as separate events but as part of an overall and ongoing program that continues to contribute to results—and to build long-term relationships with customers—over time.

The best possible way to understand any new concept is to see it at work. An excellent example of the new IMC in practice is Intel Corporation's "Intel Inside" program. As you read Intel's success story, consider how effectively the company put the key elements of IMC in place to achieve a sophisticated level of integration over time.

IMC at Work: Intel Inside

The Intel Inside program was not conceived as an IMC initiative. Rather, it was developed as the solution to a major competitive challenge Intel Corporation faced during a critical time in its organizational history. In the 1980s, the company identified its products by assigning each a number; the number 286 indicated a certain level of technology, 386 a higher level, and 486 something higher still. As the silicon chip business became increasingly competitive, Intel's numbers were adopted by other manufacturers to signal the technological capability of their products. Competitors began to identify their chips as "386-type." Intel tried to protect its numbers from competitive infringement by attempting, in effect, to trademark them as brands. However, the federal courts objected, and the numbers Intel had devised essentially became the de facto names of certain levels of technological development in silicon chips.

Intel needed a way to both differentiate its offering and protect its investments in research and development (R&D) and its intellectual property. The company created the Intel Inside logo to signify that the chips inside various brands of computers were manufactured by Intel. As the firm developed more advanced technologies, such as Pentium and Celeron, those products also carried the logo. Intel's success was phenomenal. For instance, in 1991—immediately preceding Intel Inside—the company's market capitalization stood at about $10 billion. By 2001, Intel's market cap had grown to $260 billion.[1] If even a tenth of the increase in market value can fairly be attributed to Intel Inside, the net result of the marketing, communication, and branding program accounts for more than $25 billion over a ten-year period. By 2002, *Business Week*'s annual "Top 100 Global Brands"—a survey conducted by Interbrand using a proprietary valuation method—pegged Intel's brand value at $30.6 billion, making it the world's fifth most valuable brand, topped only by Coca-Cola ($69.6 billion), Microsoft ($64 billion), IBM ($51.2 billion), and General Electric ($41.3 billion).[2]

While it began as a way to differentiate products from competing brands, Intel Inside involved far more than the creation of a logo. What did Intel do to build not only market value but consumer value as well? How did Intel go from being a rather late entry in the silicon chip business to the icon of the industry? More important, how did Intel build marketplace value for a product that most end users had never seen and could not easily compare with competitors, whose purpose they did not understand, and whose value was virtually impossible to measure? Silicon chips, after all, are only one component of a computer. But Intel Inside succeeded in giving that component a manufacturer, channel, and consumer cachet that rocketed the company to the top of the computer chip industry. In essence, Intel Inside came to signify the development of a brand and brand value in the technology industry while at the same time becoming a household name.

At the first level of integration (see Exhibit 3.1), Intel pulled all the right levers and pushed all the right buttons. The company took a simple concept, the Intel Inside brand, and through brilliant creative and graphic design, created an image and identity that had real marketplace appeal. In an arena where many computer purchasers felt uncomfortable making product choices, Intel provided simplicity and assurance, giving customers and consumers all they wanted and needed when making a major purchase investment.

The critical ingredient was the integration of Intel's marketing and communication activities. The Intel Inside logo was used throughout all marketing and communication activities and provided the basis for the entire program. Every piece of advertising, direct marketing, pack-

Exhibit 3.1 Early "Intel Inside" Ad

aging, public relations, and internal and external communication was developed to have the same look and feel and shared the same strong graphic elements. Everyone—consumers, manufacturers, channels, the financial community, shareholders, and employees—was exposed to the new look. In short, Intel Inside was totally integrated at the tactical level—a perfect example of the "one sight, one sound" concept. Exhibit 3.1 shows an early Intel Inside ad. A comparison with ads that you will find in many magazines today shows how consistently Intel has used the same tactic over time.

The success of Intel Inside, however, went far beyond achieving "one sight, one sound, one concept." It's real value came from the way the program was able to span several traditional sales and marketing boundaries. It "pushed" the product concept into the marketplace and at the same time "pulled" it through manufacturers and channels. Key to achieving this was the substantial incentive package Intel gave computer companies such as Dell, IBM, Toshiba, and Gateway to include the Intel chip in their products. Intel encouraged every manufacturer using its chip to identify that use with an Intel Inside sticker on the computer's outer housing. Through various co-op advertising agreements, Intel was able to provide incentives for manufacturers to advertise Intel processors as an integral part of their products.

Aggressive incentives did not stop at co-op advertising but continued through distribution channels. Intel offered geographic marketing development funds, in-store displays, and similar programs to encourage retailers and distributors to display, promote, and sell the value of Intel Inside, regardless of computer manufacturer. Intel's goal was to make the manufacturer/channel combination as seamless as possible.

Finally, Intel invested substantial amounts in consumer marketing and communication programs to convince consumers and end users that they need only look for the Intel Inside logo to assure themselves they were getting the most advanced, most dependable chip technology and, by implication, the best computer available. This end-user program was particularly important since many buyers, particularly first-time purchasers, didn't understand the technology involved and had difficulty evaluating specific chip innovations in terms of price value. However, if the prospective buyer knew there was an Intel chip inside, many of their questions were resolved or their fears diminished.

Through a single, integrated approach, Intel was able to push its product to and through computer manufacturers, into the distribution channels, and then on to the final purchaser. Exhibit 3.2 demonstrates how the program progressed. Intel Inside started inside the organization with an internally integrated team of sales, marketing, and production groups. It then integrated and aligned all the various external Intel partners such as the computer manufacturers, the channels and distribution systems, and those involved in external communication programs as well. All were focused on influencing the end user of the product to make a final purchasing decision.

It is important to note that Intel, like other successful IMC initiators, recognized that integration must first take place *inside* the organization. Here, that meant bringing engineering, production, operations, logistics, finance, and so on together and getting them focused on the one key element they had to support—the Intel Inside brand and communication program. This required training and development and, most of all, ongoing senior management commitment to the concept and its execution.

Next, Intel had to align its immediate customers, primarily computer manufacturers, behind the program. Then came channel partners, such

Exhibit 3.2 External and Internal Alignment System

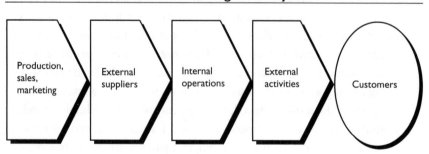

**Integrating the system,
not the pieces and parts**

as computer retailers, distributors, value-added retailers, catalog sellers, and all the forms and methods by which a consumer or customer or prospect could obtain a computer with an Intel processor. Finally, Intel focused on external communication programs, including advertising, promotion, point-of-purchase, public relations, trade dress, packaging, and all other communication channels through which Intel Inside reached the ultimate consumer.

It is important to remember that while consumers were the last to be exposed to the program, they were the most critical group. After all, if Intel couldn't convince people to dig down in their pockets to buy a computer with Intel Inside, then the entire program would fail. Intel Inside worked because at all stages it was focused on the ultimate consumer; it was a totally integrated program that brought all the participants in the value chain together to deliver value to that final purchaser.

It is clear from the Intel Inside example that IMC is far more than a marketing or communication tactic or technique. It is a process or system that encompasses the activities not only of the firm but of all its internal and external contacts. Unlike other marcom efforts, IMC is clearly strategic in nature, oriented around the firm as a whole rather than around marketing activities.

How well did Intel Inside measure up to the four-part definition of IMC? First, Intel certainly viewed its program as a strategic issue rather than the domain of marketing alone. Second, the program involved all parts of the organization, including external partners and channel members. The same concept was delivered across all markets, segments, customers, and prospects. Third, the program was developed, executed, and measured against objectives. Finally, Intel Inside has been a long-term and ongoing commitment.

Eight Guiding Principles of IMC

Case examples like Intel Inside help identify certain elements that underlie a strategic, value-oriented IMC approach. Here, we will examine eight guiding principles of IMC that are key to developing and executing an integrated program. The principles evolved from practitioner examples as well as from solid theory and comprehensive research into media and channel organizations and consumer product companies. The principles are global, crossing national and cultural boundaries. They represent the core concepts an organization must embrace and practice—both internally and externally—in order to succeed in the customer-focused, interactive global marketplace of the twenty-first century.

Guiding Principle 1: Become a Customer-Centric Organization

The ultimate end user, customer, or consumer must be at the center of any type of integration. In the increasingly complex global marketplace, the term *customer focus* has taken on many meanings. For the purposes of IMC, a customer-focused (or customer-centric) organization is simply one that considers the ultimate purchaser or consumer of the product first, foremost, and always. Although important, wholesalers, retailers, and other intermediaries are not as critical to a customer-centric organization as those who eventually buy or use the product. The intermediaries are simply that—middlemen in a value chain—and while they have a role to play, it is secondary to that of the ultimate customer.

Over the years, several organizational concepts have drifted in and out of popularity. Some focus on building shareholder equity in the form of dividends and increased share prices, while others favor building the organization for the benefit of employees or the community at large.

Our view is simple but clear: the organization must focus on its end-user customers and consumers. Those are the only people or groups that can provide income to the firm. Customer-generated income flows enable the company to provide employee benefits; reward shareholders for their investment and risk; and provide society with the benefits a well-run, socially responsible organization can generate. Unless the firm is financially successful, it cannot reward employees, shareholders, management, or society. Therefore, the approach in this book is unambiguous: the company must focus on its ultimate customers, for they are the only ones who provide the resources and therefore the rewards for everyone involved.

Most organizations are structured on a hierarchical basis, a "command-and-control" approach that can be traced back to the Roman legions. Within the hierarchy, managers focus on activities, elements, or units that perform certain activities and over which they can exert some direction and control. Each of these separate fiefdoms or silos is focused on what it does best but not necessarily on the customers the organization ultimately serves. Further, between each silo there is little cross-functional interaction that helps align the various elements to benefit customers. The firm is, in essence, inwardly focused. Employees are taught that success is based on the efficient completion of various activities or tasks, not whether customers are happy or satisfied.

Unsuited to siloed organizations, IMC thrives in organizations that revolve around the customer. Exhibit 3.3 clearly illustrates the difference. In a customer-centric organization, the customer is at the center. All functional activities, elements, and units are directed toward and focused on providing customer benefits, filling customer needs, or satisfying customer requests. The key goal of the firm is to serve and satisfy the customer and build loyalty and ongoing flows of income from those customers.

Because of their common focus, members of a customer-centric organization work together to provide the best customer products, services, and solutions. For example, to provide total customer satisfaction, there is a clear need for manufacturing to talk with logistics and distribution. Similarly, there is a natural reason for accounting to interact with marketing and so on. Thus, once the firm adopts the concept of becoming customer centric, there is suddenly a need for total integration of the various functional groups within the firm. Integration at all levels becomes the norm rather than the exception.

Perhaps there is no better example of a customer-centric company than Dell. From consumers to large businesses, Dell's business model and culture is completely driven by the needs of its customers. For instance, the firm uses its Premier Dell.com service to customize products and services for large corporate clients. A client can log on to a

Exhibit 3.3 Traditional vs. Customer-Centric Integrated Organizations

Traditional organization

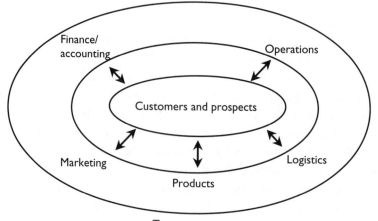

Integrated organization

custom-created Premier site and shop for desktops, notebooks, servers, storage, and related services. The client company can view its contracted prices for Dell products, see a list of company-approved components and accessories, review past purchases, and find contact information for Dell service representatives. By allowing end users to view pertinent information about their company's contracts with Dell, Dell establishes one-to-one relationships with the people who use its products and services firsthand.[3] After purchasing a Dell computer online, Dell customers receive immediate confirmation of their order and delivery date. Additionally, if a customer has questions or experiences problems, help is only a phone call or an E-mail away. As follow-up, Dell sends an E-mail to the customer to assess satisfaction. The organization has successfully set up a multichannel customer service feedback system that differentiates it from many other computer marketers.

Guiding Principle 2: Use Outside-In Planning

Achieving a customer-focused system is generally impossible unless and until the organization fundamentally changes its marketing planning approach. This is because customer focus means more than servicing existing customers; it means that the company has succeeded in structuring its business systems—from budgeting and planning to operations to delivery to performance evaluation—around its customers and prospects. This is often a radical change for many enterprises.

The most common method of planning and budgeting for marketing is shown on the left-hand side of Exhibit 3.4. We call this the inside-out planning approach. It starts with what the organization wants to achieve and then forces various activities into a series of steps that will hopefully produce the desired results. Planned volume or financial goals drive the marketing and communication investment or spending levels. If anticipated goals are achieved, the firm is then willing to use a portion of sales to buy further marketing and communication activities.

Clearly, in the inside-out approach there is no recognized connection between marketing spending and expected sales results. In fact, just the opposite is true—sales success creates marketing funds. This is a most illogical approach but one that is widely practiced in all types of

Exhibit 3.4 Inside-Out Planning vs. Outside-In Planning

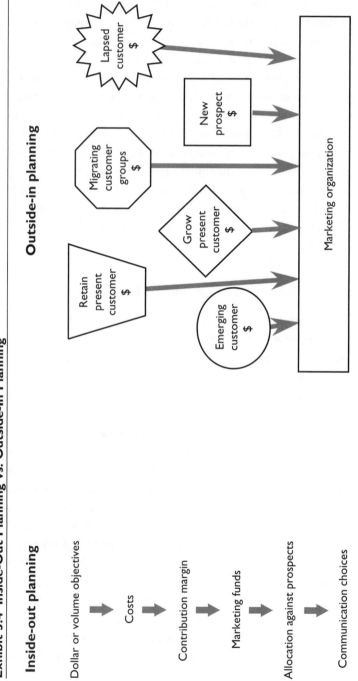

Outside-in planning

Lapsed customer $

New prospect $

Migrating customer groups $

Grow present customer $

Retain present customer $

Emerging customer $

Marketing organization

Inside-out planning

Dollar or volume objectives

Costs

Contribution margin

Marketing funds

Allocation against prospects

Communication choices

organizations. Since there is no assumed relationship between marketing and sales, management has little expectation of any measurable financial return on its marketing and communication investments. In fact, the management view is generally "If the marketing expenditure can be reduced, so much the better for the bottom-line results of the company. Funds not spent are funds retained, and funds retained can be taken to the bottom line."

While this approach is filled with flawed assumptions, it is the methodology most companies around the world use to develop, implement, and fund marketing and marcom programs. The IMC alternative is to flip the inside-out model to create the outside-in approach illustrated on the right side of Exhibit 3.4. Here, the marketing or communication manager views customers and prospects not as units of expense but as income flows to the firm. The goal is to manage the creation of demand and income flows rather than products and costs.

In the IMC approach, the key marcom task is to generate and retain customer and prospect income flows using various marcom tools, programs, and activities. While here we discuss the management of income flows as the primary task of marketing and communication people, in truth, it is the responsibility of the entire firm, all employees, all functional groups, all elements to develop, cultivate, and maintain those customer income flows over time.

Guiding Principle 3: Focus on the Total Customer Experience

Closely linked to the customer-centric requirement is the understanding that a strategic IMC approach is focused on the customer's total experience with the product and the firm, not just on marcom activities. The IMC manager's goals must move from a limited view of externally delivered, traditional marcom activities to the total relationship the customer has with the brand and firm. *Total customer experience* encompasses how the product or service performs in the marketplace, how it is obtained, the capability of channel members to provide products in a timely and efficient manner, how customer service is delivered, and what type of social impact the firm makes in the community it inhabits.

The goal of a strategic approach to IMC is to look at the customer experience holistically—that is, to determine all of the drivers that positively (or negatively) affect the experience as the customer perceives it—and then to manage accordingly. Thus, an organization must determine the following:

- Who its customers are from behavioral or other data
- What experiences they have had with the company
- What offers the company can or should make in its marketing and communication programs that will deliver the desired experiences
- How products, services, and people will be configured to deliver that experience

At this point, the traditional marcom manager is apt to say, "Those aren't my responsibilities. They belong to manufacturing or sales or channel partners or corporate management." Such an argument has little value in today's interconnected, interrelated, networked, and increasingly global marketplace. The company is the brand and the brand is the company. Anything and everything that sends a message, provides an experience, or relates to the product or service is something that must be considered, managed, and measured.

The formal marketing and communication programs the company develops and delivers to customers and prospects are only a tiny sliver of the overall and ongoing communication the customer has with the brand and the company. The firm is continuously communicating with its customers and prospects in myriad ways, both planned and unplanned. The real challenge of marketing and communication management is to integrate the total communication system, not just the pieces and parts of the controlled communication the firm develops and delivers.

Put quite simply, the customer will eventually integrate the organization's communication whether the company does or not. The purpose of IMC is to lighten the load on the customer and make sure the impressions delivered are advantageous for the company.

Since brand and company integration will occur, whether planned or unplanned, it simply makes sense for an organization to practice total integration as much as possible. The only question is whether the integrated view of the firm and its products is the one the company wants the customer to have or something that can and will be detrimental to any ongoing relationship.

Strategic integration reaches far beyond traditional marketing and communication roles or activities. It is about customers and their beliefs, feelings, and experiences with the firm. That comes from all the ways the firm and the brand touch customers and prospects.

Guiding Principle 4: Align Consumer Goals with Corporate Objectives

It often appears to external consultants that marketing and communication groups live in their own world and are oblivious to the direction of the firm whose products and services they are trying to promote. The edgy and often unrelated creative executions used by the dot-com firms in the late 1990s provide evidence of that problem. Creative? Perhaps, yes. Effective marketing communication? Probably not. It is a rare company that can be creative and still remain grounded in effective business strategies.

The difficulty is in aligning the organization's goals with those of customers and then supporting those goals with the appropriate marketing and communication programs. The realities of conducting an ongoing business in a highly competitive global environment make it difficult for management to achieve balance between what the customer wants and what the firm is able to provide. It is quite possible for an organization to market itself into bankruptcy if the proper level of customer wants and needs and corresponding company goals and objectives is not selected and maintained. Achieving such a balance in the rapidly changing business environment means aligning marketing and communication goals more closely with those of the organization as a whole.

In most organizations, corporate direction comes from top management. This means that to fall in line with that direction, marketing must be privy to it. Only when marketing is fully aligned with corporate direction can relevant IMC programs be developed. The changing marketplace also leads to changes in corporate objectives. Today's business climate, for instance, prioritizes the generation of short-term cash flows above the attempt to build or acquire longer-term shareholder values. The trend toward building shareholder value primarily by increasing the market capitalization of the firm is another example. Given these two corporate objectives, there are only three strategic levers available to top management seeking to achieve them:

- Invest in or enhance products or services, that is, R&D initiatives.
- Invest in the supply chain, that is, efficient customer response (ECR) and enterprise resource planning (ERP) initiatives.
- Invest in customer relationships, that is, communication, customer relationship management (CRM), and other brand-building initiatives.

These three levers are key tools to drive the firm. In the past, R&D alone fueled growth as new and innovative products were rapidly brought to market. Today, technological advances that allow competitors to duplicate and improve innovations quickly reduce the power of the R&D lever. A singular focus on innovation is a risky way to drive overall company growth.

Faster, more efficient supply chains drive growth by taking the friction out of getting products through plants and distribution systems and into the hands of consumers. Today's organizations make substantial corporate investments in initiatives designed to assist the firm in becoming more efficient in the development, delivery, and logistics and distribution of its products and services. Such initiatives include ECR, sales force allocation models, and shortened value chains.

The third management lever is to improve or enhance the firm's customer understanding and customer relationships. In other words, firms seek to become more effective at marketing and communication to attract and retain more and more profitable customers over time.

Looking at these three levers, we can clearly see that marketing communication has a significant part to play in achieving overall corporate objectives. In the past, marketing and communication in many organizations were relegated to tactical support activities and were not considered strategic initiatives. The advent of new technologies that allow for the capture, storage, and analysis of massive amounts of customer data, making customer-focused initiatives possible and practical, carve out a new strategic role for marketing and communication as well.

If they are to be strategic, however, marketing and communication must prove their worth in terms of demonstrable returns to the organization. This is where the IMC approach succeeds and traditional marketing initiatives—even the much-touted CRM—fail. By providing demonstrable returns, we mean that IMC must go much further than traditional communication goals such as building brand awareness or recognition. It must achieve management's financial goals, too. For example, if senior management is to invest in marketing and communication, the objectives of those programs must deliver specific, measurable financial results, such as top-line growth, bottom-line growth, increased market share, increased revenue per customer, and so on. The IMC objectives, which are completely aligned with corporate goals, must do one of the following:

- Generate short- and long-term cash-flow increases greater than the cost of the marketing and communication program used to achieve them.
- Accelerate cash flows—that is, move the flow of income from customers and prospects forward in time, or increase the speed with which those cash flows are acquired.
- Stabilize ongoing cash flows. In many organizations, cash flows come in peaks and valleys, high one month and low the next. The capacity of marketing and communication to flatten those cash flows or smooth them out reduces the operational cost for the company.
- Build shareholder value by increasing the equity of the firm or the brand. Strong brand equity is recognized by the financial market and commonly increases the share price of the firm, both of which will provide value for the shareholder.[4]

In industry after industry and category after category around the globe, we have observed marketing communication programs that were unrelated to one or any of the four corporate objectives listed here. Marcom managers invest financial resources of the firm to build or buy communication programs. Therefore, it is vital that the returns achieved be identified in terms of the financial outcomes they have generated or can/will generate. This is a theme we will return to again and again throughout this book.

Guiding Principle 5: Set Customer Behavior Objectives

For all the seeming complexity of marketing and communication plans, firms want only four outcomes from them:

- **To acquire new customers**. This is a fairly straightforward marketing goal and has traditionally been the primary focus of many communication efforts.
- **To retain and maintain present customers**. One of the goals of managing present customers is (at least) to maintain them at their current level of activity and income flow. In some categories, customers are limited by the number of times they can buy a product during a given period. For example, an automobile owner generally renews collision coverage once a year, just as magazine readers will generally only need to buy one subscription each year, at least for their own use. Thus, the primary task in these situations is to ensure the retention of the customer's current business before attempting to add on additional products or services.
- **To retain and grow sales volume or profit from existing customers**. Generally, this involves getting present customers to buy more, use more, or find different uses for the products or services they are purchasing now, any of which means a growth in volume or value for the firm. The challenge here is to stimulate demand for the product or service among those people who already use it.
- **To migrate existing customers through the firm's product or service portfolio**. In this instance, the goal is to get a present customer to purchase alternative, higher priced or higher margin products or services in the firm's line. Business hotels promote the

benefits of their higher priced executive floors with concierge services, while automobile manufacturers attempt to get car buyers to upgrade to a more elaborately equipped model.

Critical to all four activities is that marketing communication must affect customer or prospect behavior. It must reinforce present behavior, assuming it is currently profitable for the organization, or it must change the behavior to encourage trial or increased usage. The key ingredient in the IMC process is influencing behaviors, because it is behaviors that provide income flows to the firm from customers and prospects. Thus, with this approach, we have already set up a generalized system of measurement by understanding two key characteristics of IMC. First, IMC is designed to influence the behaviors of customers and/or prospects. Second, those behaviors can be measured and valued in financial terms. The goal of IMC—to influence a measurable change in the behavior of customers and prospects—gives a good checkpoint against which to evaluate potential IMC programs and alternatives. We will keep coming back to this idea of behavioral influence or change as we work through the IMC process.

Guiding Principle 6: Treat Customers as Assets

Closely related to the financial issues described in principles 4 and 5 is the concept that the firm must begin to consider customers its true assets. The customer, in most instances, is the primary unit that generates income flows for the organization. Almost all of the other activities and initiatives of the organization are really cost centers. So, a key ingredient of the value-oriented IMC system is the understanding that marketing and communication managers are asset managers. That is, they are or should be responsible for the initiation, continuation, and maintenance of customers, the source of the firm's income flow.

Once the firm starts to consider customers as flows of income, it can then take the next logical step, that is, treating customers as assets. That means making investments in customers and prospects and then expecting or anticipating returns on those investments. This allows the IMC manager to move to the next step also—the viewpoint that investments in advertising, direct marketing, or public relations are not really promotional purchases at all. Instead, they are investments in the customers and prospects who receive and might react to them. For example, effective marcom managers do not purchase television advertising time with the expectation that any return will come from that activity. Instead, they recognize that the investment is made in customers who may see or hear the television commercial and either increase or continue the flows of income to the organization.

Exhibit 3.5 illustrates this idea of a closed-loop system. Investments are made in customers through various types of marketing and communication programs that generate measurable response in the form of continuing or increased income flows back to the organization. To close the loop in treating customers as assets, the IMC manager must find some way to measure the value of a customer or customer group. In the strategic IMC approach, financial value is used. We first identify the historical financial value of a customer group (box on left). Once the financial value is known, the manager can then make reasonable finan-

Exhibit 3.5 IMC as a Closed-Loop System

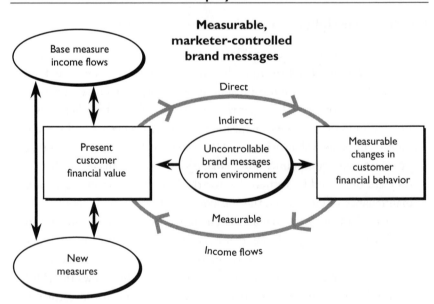

cial decisions about how much to invest in that customer group to maintain, grow, or migrate its members through the firm's product or service portfolio. Thus, if the initial value of the customer group is known, an investment of a certain amount is made against those customers. Finally, a postcommunication measurement can be made to determine the change in income flow that resulted from that investment, allowing the firm to close the loop on its marketing and communication investments. This closure step is critical in the process because it allows the IMC manager to practically and effectively meet various corporate financial objectives and tie the marcom investments to returns on those programs.

With IMC as a closed-loop system, the marcom manager can finally resolve the age-old problem "I know half my advertising investment is wasted but I don't know which half."[5] Better still, the manager can say with some assurance that with proper planning and measurement, over time he or she can effectively identify which half is wasteful and take steps to address the problem.

Inherent in the closed-loop system is the demand for incremental returns to the firm. No rational organization invests resources in an attempt to lose money, and to succeed, the firm must get back a greater return from its marcom programs than it invests. Unless there is an incremental return on the marketing and communication investment, the best the firm can hope to do is to break even—certainly not a very attractive goal in today's highly competitive marketplace. To simplify, the firm must increase returns at costs lower than the generated returns. If the firm can add $100 in new sales through a $10 investment in marketing, and if its cost of goods and overhead amount to only $50, the firm generates $40 in profit for the $10 invested. In short, it has gotten back more than it invested or has generated incremental returns.

In too many situations, marketing and communication managers have been divorced from the company's financial planning or have not attempted to relate their activities to the financial health of the firm. They have spent money and other resources as allocated by management rather than arguing for investments with which they can generate returns. If the marcom manager is to move up to the strategic level of customer investments and returns and take on the management of income flows from customers and prospects, then this incremental return approach becomes a major tool in developing and managing the IMC process.

Guiding Principle 7: Streamline Functional Activities

One of the major challenges of achieving organizational integration is sorting through the tangle of functional structures and activities through which marketing and communication have developed. Over the years, in an attempt to enhance their status, marketing and communication managers created more and more artificial distinctions between their areas of functional expertise. As we saw in Chapter 1, under the outmoded Four Ps concept, promotion was split into the three separate functions of sales, advertising, and publicity.[6] As new promotional activities became available, the managers in charge of them tried to split them off as separate entities, too. Examples include sales promotion in the 1970s; direct marketing and database marketing in the 1980s; and sponsorships, events marketing, electronic marketing, and stealth marketing in the 1990s. Today, some firms separate out electronic communication from other promotional activities, commonly with little success. In our view, too many silos within the marketing function muddy the entire marketing effort, bringing with them unnecessary battles for turf and budget. In most cases, the artificial distinctions focus on the development of delivery systems—that is delivery of the message through ads, public relations, database marketing, and so on—and not on basic improvements or enhancements of the overall marketing and communication strategy.

Thus, the major barriers to integration in most organizations have little to do with external customers at all. In too many firms, managers undermine any integration efforts by trying to separate out their functions into distinct budget or head-count centers. In many cases, managers simply don't want to give up their areas of responsibility or expertise for the greater good of either the company or the customer.

Contrast this with the perspective of the consumer. We have found that customers do not think of or describe the marketing and communication activities of the firm in the same terms that internal managers use. They simplify and aggregate. When asked about marketing communication, customers commonly say that the company is generally trying to do two things. First, it is sending out messages that it hopes the customer will remember and use when he or she next goes to purchase products or services in that area. Second, the company is sending out incentives, that is, offering some type of reward for doing something or following some type of behavior such as buying now rather than later, buying when an item is on sale, or going to the store to sample a new product. In other words, from the customer's view, the company is really dealing with only two basic marketing and communication activities: messages and incentives.

Mirroring the customer's perspective, value-based IMC rolls up all the various functional elements that marketing and communication managers have created over the years and consolidates them into these two groups:

- **Messages:** the brand concepts, ideas, associations, values, and other perceptions the firm wants customers and prospects to store away in memory
- **Incentives:** short-term offers or rewards for doing something the firm believes will be of value to both itself and the consumer or customer

This idea of focusing on messages or incentives can do much to assist the marcom manager in developing programs; it simplifies the planning and development. For example, a manager who wants to deliver a message on behalf of certain products or services using traditional disciplines can consider advertising, sales promotion, public relations, sponsorships, or any of a host of other marcom delivery methods. The same is true for incentives. An incentive can be offered in the form of a cents-off coupon (sales promotion), an advertisement that tells about a short-term offer being made in a retailer's shop (advertising), a press release with a toll-free number from which to obtain a sample of the product (public relations), or even a reduced-price ticket to a stock car race where the product might be sampled (sponsorship and/or an event). In short, by collapsing and streamlining the range of alternative communication to only messages and incentives, a much wider range of communication choices is generated.

Perhaps the greatest value of this collapse of marcom disciplines is that it forces the manager to think strategically rather than in terms of communication tactics. This is not to say tactical elements are not important. They are, but they cannot and should not drive the marketing communication effort and they have little relation to the way marketing communication is measured and evaluated.

Guiding Principle 8: Converge Marcom Activities

At the heart of any marketing and communication program, there must be convergence. Until the mid-1990s, convergence was generally considered to involve the bringing together of all communication activities under a single umbrella. Today, convergence has taken on a new meaning: the blending of traditional marcom with electronic marketing and communication activities.

As E-commerce and E-communication developed, many marketers treated them as separate and distinct marketing and communication elements. That is, they separated out website development, E-commerce, E-mail, electronic consumer research, and other capabilities into separate and unique units within the organization. In the early days, this separation may well have made sense. People working in technology-driven communication forms were generally different from those working in the more traditional areas of advertising, sales promotion, and so on. Perhaps it was important to think about, create, plan, and develop interactive marketing and communication programs separately and differently from those in traditional channels. But while this separation might still make sense within organizations, it makes no sense at all from the customer's point of view. Customers who see the brand's television commercials are, for the most part, the same ones who are accessing websites and shopping online. In other words, there is now and will continue to be convergence between the traditional and electronic forms of marketing and communication. This melding of "clicks and bricks," or the combination of location-specific physical retail and the virtual space of electronic commerce, affects virtually every organization.

With convergence must come integration. Convergence will occur, and it will come quicker than we plan or expect. That is why integration is not simply a nice idea or a money-saving approach. It is critical for every organization that hopes to become or remain viable in the twenty-first-century marketplace.

Compensation

Our review of the eight guiding principles of IMC skips one key element that makes this method valuable: compensation or the manner in which employees, managers, channel partners, and others are rewarded for their efforts and activities. Compensation is omitted for a simple reason: at present, marcom managers have little control over the compensation policies of their firms. Yet compensation is a key driver in how well the firm can integrate, how well it can become customer focused, how well it can develop and deliver on customer wants and needs, and so on. People do what they are rewarded to do. Thus, if a company's reward system is not consistent with its integrated approach, no integration will occur, no matter how much planning, effort, or enthusiasm is generated for the concept.

The primary problem at this point is that people are typically rewarded for accomplishing tasks, not for serving or satisfying customers. It is the product or internal focus that creates much of the difficulty. If customer service people are rewarded on the basis of how many calls they can handle in a one-hour period, then customer needs and requirements are placed on the second or even lower rung of the agent's priorities. If the sales force is compensated for moving a certain volume of products or units in a specific time period, then that takes precedence over learning what customers really want or need. The reward is for getting rid of product, not for serving customers. If the marketing manager is rewarded for making cost-efficient media buys, then concerns about how effective those media choices were in reaching the right audience at the right time, are pushed to a lower level of priority. If an agency is rewarded for winning awards for creativity rather than influencing behavior and thereby building customer income flows, then it is not serving the best interests of the client company. To avoid situations like these, compensation throughout the entire organization must move toward a new emphasis on gaining, retaining, growing, and migrating customers now and into the future. Marcom managers must put a financial value on their activities in order to be fairly compensated. While they may not have the responsibility for compensation, they should always lobby for an approach that will help the firm achieve full integration.

IMC: A Five-Step Process

Having a firm understanding of the eight principles that drive value-oriented IMC, we now turn our attention to the process through which a fully integrated communication program is developed. As already noted, marketing communication has historically been implemented as a series of disconnected, often unrelated activities. Ad agencies thought of their discipline as an independent unit. Direct marketers thought the same, as did public relations practitioners. Organizations also treated them as distinct disciplines. Integrated marketing communication, however, uses multiple communication methods to focus on the customer with the overall objectives of acquiring, maintaining, growing, or migrating customers in order to generate greater and most consistent income flows over time. Since IMC requires an organizationwide change in thinking, its implementation is most effectively achieved by following a clear and consistent process. Here, we introduce a five-step IMC process that has proven effective in organizations around the world over the last several years. The process is a series of interconnected, customer-focused, managerial steps that lead to and through the development and implementation of a totally integrated marketing communication program.

Exhibit 3.6 provides a simplified overview of the process. It consists of five separate but interrelated activities or steps that involve a number

Exhibit 3.6 The Five-Step IMC Planning Process

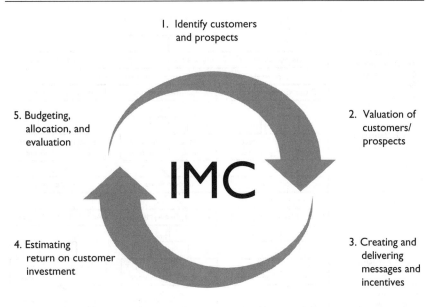

1. Identify customers and prospects

2. Valuation of customers/ prospects

3. Creating and delivering messages and incentives

4. Estimating return on customer investment

5. Budgeting, allocation, and evaluation

IMC

of the traditional functional areas of marketing and communication. They have, however, been combined in new, more effective and efficient ways so the total effect far exceeds the sum of the parts. Recall that guiding principle 6 stressed the need to create closed-loop planning systems to track the incremental gains (or losses) that result from marketing communication investment. The five-step process is structured to facilitate such tracking over both the short and long term.

A more comprehensive view of the components of each step is shown in Exhibit 3.7, on page 70, which is laid out in a process flow-chart format. It nevertheless represents a closed system in which the results of one period are used as input for the following planning cycle.

Step 1: Identifying Customers and Prospects

As guiding principle 5 indicated, IMC identifies customers and prospects in terms of behavioral data, that is, what they have done or might be influenced to do in the future. In step 1 of the IMC process, mar-

Exhibit 3.7 Details of the Five-Step IMC Planning Process

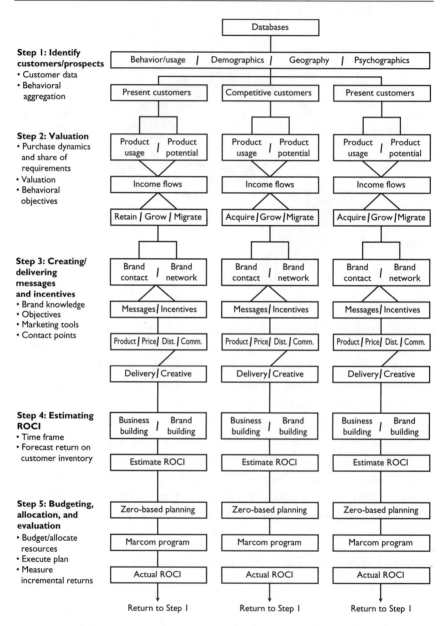

Step 1: Identify customers/prospects
- Customer data
- Behavioral aggregation

Step 2: Valuation
- Purchase dynamics and share of requirements
- Valuation
- Behavioral objectives

Step 3: Creating/ delivering messages and incentives
- Brand knowledge
- Objectives
- Marketing tools
- Contact points

Step 4: Estimating ROCI
- Time frame
- Forecast return on customer inventory

Step 5: Budgeting, allocation, and evaluation
- Budget/allocate resources
- Execute plan
- Measure incremental returns

Note: Comm. = communication; Dist. = distribution.

com managers not only attempt to identify customers according to behaviors but to understand why those behaviors occur. For this reason, step 1 involves the collection of various types of information, including demographic, geographic, psychographic, and other relevant data.

The focus is on aggregating and integrating that data to provide an understanding of persons or firms with whom communication programs are to be created. Customers are aggregated according to their behaviors in order to develop communication programs relevant to each group. As the example in Exhibit 3.7 shows, customers are aggregated into three simple groups: present customers, competitive customers, and emerging users (these are new customers who do not have strongly established relationships). This approach to defining target customer groups will be discussed in greater detail in the next chapter.

WHO IS THE CUSTOMER?

A common issue in marcom discussions is determining exactly who or what is the customer. Some manufacturers, for instance, refer to their channel partners—that is, wholesalers or retailers to whom they sell directly—as their customers, while those who buy from the retailer are referred to as consumers or end users. In some complex value chains, such as are often found in business-to-business marketing, the chain of customer relationships can be quite lengthy before the product or service reaches the ultimate end user.

In this text, we use the term *customer* to refer broadly to all types of individuals or organizations who buy or use a product or service. Where it is necessary to make a distinction between the various levels of the value chain, we use the specific term *channel customers* (to refer to intermediaries) or *consumers* and *end users* (to refer to those who ultimately consume or use the product or service).

Step 2: Estimating the Value of Customers and Prospects

Since value-oriented IMC focuses on the financial impact and effects of marketing communication, the next task is to place an estimated financial valuation on customers and prospects, that is, to identify the income flows they contribute to the firm. This step is critical, for it forms the basis on which the organization will determine against whom and how it will allocate its finite corporate resources.

Step 2 begins by obtaining a clear picture of the current usage among target customers, as well as factoring in future potential, stated in terms of current or estimated income flows to the organization. This determination is used to establish specific, measurable behavioral objectives consistent with guiding principle 5—that is, to acquire, retain, grow, or migrate customers according to the circumstances of each target group. This approach to customer valuation, which will be discussed in Chapter 5, provides the basis for the planning of marketing communication programs in step 3.

Step 3: Planning Communication Messages and Incentives

Step 3 involves planning the content of and delivery of persuasive communication to the firm's target customers. The goal is naturally to structure communication programs that are relevant and compelling and to reach customers or prospects at a time when they will be most receptive to the communication. The process begins by marketers gaining a thorough understanding of each customer group's brand contacts and brand networks—that is, where do they come in contact with the brand, and what "network" of associations to the brand do they maintain?

Guiding principle 7—streamlining functional elements into messages or incentives—is key to step 3 of the process. Inherent in this message or incentive approach are the delivery systems by which communications are delivered to customers, consumers, end users, and prospects. Having laid out appropriate message and incentive strategies, marketers can then determine how best to use their basic marketing tools (product attributes, pricing policies, distribution or channel strategies, and communication). Finally, there is the execution of the communication program, which is divided into two essential components: delivery systems to get the message or incentive to the target audiences, and the actual creative execution to be used—the words, graphics, copy platform, campaign themes, and so on.

Step 4: Estimating Return on Customer Investment

Financial values are critical in the IMC approach. By applying guiding principle 6 and treating customers as assets, the marcom manager has a pragmatic basis on which the financial effects of the company's total marketing communication program can be calculated. With IMC, managers can not only demonstrate that marcom is providing positive returns on investments, but they can drill down to specific cases to determine which elements were most effective and efficient.

Step 4 separates results into short-term (business-building) and long-term (brand-building) returns. On one hand, for example, incentives are often designed to work in the short term to generate incremental income almost immediately. On the other hand, brands are built over time; thus, marketers must also measure brand equity returns over an extended time frame.

Step 5: Postprogram Analysis and Future Planning

The final step of the process involves several steps of its own:

1. Implement the IMC program in the marketplace during the relevant period of time.
2. Evaluate the program once it has been put into action.
3. Develop a reinvestment strategy.

Within the IMC process, marketing communication is not considered a finite program, that is, it does not start and end with the organization's fiscal or financial periods. That is why the new IMC approach recognizes that marketing communication is ongoing and continuous. It is never complete and it is never over.

Moving On

Upcoming chapters describe each of the five steps of the IMC process in detail. The brief overview given in this chapter, however, gives you enough information to help you determine how well the marketing and communication programs in your firm align with the IMC process. If you agree that value-oriented IMC principles, methods, and processes make sense, read on. If not—or if your firm does not seem ready to consider taking the steps necessary to move toward integration—set this book aside. Continue to develop and implement your programs as you have always done. Come back to the book only when you and your firm are ready for a change in thinking. Hopefully, we'll see you in the next chapter.

PART II

STEP 1:
IDENTIFYING
CUSTOMERS AND
PROSPECTS

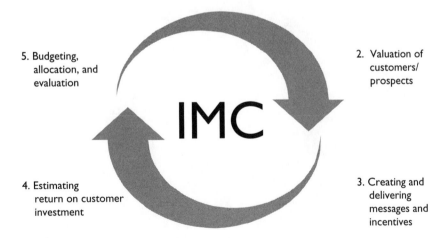

1. Identify customers and prospects

2. Valuation of customers/prospects

3. Creating and delivering messages and incentives

4. Estimating return on customer investment

5. Budgeting, allocation, and evaluation

IMC

CHAPTER 4

HOW TO DEFINE CUSTOMERS AND PROSPECTS ACCORDING TO BEHAVIOR

The first step in developing a value-oriented IMC program is to identify and define customers and prospects using a behavioral database. Implicit in this task is the idea that customers and prospects are treated as *individuals*, not as markets. People are not identified in terms of market segments, demographic groups, geographic units, social classes, or any other arbitrary grouping. Perhaps because of the lure of technology that enables sophisticated statistical analysis, marketers have traditionally focused too heavily on market segmentation based on such factors. Integrated marketing communication reverses that trend, viewing customers primarily as individual people who provide flows of income to the firm. This is as true for business-to-business organizations as it is for consumer goods manufacturers. Whether customers are buying at a discount store, at a trade show, directly from a field sales force, or simply by reordering office supplies over the phone or Internet on a regular basis, all communication must be with, for, and about people. When marketers lose sight of the individual behind the purchasing decisions, they generally lose sight of the objectives of communication. By focusing on people rather than markets or segments, IMC avoids falling into that trap.

Aggregating Individuals into Behavioral Groups

Value-based IMC is based on customer or prospect *behavior*. Marketers aggregate or combine customers and prospects who are similar in how they use a product or who are alike in enough ways to make generalized messages or incentives practical. This aggregation process allows marketers to make use of the efficiency of various forms of traditional media while still focusing on specific, behaviorally defined groups of customers and prospects (and, in some instances, even individuals). It is easy to see from Exhibit 4.1 how aggregation differs from traditional market segmentation in that it starts with identifiable individuals and aggregates them into like-behaving groups.

As it is commonly practiced, segmentation starts with the entire market and then, by analysis or other rules of separation, breaks the total

Exhibit 4.1 Market Segmentation vs. Aggregation

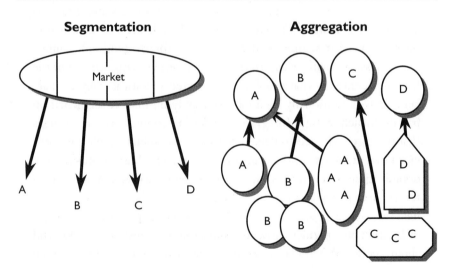

down into manageable groups for marketing and communication purposes. For example, the U.S. census has traditionally reported the makeup of the population based on demographic and geographic factors. The demographics identify various population groups by age, gender, education, income, and so on. The census also reports on population segments by geography, that is, states, cities, rural or urban areas, and so on. Because the information is initially gathered by the government and then made available to the public, it is relatively inexpensive and easy for marketers to obtain.

While census information is useful for classification purposes, it doesn't provide much insight about customers or prospects. To supplement census data, many organizations either conduct survey research or enhance their geo-demographic data by appending additional information, often from third-party, syndicated suppliers. This is useful as well, but it assumes that a market consists of a homogeneous mass that can be segmented based on age, gender, income, geography, and the like.

Business-to-business marketers also use segmentation, in their case based on Standard Industrial Classification (SIC) codes. Also gathered by the government, this data classifies business organizations by industry or business type, number of employees, firm turnover, and other factors. While such data may be interesting and useful in developing a broad understanding of the market, it is not often helpful in understanding the value of customers or prospects for marketing or communication purposes.

Integrated marketing communication moves beyond the concept of segmentation. Instead, it aggregates groups of individuals based on their behaviors in the marketplace. In essence, customers group themselves based on what they do, not on an artificial classification scheme the marketer develops. In other words, one must start with people—identify their actions and activities and then turn those into naturally occurring market groups. For instance, marketers can identify which groups of customers or firms buy, how they buy, when they buy, how much they buy, and how much they may buy in the future.

Companies frequently develop aggregation plans based on the strength of the relationship between the customer and the brand. A company might, for example, start by aggregating customers and pros-

A One-to-One Future?

One-to-one marketing is a highly individualized approach to marketing that uses customer databases to transmit customized marketing messages, offers, or products based on a customer's past behaviors or stated preferences. Don Peppers and Martha Rogers, originators of the term, explain it as the ability to "treat different customers differently."[1]

While we subscribe to the concept and principles of one-to-one marketing as a valid approach in a complex, global, and networked marketplace, we find it relevant for only a limited number of categories. One-to-one marketing simply is not practical nor financially feasible for many organizations. As a general rule, unless the marketer has direct and ongoing contact with the customer or prospect and the product or service can be "customized" relatively easily and inexpensively, one-to-one is often not the most practical way to implement a communication program. This obviously raises the question of whether or not all communication must be targeted, specific, and direct. And the answer is no. Indeed, in the following chapters, we make a strong case for the use of broadscale, generalized brand value propositions and approaches that can best be implemented by mass media systems.

pects into three simple groups: present customers, competitive customers, and emerging users. All present customers may be treated as a single target or may be broken down further into subcategories such as high-volume/high-profit users versus occasional or low-profit users. Similarly, competitive customers may be subdivided into those who are extremely loyal to a competitor and those whose previous behavior indicates they are switchers. Emerging users present special communication challenges. These are users who are new to a category (such as new mothers, college students who have just moved into a dormitory, and recent retirees) and therefore do not have a strongly established relationship with any competitor. Since they are new to the category, however, they may have special informational needs and may have to be reached through different venues or channels than those already established.

Once customers and prospects have been defined and aggregated according to their behaviors, the marketer can enhance this behavioral information by using traditional tools, such as demographic, geographic, or psychographic information. These data help explain the behaviors that have *already been observed* and help marketers understand why those behaviors most likely occurred.

We believe that aggregation is a far richer and more insightful approach than traditional methods of segmentation, because it treats customers as people rather than simply as census segments. We have found—and the same has generally been proven in the marketplace—that data on what customers do, how they perform, or what their past

---

BEHAVIORS AS PREDICTORS

New research provides marketers with good reason for using behavioral data as the basis for communication plans. Researcher Andrea Ovans has found that people's reported purchase intentions or their reported purchase behavior are not very accurate representations of what they actually do in the marketplace and are even less useful for predicting what they might do in the future. For example, using data from two hundred products and sixty-five thousand consumers in previously published academic and industry-sponsored studies, Ovans found that purchase intentions were weak predictors of future behavior. According to her research team, ". . . people aren't generally reliable predictors of their own long-term purchasing behavior for any type of good, new or old, durable or not."[2] Thus, whenever and wherever possible, it is advisable to use behavioral data, which tells what customers have truly done in the past, not what they say they will do in the future.

histories are in relation to products or services are much more useful than data on their age, gender, income, or neighborhood. Further, behavioral data, particularly in established Western markets, are much more easily obtained today than in the past. In many cases, marketers have already captured the names and addresses of their best customers or have been able to obtain that information from third-party sources.

Finding the Data Marketers Need for IMC Planning

An overriding goal during step 1 of the IMC process is to gain meaningful insights into the needs, wants, and wishes of those individuals or companies the firm wishes to serve. Customer data is the source of such insights. One of the major changes in the way business is conducted today is the tremendous amount of data the marketer has typically gathered on his or her firm's customers and prospects. The growth in data capture, manipulation, and interpretation has been dramatic in the past twenty-five years. So, the problem is not due to lack of data. Nor is it difficult to obtain more data from customers and prospects; that information seems to come to the firm in an unending stream. Instead, the data challenge is to organize all the information the organization has and make it accessible to those who need it.

Most firms have "islands of information" spread throughout the organization. There is some data in the market research department; some in the sales department; and other types in the customer service, accounting, and communication departments. The problem is that few firms are successful in systematically connecting these islands of information to achieve a comprehensive, insightful view of their customers. How should organizations go about connecting the various sources of information they have on customers and prospects, and in what ways do they use it? The experiences of BMW provide some of the answers.

Customer/Prospect Data Sources

Customer and prospect data come from multiple sources. Firms that excel at handling data are generally the best at developing effective and

---

SHARING THE CUSTOMER WEALTH

According to dunnhumby associates limited, a London-based database consulting group, BMW in the United Kingdom has been collecting and integrating various forms of customer data since the early 1980s. The company collects information from a variety of sources, including new and used car buying records, warranty and service records, BMW financial services records, direct mail and Internet sources, and external information such as competitive sales data sources. BMW is able to create a marketing database that gives it big advantages in the marketplace by allowing the company to better understand its customers and helping to inform its employees as to what is going on with its products in the outside world.

The database is used for many different purposes. Often it is used to predict when customers are likely to change their cars. Armed with this data, dealers can talk to consumers and help them plan their next purchase. Information is also used in advertising; dunnhumby reports that response rates to various BMW campaigns have tripled in the past few years. This improvement occurred because analysts are able to segment and target customers accurately and contact those customers who were willing to respond.

Lastly, to keep up with their reputation for excellence in customer service, BMW gives the information from the database to the front-line employees at call centers. Operators are armed with details of customers' lifetime value, as well as their customer contact with BMW—regardless of the channel they used to buy their cars.[3]

---

efficient integrated marketing communication programs. Certainly that was the case with the best IMC firms benchmarked in the leveraging customer information (LCI) study discussed in Chapter 2. There, we introduced a three-part model of how organizations capture, manage, and apply customer data (see Exhibit 2.4). Here, we review each component of the model in greater detail.

The left-hand column in Exhibit 2.4 lists the various sources that organizations commonly use to gather customer and prospect information. Data sources are placed on a continuum bounded by whether the information generally comes from internal or external sources. For purposes of developing a comprehensive IMC program, most firms use a combination of the two. Each type of data has particular benefits and characteristics. While the list in the diagram is by no means exhaustive, it covers the primary types of data typically gathered by best practice organizations in the LCI study.

This incredibly rich range of information can be overwhelming. Further, although data are plentiful, it's often the case that few have been turned into customer knowledge. Thus, the question is often where to start. As suggested earlier, the most valuable information about customers or prospects is what they have done in the past. That is, what were their behaviors, purchases, or activities related to the product or service for which the IMC program is being planned?

We have found behavioral data almost always provides more valuable insight about what customers might do in the future than any other type of information. People and firms are creatures of habit. What they have done in the past, they are most likely to do in the future. This is not to say that attitudinal data—how people feel about a company or brand—have no value. Generally, however, such information lacks predictive ability. For example, people are notoriously poor at predicting what they would do in a future scenario (see the references to Ovans's research earlier in this chapter). So, rather than using attitudinal data to foretell what customers might do in the future, marketers use it to explain why those customers did what they did and why they might perform that way again in the future.

Understanding Customers and Prospects

Many companies gather literally mountains of data, often simply because the information is available or because they can. In the spirit of trying to understand customers, firms often gather all the data possible, seemingly with the idea that they will or can "sort it out later." In today's marketplace, gathering data is much like trying to drink from a fire hose. Since there is so much data available, the company becomes overwhelmed and, in many cases, simply freezes in place. The alternative is that it looks for the ultimate database or technology and, in the course of defining and refining data, never gets around to using any of the results!

When looking at collected information from an IMC perspective, marketers need to separate data according to tactical and strategic value. Data to support tactical decisions are based on how marketing activities should be carried out, meaning media forms, delivery systems, messages, offers, and so on. Strategic information and data allows an organization to make decisions about what should be done. To decide whether data is worth gathering and keeping, marketers can use this simple three-part test:

1. Will these data help our company become more relevant to customers and prospects? Will we be able to offer products or services they might logically want or need, not just the products or services we have to sell, and be able to communicate with them in a meaningful way?
2. Will these data help us become a learning organization? Will we be able to understand a customer's actions and use that knowledge to create a satisfying experience for the customer in the future? Will these data help us learn from our mistakes and take advantage of our successes? Can the data we are capturing help us to change and grow with the customer and his or her needs and wants in the future?
3. Will these data help us better allocate our finite resources now and in the future? Will the data enable us to make better marcom decisions? Can we determine what works and what doesn't and, more important, why? Will the data we are capturing, managing, and analyzing help us be better stewards of this firm's finite resources in the future?

If the data in question are valuable in one or all of these three key areas, then it is most likely worthwhile to capture, manage, and analyze that data.

DOES ATTITUDE NECESSARILY INFLUENCE BEHAVIOR?

Any study of customer behaviors inevitably raises the issue of the extent to which attitudes lead to certain behaviors. The controversy, which repeatedly crops up in the marketing and communication community, stems from a hypothesis originally developed over forty years ago in an attempt to explain how advertising works. The original hypothesis suggested that communication exposures moved consumers through some sort of mental process, such as moving from awareness to knowledge to preference and so on, at some point resulting in behavior. This hypothesis has never been proven in the marketplace. It is this inability to connect attitudinal change to marketplace behaviors that has created much of the controversy. To put this argument to rest, let's briefly review a well-known marketing concept, the hierarchy of effects model, first developed by Robert Lavidge and Gary Steiner in 1961.[4]

As shown in Exhibit 4.2, the hierarchy of effects (or traditional advertising-based) model assumes that individuals go through a series of attitudinal stages on the way to a purchasing decision. Exposure to an advertising message is thought to move them along a continuum from awareness to final behavior or purchase. The model further assumes that marketing communication is the tool that drives that movement. Therefore, the more messages or exposures provided to customers and prospects, the faster they will move along the continuum and ultimately purchase the marketer's product or service. Acceptance of the hierarchy of effects model has led to many key assumptions in marketing and media planning, including reach and frequency, share of voice, and others (see Chapter 8).

Despite the intuitive appeal of this traditional model, there are a number of problems associated with it. Since it was developed more than four decades ago, when fewer marcom vehicles and less competition existed, the model ignores the impact of competitive messages and forms of communication other than the ones being measured. However, the greatest challenge to the model is that it is hypothetical and, despite its acceptance, there is practically no scientific evidence that it correctly assesses the way the human mind responds to advertising or marketing communication.

The critical element in understanding the impact of marketing communication is to understand that it is consumer behaviors, not attitudinal changes, that result in sales. Thus, IMC focuses on the use of consumer behavioral data and then explains those behaviors through attitudinal information or material. We have, in essence, started at the other end of the hierarchy of effects and worked backward—a most dramatic change.

To be of strategic value within an IMC program, marketing communication must affect the present or future behavior of customers and prospects. Marketers do not presuppose that this will occur, nor do they presuppose the manner in which such a product or service purchase will occur. They take the behaviors as givens and then try to reinforce or change them. Therefore, by having some knowledge of the customers'

Exhibit 4.2 Hierarchy of Effects (Advertising-Based) Model of Communication

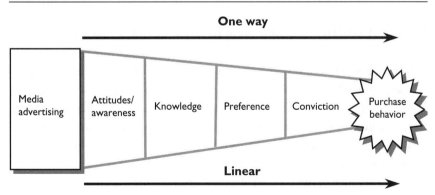

"Acting on consumers"

previous behavior, marketers know what to try to influence in the future and what to measure against in future evaluation of their programs.

An excellent example of this approach to managing customer behaviors is the process developed by dunnhumby associates limited.[5] Working with a number of its clients, dunnhumby has taken customer purchase data from organizations such as supermarkets, automobile manufacturers, and clothing retailers to create huge multidimensional matrices that plot customer behavior on three or more dimensions. The firm then populates those matrices with actual customer behavior, or the purchasing behavior of individual customers over time. This information commonly comes from the behaviors captured in some type of customer loyalty program.

By placing its customers in these matrix boxes, dunnhumby can then identify other matrix boxes that might be most beneficial for both the marketer and the customer. Since the marketing organization knows the current matrix box the customer occupies, marketing and communication programs can be developed and designed to "migrate" that customer or group of customers into a more desirable position in the matrix. In some cases, for example, with supermarket customers, it is possible to view the movement of customers from one matrix box to another on a weekly basis. Thus, the marketer has real-time results to see how well the various marketing and communication programs are performing.

Understanding Databases in an IMC Context

Over the past ten to fifteen years, the siren call of the database has been heard by marketers all round the world. In the mid- to late 1980s, it was believed that an organization that had no customer database or could not relate to its customers on a one-to-one basis was doomed to fail. This has not proven to be the case. We found a number of best practice firms in the LCI study that were either working with legacy computer systems or had cobbled together computer and information systems and methodologies that allowed them to recognize, understand, market, and communicate with their customers and prospects. Indeed, as seen in Chapter 2, powerful firms have been able to overcome technological deficits through strongly focused customer-oriented cultures within their organizations.

When direct marketing and database marketing were at the peak of their popularity, many companies yielded to the promised benefits of data capture and management. They invested huge sums of money in buying or leasing computers, installing sophisticated software, hiring information technology people, and gathering every bit of data available. They then stuffed all the data into a computerized system and sat back and waited for success to happen. Unfortunately, success was elusive. The reason? The focus was on the data and technology, not on the application of data to gain customer and prospect insights or influence their behaviors. This is not to say that all database systems are bad or useless. It is, however, a reminder that the purpose of a database is simply to provide information and knowledge to a firm's managers, not to solve their marketing problems.

The IMC attitude toward databases is simple. Some companies need one, some don't. Indeed, some firms can exist very nicely, thank you, even in the Web-based, electronic marketplace of the twenty-first century, with relatively limited amounts of information on customers and prospects (usually just what they buy and when they buy it). The key to success in understanding customers and prospects is not how much data the organization has, but how the available data are used. The IMC view has always been that as soon as two pieces of data of any kind on a customer or prospect are gained, those bits of data should be used to better understand the customer or prospect or to build better, more relevant marketing and communication programs. In short, if the information doesn't make the customer's life better, why gather it at all?

Data Audits

The first step in the development of a relevant database is usually a data audit. In more than twenty years of working with all types of organizations around the world, we have yet to find a firm that needs more data. What we have found are many, many organizations that have all the data they need but (a) don't know the information exists within the firm, (b) can't access it for marketing and communication purposes, or (c) can't combine or analyze it so it provides new or useful customer insights. As a result, the common assumptions of a manager who wants to develop an IMC program are first, that the company must build a database and second, that the company must gather more data through research, purchase from an outside vendor, or some other method of data acquisition. Our advice? Resist the temptation! Most likely, you have most of the data you need inside the firm. So, go and find it. We call that a data audit. Data audits generally start with a review of what is already available in each of the areas shown in Exhibit 4.3.

Wherever the firm touches a customer, data is usually created and available. So, start inside. Talk to sales. Talk to accounting. Talk to customer service. Ask them what data they have on customers and prospects. Chances are you will find what you need fairly quickly and often at little cost. The challenge, of course, is how to bring all the information together once you've found it.

Qwest, formerly known as US West Direct, offers a brief illustration of how this works. Qwest wanted to change the way it sold advertising space in its Yellow Pages product. Traditionally, sales representatives sold space based on the type of advertisements that were available: size, color, coupon, and so on. To better understand the needs of its customers, the company conducted a survey. Based on the results, customers were aggregated into clusters. Qwest marketing managers found customers who wanted to grow their business, customers who wanted smaller ads in many locations because they offered niche services/products, business-to-business customers, and customers who were ambivalent about the location of their advertisements in the publication. Within the clusters, managers also found that customers had similar needs. As a result of these simple findings, sales representatives were trained to ask only a few questions and quickly place the customer in the appropriate group. The sales message was changed to focus on customer needs rather than the product. Based on one study, Qwest was able to improve advertising sales and significantly reduce costs because the sales process became much more efficient.[6]

Exhibit 4.3 Internal Data Sources by Department

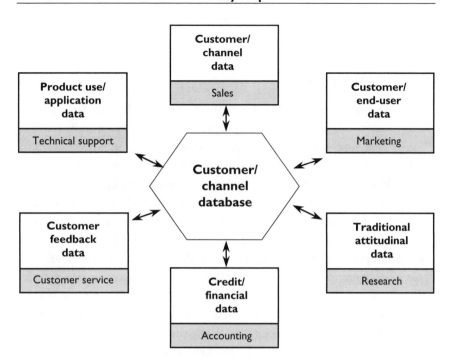

Another example comes from Time, Inc., the publishing branch of AOL Time Warner, the largest media and entertainment company in the world. With its marketing information department (MID), Time, Inc., sustains several subscriber databases that interact with each other. The company is constantly trying to maximize the effectiveness of its marketing campaigns with existing in-house data as well as mounting external efforts to contribute to targeting and attracting new readers and subscribers. For example, if a customer subscribes to both *Time* and *People*, the company attempts to cross-sell another magazine or related product that the customer would like. Employees in MID are responsible for managing and manipulating the company's data to ensure that new offers, billing, renewals, and other efforts are completed with maximum accuracy. These employees are also responsible for improving lists by gaining new prospects and delving deeply into the database to gain more insight about existing readers and subscribers. The company is a good example of a firm that effectively integrates and uses multiple databases to communicate with and gain more insight into the behaviors of their current and future customers.[7]

Types of Databases

Having made a case that databases are nice to have but not absolutely necessary for developing an IMC program, the question naturally arises as to what type of information gathering or aggregation is most useful in the development process. Exhibit 4.4 helps answer this question. Developed by Targetbase—a database marketing service firm located in the Dallas suburb of Irving, Texas—this framework has proven to be a practical way of assessing the level and sophistication of the database an organization needs to develop an effective marcom program.

The type of database required depends on the type of marketing program being developed. The vertical axis of the chart shows the value of the customer to the organization. The horizontal axis is a continuum showing increasing levels of database sophistication corresponding to increasing levels of customer value. While this example primarily views the database as an investment by the firm, it also indicates the level of data management needed, ranging from a simple list of customers to a high-end marketing database that will allow the organization to develop personal services for highly valued individual customers and some level of mass customization development for the products and services being offered.

Highly integrated marketing communication programs require a midlevel to high-end database. This does not mean that integrated programs cannot be developed without a major investment in technology. What it does mean is that to develop truly interactive integrated programs, a fairly comprehensive database is required. Of particular interest is the concave line identifying the area where a database would likely provide no real value to the organization. If, for example, a firm's only interest is in reaching the first level of integration—that is, combining and coordinating the various types of outbound marcom activities— then a sophisticated database likely would not pay for itself, or at least there would not be sufficient increases in incremental returns to the organization to justify the cost of a database.

Exhibit 4.4 Finding the Right Type of Database

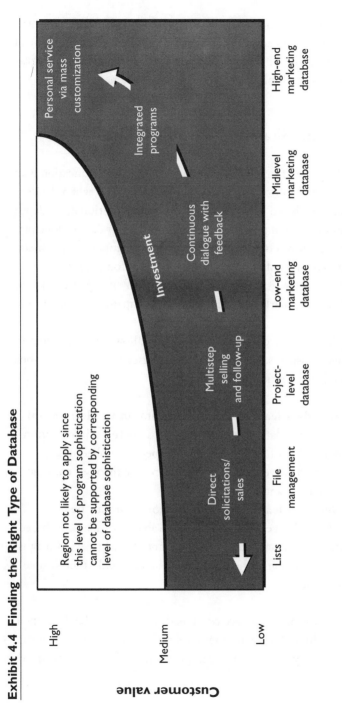

Sophistication of database technology

A more critical question, beyond the need for a database, concerns how data on customers and prospects can be applied to gain additional insights into behavior. This typically requires aggregation or integration of data from multiple sources, the topic of the next section.

Combining and Sharing Customer Data

While much of the effort in customer and prospect identification is in obtaining data and information, the real insights come when data are combined and analyzed in some way to provide additional, in-depth detail on customers and prospects. The combining of data is done primarily to get a more complete picture of the customer or prospect. Often when two bits of data are combined, a third, fourth, fifth, or even sixth bit of knowledge is created. It is this type of synergistic reaction that really helps the marketer understand the company's customers and prospects.

To gain the valuable customer insights that allow a firm to identify customers and prospects, all available data are used to create a four-box matrix around two continuums:

- **Measurable data leading to implied data on the horizontal axis.** Quantifiable data provides concrete, structured information on a large number of customers and prospects. Implied data is derived through survey methods of research or through episodic customer contacts and comments.
- **Observable data leading to information that can be projected on the vertical axis.** Observable information is based on actual, traceable customer behaviors and data. Projected data is based on information gathered through surveys and other sample-based techniques.

When the two forms of data are combined, a matrix can be developed, as shown in Exhibit 4.5. Here, examples of various types of data that companies typically gather have been placed in each of the four quad-

Exhibit 4.5 Observable/Measurable Data Matrix

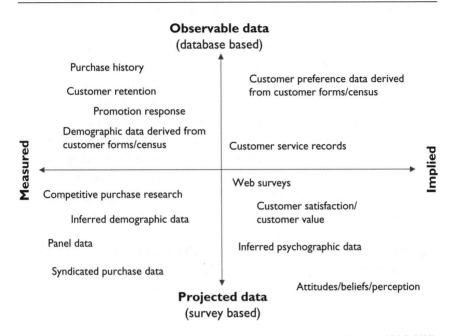

From "Leveraging Customer Information," American Productivity and Quality Center (Houston: APQC, 2000). Used with permission from American Productivity and Quality Center.

rants. Although the matrix shown is not exhaustive, it does illustrate the types of data an IMC manager might find in his or her organization. It also provides one approach to organizing data for analysis and planning.

Of course, data is only valuable once it is analyzed in some way and customer and prospect insights are developed. This is generally done through some type of data gathering, management, and integration process. Look again at the IMC model in Exhibit 2.4. Bringing all the data in the organization together into some type of useful and usable information about customers is done with organizational and technological enablers. *Organizational enablers* are those things found in the firm that make data integration and insight possible. They generally include the culture of the organization (the extent to which it is customer focused; the level of support from top management; the level of cooperation between groups, units, strategic business units [SBUs], and so on). *Technological enablers* include the compatibility among computer hardware and software, data transfer systems, data-gathering facilities, and so on. Both types of enablers are necessary for successful integration.

For many organizations, customer insight comes as a result of the ways in which data are linked. Links may be either hard or soft. Hard links are activities that enable the physical matching of various kinds of data, such as matching customer buying records with third-party demographic data. Soft links are those types of activities that involve human intervention or activities to ensure success. Customer profiling, customer scoring, and the design of samples for data gathering are all soft links. All these methods are highly dependent on the skills and capabilities of the persons designing or developing various models and algorithms to provide useful outputs.

Finally, at the center of all data gathering are the management and integration activities that bring together data from all sources, ready for the kind of analysis that will generate valuable customer insights. This is the topic of the next section.

Generating Customer Insights

All the marketer's efforts to this point have been leading toward achieving customer insight. Look once more at Exhibit 2.4. The right-hand column lists ways that aggregated data are applied to shape business activities and strategies. These outputs or applications are arrayed on a vertical continuum ranging from strategic to tactical. Obviously, the primary tactical output of importance to the IMC manager is the segmentation or aggregation of customers and prospects, which is shown at the top of the continuum. From the aggregation of customers and prospects, it is then possible to develop message delivery, service delivery, and so on. At the other end of the continuum, business strategy output, the analysis of customer data can be used to develop various methods of long-range planning and even the development of a "balanced scorecard."[8]

Moving On

What is obvious from reviewing the right-hand column of Exhibit 2.4 is that the gathering of customer and prospect data in its many forms and from various sources is simply an attempt by the organization to develop a better method for customer contact management. In truth, that is what the new IMC is all about—better management of every contact (planned and unplanned) the firm has with its customers and prospects. We will say more about this idea of contact management in later chapters, but for the present, it is clear that the analysis of the data the organization gathers on customers and prospects has a great deal to do with whether marcom programs can be integrated. It also determines whether the integration of those programs can be made relevant to the individuals on whom marcom efforts are focused.

PART III

STEP 2: ESTIMATING THE VALUE OF CUSTOMERS AND PROSPECTS

1. Identify customers and prospects

5. Budgeting, allocation, and evaluation

2. Valuation of customers/ prospects

IMC

4. Estimating return on customer investment

3. Creating and delivering messages and incentives

CHAPTER 5

HOW TO DETERMINE FINANCIAL VALUES OF CUSTOMERS AND CUSTOMER GROUPS

The goal of step 2 of the IMC process is to determine the financial value of customers and prospects in order to make intelligent marcom investments. By setting this goal, it should be clear that value-based IMC differs from traditional approaches to marcom planning. Inherent in the IMC methodology is the premise that marketing communication can be raised to the level of a strategic corporate activity, not just operated as a functional tactic used on a hit-or-miss basis. As a strategic tool, IMC must be viewed as an investment the organization makes rather than as an expense it incurs. And finally, it clearly illustrates why customers are the most critical element in the firm's value chain. Customers, their value, and the income flows they create are the basis for organizational investments simply because they are one of the primary elements that generate financial returns for the organization.

Customers, in a strategic sense, have asset value for the company. While message creativity and communication delivery systems are still critically important to the success of any marcom program, they play a new role in organizations that practice IMC (see Chapters 7 and 8).

This chapter looks at customers as assets that provide firms with real and ongoing financial returns on their communication investments. Further, we provide the basic elements that allow the IMC manager to move from simply being the one who allocates corporate communication resources to the role of a steward of customer income flows.

Determining Financial Value

Step 2 of the IMC process requires the IMC manager to develop a methodology for determining the financial value of customers and prospects. This starts by understanding the purchase dynamics of each aggregated customer group and the share of their purchasing in the category that is directed to the firm or brand. The approach is based on an understanding of the current level of demand for the firm's products or services and must include an estimation of projected potential demand. As discussed in Chapter 3, a customer's demand is stated in financial terms—that is, anticipated income flows—and not volume, product units, or capacity measures. Using this financial view of customer value, the IMC manager establishes appropriate behavioral objectives for each customer group. For some groups, it may be acceptable simply to maintain current spending levels, while for others, the company may wish to increase spending or migrate customers to a different, more profitable line. For those who are not users of the product, the plan may be to obtain a trial purchase in anticipation of acquiring them as ongoing customers sometime in the future. Underlying all of these scenarios is the need for an initial baseline valuation to provide the financial footing from which the manager will determine the returns on customer investments in steps 4 and 5.

To determine returns, the manager must first have some idea of initial customer value. This is critical, for it provides a baseline to determine how much the firm is willing to invest in any customer, prospect, or group over various periods of time. It further enables the manager to measure the returns the company did or might achieve on the investments made in those customers.

Seeing Customers as Assets and Communication as an Investment

Because of accounting conventions, most organizations currently treat marketing communication as a corporate or business unit expense. The firm determines how much it is willing to spend on marketing programs for a period of time, usually a fiscal year, and then sets that amount as a budget item or at least as an expected expense. A budget management system is then developed, and management controls and financial constraints are established to control the flow of expenditures.

All this is done because, in most organizations, marketing communication is a cost-centered activity, that is, an expense that must be managed, apportioned, and monitored. Budgets are set up so that there are constraints on the marketing or communication managers that prevent them from spending more than the planned and approved amount. If budget savings can be achieved through consolidating, optimizing, or simply not spending the amount initially budgeted, then those savings become expense reductions and drop immediately to the firm's bottom line.

Since marketing communication is considered a cost function, there is generally little expectation by senior management that there will be any financial returns from the marcom investment. This is true even though management commonly asks marcom managers to "prove the value" of their marketing and communication programs. The challenge is to show that sales or margins, volume, or some other financial measure improved as a result of an investment in a marcom program. This is a critical element in the IMC process and is covered in more detail in steps 4 and 5.

Look again at the step 2 portion of Exhibit 3.7 on page 70. In step 1, customers were aggregated by their behaviors into present, competitive, and emerging categories. Step 2 lists the behavioral objectives marketers hope to gain through the communication initiative. Obviously, each of these customer or prospect groups generate differing flows of income to the firm. Some cost more to manage than others, so they may be less profitable. Some are more expensive to acquire than others, so their income flows take longer to become profitable. Lost customers generate zero cash flows and attracting them back may require additional investment. When marketers view customers and prospects in terms of characteristics like these, they can start to consider the various types of marketing and communication programs needed to influence the behavior of each. Further, they begin to see that differing levels of investment in marketing communication will likely be required and will likely generate differing levels of return.

Viewing customers and prospects as current or prospective income flows to the firm is the key element in understanding the value-based IMC approach to marketing communication. The questions marketers ask now are as follows:

- What customer behaviors are to be influenced and with what result?
- What customers and prospects are to be acquired and at what cost?
- Who will return what value?
- Which customers are to be retained?
- Which customers are to be migrated to a more profitable line as a result of the firm's marcom investments?

In attempting to answer questions like these, it again becomes clear that the goal of marketing communication in an IMC approach is to influence customer income flows as a result of marcom activities. Customers are clearly positioned as assets of the organization, no different from any other asset that generates income and profit. Plants and factories are built with the idea that their output will generate future income flows for the firm. Investments in research and development and information systems are made in the expectation that their outputs—in the form of innovations, product enhancements, or cost savings—will generate positive income flows for the firm. Integrated marketing communication treats marcom activities in the same way. Thus, the assets of the organization must be used to generate income flows and profits; customers are assets because they generate income flows and should be managed as such. This is a lesson that has been well learned by companies such as FedEx, Prudential Insurance, Marriott Hotels, and the British supermarket chain, Tesco.

THE TESCO WAY

Today, grocery stores around the world use loyalty programs of some kind or other to collect data on shoppers. Yet in most cases only a very small amount, if any, of that data is ever used, and rarely is it applied in a way that can truly influence loyalty. An important exception is Tesco, the United Kingdom's leading supermarket chain. In 1994, Tesco decided its Clubcard program needed improvement. With the data analytical firm, dunnhumby associates, Tesco decided to take advantage of the data provided by Clubcard users and learn about customers' values, behavior, and needs.

Tesco's Clubcard collects data on how much customers spend, as well as where, when, and what products they buy. Based on Clubcard and merchandising information, Tesco aggregates customers into precisely defined, relevant marketing groups. Using the segmentation scheme, the company can manipulate price, product, and promotion to fit various groups of customers. According to dunnhumby,

> By understanding what matters to shoppers on a budget, for example, they can be really competitive on the products they buy. By understanding what promotions work for customers, Tesco and listed suppliers can reduce the volume of promotions in-store, yet increase overall returns. The range of products on the shelf is tailored using knowledge of how customers shop across brands, with a subtlety that product data alone can never reveal.

Originally, promotions and coupons that were sent to families varied depending on the data. In 1995, only six variations existed. Today, more than one hundred thousand variations are changed weekly. Customers receive targeted offers based on what they do and do not buy, their spending levels on particular products, their responsiveness to other offers, and much more.

Tesco is now one of the most successful grocery stores in the world, and retail chains everywhere try to emulate its use of customer data. The company's ability to apply data from all areas of the store has been the distinguishing factor that has contributed to its success.[1]

Developing a Customer/Prospect Valuation Methodology

A useful customer valuation methodology must provide a view of historical, current, and future financial value. In too many cases, traditional financial valuation methodologies have been limited to historical data, that is, what the customer was worth in the past. Past value has then been used to forecast what the customer or prospect might be worth in the future. While these approaches are valuable, they do not take into consideration the limitations on customer retention and growth. In other words, they assume the marketer is in control of the customer and the marketplace as well as marketing activities.

Traditional valuation methodologies further assume that all customers are equal or have equal value. For almost every product category that has been studied from a marketing standpoint, that is simply not true. Some customers and prospects are worth more than others. They spend more in the category. They are more profitable. They are more loyal. They are simply better customers than the general customer pool.

For example, in most product categories there is what is termed the "80/20 rule," or the Pareto rule (named after Italian economist Vilfredo Pareto). The rule simply states that 20 percent (perhaps a bit more or less) of customers commonly contribute approximately 80 percent of the firm's sales, profits, or income. The importance of the 80/20 rule cannot be emphasized enough for it forms the basis for almost all market aggregation. That is, in almost every company, a relatively small group of customers is critically important to the success of the company. In *Not All Customers Are Created Equal*, Garth Halberg quotes research indicating that within the yogurt category, 16 percent of U.S. households account for 83 percent of all purchase volume.[2] Similarly, he cites research by Folger Coffee Company indicating that 15 percent of households account for 70 percent of sales volume. A credit card marketer with which we are familiar took the analysis a step further to examine profitability by customer group. It discovered that a mere 12.8 percent of its active cardholders accounted for 90 percent of profits.

Table 5.1 shows that the Pareto rule holds true for services as well. The table captures customer data from a resort hotel over a recent one-year period. Each of 19,420 customers was first classified by the total amount of money spent in the hotel during his or her stay. Customers were arranged in descending order from those who spent the most to those who spent the least. Then, all of the classified customers were aggregated into ten equal groups of 1,942 members. (This division by tens is termed *decile analysis*.) This exercise clearly illustrates that some customers are much more valuable financially to the hotel than others. Indeed, 30 percent of the customers, the first three deciles, accounted for nearly 80 percent of total spending. Decile analysis is a commonly used approach to categorize customers. We discuss this approach in more detail in later sections of this book.

Note that this analysis is limited to customer spending. There is no data on age, gender, size of family, previous spending, geography, or other information to help explain these spending patterns. But since behavior and financial value of behaviors are at the heart of IMC, this is an excellent starting point for placing values on customers as assets.

Customer Brand Valuation

Targetbase, a database consulting group based in Irving, Texas, has developed an innovative approach to valuation that goes far beyond simple decile analysis. The method seeks to define an overall customer brand value (CBV).[3] Targetbase starts with the financial value that a customer (or group of customers) could represent to the brand's profitability. As shown in Exhibit 5.1, four factors underlie the CBV valuation.

Table 5.1 Decile Ranking of Hotel Customers by Total Revenue

Decile (%)	No. of Guests	Cumulative No. of Guests	Total Revenue	Cumulative Revenue	% of Total	Minimum Expenditure	Avergage Expenditure
10	1,942	1,942	$13,501	$13,501	57.5	$2,322	$6,952
20	1,942	3,884	$3,257	$16,758	71.4	$1,248	$1,677
30	1,942	5,826	$1,987	$18,745	79.9	$843	$1,023
40	1,942	7,768	$1,402	$20,148	85.9	$613	$722
50	1,942	9,710	$1,045	$21,192	90.3	$468	$538
60	1,942	11,652	$790	$21,983	93.7	$348	$407
70	1,942	13,594	$602	$22,585	96.3	$278	$310
80	1,942	15,536	$487	$23,072	98.3	$226	$251
90	1,942	17,478	$349	$23,421	99.8	$100	$180
100	1,942	19,420	$40	$23,460	100.0	$0	$21
Totals	19,420		$23,460				

30% of customers = 80%+ of total revenue

Exhibit 5.1 Calculating Customer Brand Value

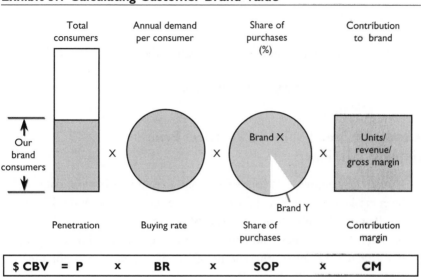

Used with permission from Targetbase, Inc.

- **Penetration (P).** The number of customers the firm has as a percentage of the total number of customers in the category.
- **Category buying rate (BR).** The average annual (or other time period) demand for the product, service, or brand per the customer.
- **Share of purchases (SOP).** The proportion of total customer purchases that the marketing organization enjoys. In other words, what percentage of all purchases in the category do customers give to the marketer's brand or firm? For example, if customers spend $100 per year on duct tape, what percentage do they spend on the firm's brand of tape?
- **Contribution to margin (CM).** How much of the total purchases made by the customer results in income flows at the company's contribution margin line? This is the key element in the evaluation, since it gets to the actual financial return to the organization, not just the dollar amount of the product sale at retail. Since the firm invests net dollars to purchase various forms of marketing communication, it is important to know how many

net dollars the organization actually receives once all costs have been taken out.

Customer brand value is calculated using the following formula:

$$\mathbf{CBV = P \times BR \times SOP \times CM}$$

Customer Brand Value in Practice: Printer Supplies Marketer

While the example that follows is from a real organization, data has been masked and simplified for the purposes of this illustration. Hampton Printing Supplies Company (HPSC) makes cartridges for desktop printers, fax machines, and other printing equipment. The company has targeted the small office/home office market and uses a combination of retail distribution and direct marketing sales to customers and prospects. The company has high brand awareness but has seen the category become increasingly saturated and "commoditized" as other companies have entered the field. A new marketing director believed the company could better manage and direct its marketing resources against the most valuable customers in its segment. As a result, she raised several key questions typical of issues confronting many marketers:

• Which product owners are most important to HPSC now and into the future?
• What actions do we want them to take?
• How much should we invest in them?

Using an in-house database as well as external industry data, the marketing team identified 100,000 owners of compatible printers within its Southeastern region. They then found that 40,000 of those owners had purchased Hampton brand cartridges at least once within the past year. They estimated that there were a total of 200,000 printers in the region (that is, an average of two printers per customer) and that each printer required an average of 12 refills per year. Thus, the annual demand per printer owner was 24 cartridges per year.

The marketing director estimated that the company received a 65 percent share of purchase (SOP) among the 40,000 owners who had purchased the Hampton brand in the past year. That is, among Hampton customers, some were entirely brand loyal, while others rotated their purchases among two or three cartridge manufacturers. Customers sometimes found that retailers were out of stock and thus would purchase another brand rather than wait for a delivery of Hampton products. Or some price-sensitive buyers would stock up on a competitor's brand when it went on sale. On average, Hampton customers purchased 15.60 cartridges per year from the company while also buying 8.40 cartridges per year from competitors.

The marketing director knew that previous communication efforts had concentrated on increasing market share and the number of units sold, regardless of the impact on profitability. To present top management with an alternative strategy, her plan was to frame the discussion not in terms of units or volume, but in terms of profitability to the company.

Working with the company's chief financial officer, she determined that the gross margin for cartridges was $6.50 each, in line with industry average. That meant that the typical buyer in the region was potentially worth $156 in profit each year (24 purchases $\times$ $6.50). The problem was that Hampton buyers gave the company only 65 percent of their total purchases. Thus, in reality, each customer was worth an average of only $101.40 ($156 $\times$ 65%). The remaining $54.60 in gross margin sales went to competitors.

Here, we summarize the data covered so far:

Penetration (P)
Total identified customers in market = 100,000
Number of Hampton brand customers = 40,000
Penetration of Hampton brand (100,000/40,000) = 40%

Buying rate (BR)
Average printers per customer = 2
Average refills per year per printer = 12
Average annual demand per customer (2 $\times$ 12) = 24

Share of purchase (SOP)

Hampton brand share of purchase = 65%

Hampton demand per customer $(2 \times 12 \times .65) = 15.60$

Contribution margin (CM)

Gross margin per unit sold = $6.50

Value of a customer ($P \times BR \times SOP \times CM$)

Average value per category customer $(2 \times 12 \times 6.50) = \$156.00$

Average value per Hampton customer

$(2 \times 12 \times .65 \times 6.50) = \$101.40$

The marketing director immediately saw two areas of opportunity:

- To increase the company's penetration among buyers in the region—that is, to go after the 60,000 printer owners who do not use the Hampton brand
- To increase Hampton's share of purchase, meaning to capture more of the 35 percent of Hampton-buyer purchases that is going to competitors

The marketing director, however, found these two alternatives too broad. Her resources were too limited to chase after the entire marketplace. She felt that by analyzing the company's in-house customer database she could better pinpoint specific opportunities. She aggregated customers in the database first by usage and found three distinct groups:

- **Heavy users.** Twenty percent of buyers purchased 34 or more units a year, with an average of 42.4 cartridges.
- **Medium users.** Sixty percent of buyers bought 14 to 33 cartridges per year.
- **Light users.** Twenty percent of buyers bought 13 or fewer units per year.

Next, she aggregated those customers according to their buying behavior, that is, how loyal they were to their primary brand or brands. Again, she developed three groups:

- **Loyal users.** Fifteen percent gave all or most of their share of purchases to their preferred brand.
- **Switchers.** Fifty percent rotated their purchases between two or three preferred brands.
- **Price buyers.** Thirty-five percent bought cartridges only when they were on sale, regardless of brand.

From here, the marketing director developed the strategy formulation matrix shown in Exhibit 5.2. She simply crossed the usage data by the buying behavior aggregation. (Again, we are using simplified data for this example and assume even distribution of each segment across the matrix.) By incorporating CBV analysis information computed earlier, she was able to determine the potential reward for each group along with the appropriate behavioral goal.

The matrix suggests three alternatives:

- **Group A.** These buyers represented highly loyal, heavy users who gave most of their purchases to their preferred brand. Because each customer used an average 42 cartridges per year, they represented a significant financial value, that is, $273 in gross profit per customer each year rather than the $156 of the "average" customer across the entire market. Unfortunately, this group represented only about 3 percent of the buying universe. Thus, the marketing director did not feel it offered significant growth opportunity for her investment. The

Exhibit 5.2 Strategy Formulation Matrix

	Heavy Users (20%)	Medium Users (60%)	Light Users (20%)	Total
Loyal users (15%)	3,000[a]	9,000	3,000	15,000
Switchers (50%)	10,000	30,000[b]	10,000	50,000
Price buyers (35%)	7,000	21,000	7,000[c]	35,000
Total	20,000	60,000	20,000	100,000

a. Each customer is potentially worth $42 \times \$6.50 = \$273$ in profit.
    Goal: Acquire and retain

b. Each customer is potentially worth $24 \times .65 \times \$6.50 = \$101.40$ in profit.
    Goal: Convert to loyal users

c. Each customer is potentially worth $7.5 \times \$4.50 = \$33.75$ in profit (at best).
    Goal: Retain as cost-effectively as possible

goal for this segment, then, would be to acquire those who were not already using Hampton products and—most importantly—make sure the company retained those it already had. The marketing director knew that it would be difficult to switch those who were strongly loyal to another brand, so she questioned whether she could better deploy marketing resources elsewhere.

- **Group B.** This group represented individuals with lighter than average consumption, only 7.5 units per year. When they did need a refill cartridge, they appeared to buy a brand only if it was on sale. Such customers, the marketing director thought, offered little financial opportunity to Hampton. Assuming that it would take a $2.00 discount to incite their purchase, thus reducing the HSPC gross margin from $6.50 to $4.50 per cartridge, each customer would represent a profit of only $33.75. And that would occur only if customers gave all of their purchases to Hampton. While the marketing director did not want to walk away from this segment, she recognized that she must retain those buyers she could using the most cost-effective means possible.

- **Group C.** This large group was attractive to the marketing director because of its size and therefore the opportunity for potential profitable growth. The economics of this group are similar to the average Hampton buyer, that is, each customer represents about $101.40 in profitability. Because of the size of the group, however, the marketing director recognized she would have to fight hard to protect and increase her share among these current users. Additionally, because these customers were not highly loyal to other brands, she felt she likely stood a better chance of converting these switchers to the Hampton brand than converting some of the other groups.

As the experiences at HSPC clearly illustrate, CBV allows the IMC manager to identify which customers are most valuable, which have the greatest potential, which must be protected and their income flows retained, and so on. With this type of valuation analysis, which is not particularly complicated or difficult, marketing and communication managers can start to build a basic platform for their marcom programs that encompasses what the program should be designed to achieve, how much they would or could be willing to invest, how returns could be measured, and—most importantly—how the firm should or could invest its finite financial resources among marketing communication target customers and communication alternatives.

Customer brand value is particularly suited to categories in which an identifiable group of customers and prospects makes ongoing purchases of a product or service according to reasonably predictable consumption and repurchase patterns. Thus, it is extremely useful in planning for products such as consumer packaged goods, industrial supplies, gasoline, airline travel, and so on. It is less useful in categories where purchase is spontaneous or difficult to anticipate or where customers do not spread their purchase among more than one provider, such as financial services, automobiles, home furnishings, or management consulting services.

Creating Customer and Marketplace Value

To this point, we have viewed customers and prospects primarily as passive entities that can be manipulated at the whim of the marketing communicator. In other words, the marcom manager has all the tools, all the expertise, and all the skills and capabilities to create communication programs that will manage the behavior of customers and prospects. While this is a commonly held belief, nothing could be further from the truth. Value is in the eye of the beholder. It is the customer who determines what value the product or service offers him or her individually. It is customers or prospects who determine whether or not the price/value relationship is appropriate for their use or for use by their company. It is customers or prospects who decide on brand or company loyalty. In short, the customer, not the marketer, is in control of the marketplace. The faster organizations move toward networked, interactive, and dialogue-driven marketplaces, the more true this will become.

How, then, does the marketer create value in the eyes of the customer? In most marcom planning approaches, it is assumed that certain forms of customer value are inherent in the product or service the organization is vending. Therefore, historically, the task of the marcom manager has been to identify those values and communicate them to customers and prospects. Or, in some cases, the benefits or values may be latent in the product or service and the communicator must identify them and then use them to persuade customers and prospects of the desirability and value of the product or service. In either case, value is determined by the marketer, or—at least—the marketer determines in advance the value the customer or prospect should consider or the features that should be of value. The focus of traditional advertising on finding a unique selling position, or "inherent drama," in every brand is based on the age-old assumption that the marketer is in control of the offering and its value. The marketer determines what the composition of the product or service will be, how it will be distributed, what price will be asked, who will be told about the value, when the value will be communicated, and so on.

Associated with this assumption is the common marketer belief that any product or service can be "sold" to consumers if the marketer has enough money, is clever enough with the marcom program, and is given sufficient time. That's why much of the present promotional planning is based on such notions as "creativity," "share of voice," "ubiquity of distribution," and other factors over which the marketer has control. As noted in Chapter 1, the outdated but seemingly immovable Four Ps marketing model is all about control. If the marketer can get the product, price, place (distribution), and promotion right, the customer will buy and continue to buy over time. In short, it is a marketer-controlled system in which the marketer assumes power over all marketplace elements: money, raw materials, manufacturing technology, information technology, channels, media, and communication. The consumer is little more than a pawn to be manipulated by the marketer and influenced by the company's communication programs.

The reality, however, is that in today's interactive environment, control is quickly slipping away from the marketer. In the new marketplace, driven by the Internet, mobile and wireless communication, instant messaging, and other technological advances, customers have the upper hand. They can view, shop, and buy from all types of alternative systems, ranging from bricks and mortar retail outlets to E-commerce sites. People are no longer restricted to goods and services that are immediately available geographically or during certain time periods. Indeed, customers and prospects are able to identify, evaluate, and purchase products and services from all over the world using their own time frames and through processes they set up. Control over time and distance, once the domain of marketers, simply disappears or shifts into the hands of individual customers and prospects.

The companies that have been successful in pleasing this new breed of customers have enhanced the value of their brands in the eyes of consumers, often by finding ways to personalize mass-produced products. Lee Jeans stores, for instance, will take a customer's measurements and make a pair of jeans especially for that individual, exactly the way he or she wants. A customer can order a Dell computer with the specific components that he or she needs. In Asia and Europe, the wide variety of cell phone covers and personalized rings is Nokia's way of personalizing the cell phone. Even My Yahoo attempts to personalize its brand of Web services for the customer.

As well as control over the product, traditional marketing also sought control over the value chain. In *Competitive Advantage: Creating and Sustaining Superior Performance*, Michael Porter describes the traditional process whereby the marketer, the channels, and the media commonly created "value chains" in which desirable features and elements were added along the way as the product or service moved from seller to buyer.[4] According to Porter, in the traditional value chain, the marketer or marketing system and its partners delivered customer value for the basic product or service through assembly, distribution, stocking, and other methods. In each step, it was assumed the marketer added value for the ultimate customer. Of course, the value-adding organization expected to take a margin or generate some income for its efforts. Therefore, the actual product itself, by the time it was available to the end user, commonly cost three to twenty times more than it actually cost to manufacture. Traditional marketing further assumes the value chain is linear, that is, it flows from the manufacturer through all the value-adding steps on the way to the end user.

The problem with this view, of course, is that in many cases some of that costly "added value" is not wanted or needed by the consumer. In today's interactive marketplace, the consumer—not the marketer—controls much of the value chain. For example, the end user may decide that buying a book through a local bookshop really provides little extra value. As an alternative, amazon.com offers wide selection, competitive service, and an easy purchase and delivery system. Similarly, a wooden door manufacturer may decide to choose from a wide variety of suppliers for a certain standardized group of hinges and door hardware. FreeMarkets On-Line will organize a widely dispersed group of suppliers, qualify them in terms of their capacity to provide the required hardware at the necessary quality level, and then set up an online auction in which various suppliers bid for the door manufacturer's order. Here, roles are reversed. The hardware manufacturer does not target and market to its ultimate customer, the door maker; instead, with the help of FreeMarkets, the customer is in control of the buying process. Potential sellers are then left to make bids to provide that value at the price they are willing to offer.

The automotive industry offers another good example that recognizes the shift of power from seller to buyer. In 2000, DaimlerChrysler, Ford Motor Company, and General Motors announced efforts to work together to form a single global business-to-business supplier exchange. The results of their efforts emerged under the name of a new company called Covisint, with the goal to become the central hub where original equipment manufacturers (OEMs) and suppliers of all sizes could come together in a single business environment using the same tools and user interface. When the company was formed, Covisint was envisioned as an Internet leader, similar to eBay, with a bidding and purchasing system for everyone who sells products to the automobile industry. The company would help increase supply chain efficiencies and reduce costs for both the supplier and the automobile manufacturer. While there have been several challenges for the newly formed company, it was formed with this twenty-first-century concept: there is an increase in power and knowledge for both suppliers and manufacturers when they combine and cooperate.

Learning the Five Rs of IMC

This switch in the determination of "value add" that reverses the traditional value chain is critical to understanding IMC. Since IMC puts

the customer at the center of the organization, it changes the entire concept of value. No longer is value added sequentially as in the traditional
model. Instead, the customer determines value and selectively adds that
value from the marketing system using only those elements that provide the greatest value to him or her. One might refer to this as a
demand chain rather than a supply chain. In Exhibit 5.3, we visualize
this "customer value add" as a series of circles surrounding the customer
or prospect from which he or she or the firm can select, combine, and
organize products and services in ways that create the greatest personal
or organizational value.

At the center of the system is the customer or prospect. Surrounding the customer are the traditional marketing value-add systems,

Exhibit 5.3 IMC Circular Value Add

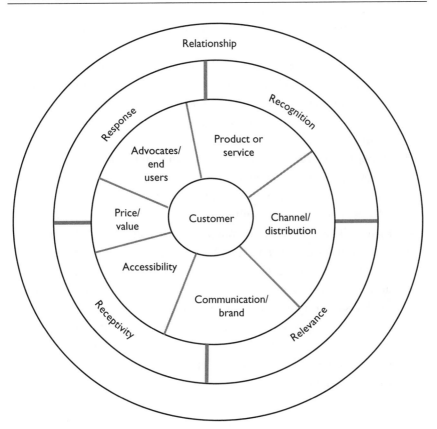

including product/service specifications, price, channel or distribution system, communication and information, and so on. The initial value-added elements shown include the traditional Four Ps. However, we have added others that become more relevant, such as the influence of advocates, endorsers, and communities of interest, as well as accessibility, or the ways in which the product or service can be obtained. While the added values we have shown in the first ring around the customer are not exhaustive, they are illustrative of the new concept of the customer or prospect selecting the value to be added and essentially creating much of the value enhancement for themselves.

The second concentric ring includes the first of what we call the new Five Rs of IMC. Where traditional marketing focused on the Four Ps—product, price, place, and promotion—IMC concentrates on the following:

1. **Relevance.** This term is used to determine how relevant the marketing firm can be to the customer in terms of making products and services the customer wants and needs. Beyond this, the marketer must further provide relevant, compelling, and meaningful communication as well as relevant, competitive pricing and relevant distribution systems through which the customer can acquire the product or service.

2. **Receptivity.** This term has two meanings in the context of strategic IMC. On one hand, marketers want to be able to reach customers and prospects when they will be most receptive to the message. That is, if a marketer is selling hamburgers, the best time to reach them will be when they are hungry. So, the question is when and at what point of brand contact will the customer or prospect be most receptive to the message or incentive? Receptivity also encompasses how open the organization is to new ideas, new concepts, and new methods of doing business. Inherent in this is the idea that IMC is not simply about how the company wants to communicate; it is, instead, about how the customer wants to communicate or be communicated with. This requires receptivity to new approaches on the part of the marketer.

3. **Response.** There are two aspects to this term in the IMC context. First, response raises the question of how easy it is for the customer or prospect to respond to the company's offerings. Is the company easy to do business with, and does it effectively facilitate the transaction process at every possible point of contact? Second, response refers to how well the organization can sense, adapt to, and answer the needs and wishes of its customers and prospects. In an interactive marketplace, the key skill of the marketer is no longer his or her ability to plan, develop, and implement marketing and communication programs. Instead, it is to be able to respond appropriately to customer needs and wants.

4. **Recognition.** As with receptivity and response, recognition has dual meanings. First, it reflects the firm's ability to recognize a customer at important points of contact and to immediately connect to the firm's stored knowledge about that customer. In other words, when a customer calls its toll-free number, can the answering representative immediately draw on the customer's transaction and service history to facilitate the call? Or does the company recognize a returning visitor to its website, and does it have the ability to link that visit to previous activity? Second, recognition has to do with the customer's ability to recognize and select the organization's brand from a given array of alternatives. Are prospects and customers aware of the brand? Do they associate it with particular needs and uses? Are they able to understand what differentiates this brand from those of competitors?

Exhibit 5.3 shows the first four Rs as surrounding the customer or prospect. Depending on how the customer or prospect wants to obtain value through the first circle, the second circle illustrates the types of additional value he or she can receive from the company because of its organizational structure, company focus, willingness to change, and so on. In short, the first four Rs reflect the additional value the marketer wants to provide for the customer.

At the outer edge of the new value-add circle system is the single element of relationship, the fifth R.

5. **Relationship.** This term has come to mean many things in marketing. Trends like customer relationship management (CRM), customer relationship marketing, and one-to-one marketing all revolve around *relationship*. Unfortunately, as it is used in marketing, the term essentially suggests the marketing firm can create a relationship with customers based on data, analysis, and various forms of communication primarily based on the use of information technology. In value-based IMC, the customer is the one who creates the relationship, not the marketer. It is the customer who decides with whom he or she will do business and under what time and situation constraints. The power of the customer is key in understanding the customer-centric view of IMC: the customer decides, the marketer responds.

Let's look at a real-world example to review the Five Rs. The online community website, women.com, offers editorial content and E-commerce services on issues that are important to women. Through chat rooms and bulletin boards, the site can obtain insights about consumers, including demographic, psychographic, and behavioral information. This information is used to understand how the customer thinks. By collecting more than just demographic data, the site can offer advertisements, promotions, and editorial articles tailored to individual consumers. In this way, women.com achieves both *relevance* and *recognition*. The member can access the site at a time that is most convenient for her, when she is most interested in receiving information, which equates to *receptivity*. The site builds a dialogue with the consumer, in which the consumer talks and women.com listens and learns, achieving *response*. A brand such as women.com that listens and has a *relationship* with the consumer is more effective than a brand with no relationship at all.

Using the Five Rs of IMC rather than the Four Ps of traditional marketing changes the way in which managers think about and develop marcom programs. Just as we suggested changing the model of how customers and prospects are valued by the firm, so too must the planning of marketing and communication programs change.

Three Key Questions

After working through steps 1 and 2 of the IMC process, the marcom manager should be able to answer three critical questions based on the customer and prospect data assembled so far:

- Who are the firm's best customers, and why?
- Who are the firm's best prospects, and why?
- What information does the marketer need to be more relevant to customers and prospects?

Moving On

A marketer who can answer these three questions is almost ready to move to step 3. Before we do that, however, it is important to summarize the approach to customer valuation. Valuation starts with the marketer's view of customers, particularly in terms of customer income flows and their contribution to margin. Defining customers in these terms tells the marketer who the company's most important customers and prospects are or might be. But to develop effective marcom programs, the marketer must also understand the customer's view of the brand, product, or firm. This introduces a reciprocal view of the marketplace, requiring the marketer to look at value through the eyes of the customer, not just from the standpoint of the organization. The strategic, value-based IMC approach demands this total view of the customer if effective marcom programs are to be developed and delivered. Therefore, before moving on to step 3, we will discuss the concept of reciprocity and how it relates to the challenges of integration. This is the topic of the next chapter.

CHAPTER 6

THE PARTNERSHIP OF INTEGRATION AND RECIPROCITY

T o this point, we have focused primarily on the marketing manager's approaches to integration. We've looked at the marketer's
goals and presented methods by which a firm can determine which
customers or prospects are potentially the most profitable for its marcom investments. Along the way, we've noted that a value-generating
approach to communication is not just about what the marketer wants
to achieve. It is about interactivity, that is, creating a dialogue between
the company and its customers and prospects. We have also discovered
that real success comes from long-term relationships, not just short-
term sales bumps.

Interactivity is all about sharing—the dynamic sharing of value,
meaning, and information between marketer and customer, between
marketer and channels, between management and employees, and
between the organization and its shareholders and stakeholders. Yet
most marketing approaches are not based on sharing, but on winning.
Even the terminology is a giveaway: "target markets," "gaining market
share," "outflanking the competition, "blitzing with advertising," "slash-
ing prices," and hundreds of other euphemisms that imply conflict in
which the marketer wins and someone else loses. How can the market-

ing and communication approaches developed over the last sixty years hope to move marketers away from an attitude of winning to one of sharing?

The answer, of course, is they can't! What's needed is a new way of thinking, a new corporate culture, and new approaches to marketing and communication. This chapter tackles the challenge of creating programs that bring marketers and buyers together in a two-way relationship characterized by sharing and reciprocity.

The Need for a Reciprocal Marketer-Consumer Relationship

Historically, marketing and communication's primary value to a firm has been to identify and communicate some competitive advantage that differentiates its offerings from competitive brands. Developing competitive advantage has not always proven to be in the best interests of the consumer, resulting, for example, in overpricing, reductions in product quality, or fictitious product changes. This happens when the marketer focuses on developing competitive advantage rather than on increasing value in the eyes of the customer. In an interactive marketplace, the customer controls much of the power of choice and selection and has an almost limitless availability of brands and solutions. The world is approaching what economists have called "perfect marketplace knowledge." This power switch means that competitive advantage loses its meaning and the marketer must instead emphasize *shared values* with customers and end users. The section that follows provides the theoretical base that explains why.

An Aristotelian Beginning

In fourth-century Greece, Aristotle and his students identified two types of justice: *corrective justice*, or the proper punishment of criminal acts, and *distributive justice*, or the equal sharing of inputs and values or rewards among participating individuals and groups of people. Aristotle wrote:

It follows therefore that justice involves at least four terms, namely two persons for whom it is just and two shares which are just. And there will be the same equality between shares as between the persons, since the ratio between the shares will be equal to the ratio between the persons, for if the persons are not equal, they will not have equal shares; it is when equals possess or are allotted unequal shares, or persons not equal shares, that quarrels and complaints arise.[1]

He went on to say:

Justice is therefore a sort of proportion; for proportion is not a property of numerical quantity only, but of quality in general, proportion being equality of ratios, and involving four terms at least.[2]

Aristotle was describing the basic elements of what today might be called buyer-seller relationships, or even better, customer relationships. As long as each party believes the value of their rewards from the relationship are equal to the value of their inputs, both will be satisfied. When there is a perception of unequal input or unequal sharing of rewards, the relationship will break down.

Adams's Inequity in Social Exchange

With this Aristotelian foundation, J. Stacy Adams, a behavioral scientist at General Electric Company in 1963, developed the concept of *economic distributive justice*:

. . . distributive justice among men who are in an exchange relationship with one another obtains when the profits of each are proportional to their investments. Profit consists of that which is received in the exchange, less cost incurred. A cost is that which is given up in the exchange, such as forgoing the rewards obtainable in another exchange, or a burden assumed as a specific function of the exchange, such as risk, which would include not only potential real loss but the psychological discomfort of uncertainty as well. Investments in an exchange are the relevant attributes that are brought by a party to the exchange. They

include, for example, skill, effort, education, training, experience, age, sex, and ethnic background.[3]

Schematically, for a dyad consisting of A and B, distributive justice is realized when the relationship between them exists as follows:

$$\frac{\text{A's rewards} - \text{A's costs}}{\text{A's investment}} = \frac{\text{B's rewards} - \text{B's costs}}{\text{B's Investment}}$$

Adams further states:

When an inequity between the proportions exists, the participants to the exchange will experience a feeling of injustice and one or the other party will experience deprivation. The party specifically experiencing relative deprivation is the one for whom the ratio of profits to investments is the smaller.[4]

Adams develops his concept by offering a theory of inequity. His premise is that whenever two individuals exchange anything, there is the possibility that one or both of them will feel that the exchange was inequitable. Therefore, inequity for a person in the relationship occurs whenever he or she perceives that the ratio of his or her outcomes to inputs and the ratio of the other person's outcomes to inputs are unequal. Given that circumstance, according to Adams, the person perceiving the inequity may do one of six things[5]:

1. The person feeling the inequity may vary his or her inputs, either increasing or decreasing them, depending on whether the inequity is advantageous or disadvantageous.
2. The person feeling inequity may alter his or her outcomes, that is, either increasing or decreasing them, depending on whether the inequity is advantageous or disadvantageous to him or her.
3. A third alternative is to distort the inputs or outputs cognitively. In other words, the person feeling inequality may cognitively

distort his inputs and outcomes, the direction of the distortion being the same as if he or she had actually altered his or her inputs and outcomes.

4. The person feeling the inequity may simply leave the field by severing the relationship.

5. In the face of injustice, the aggrieved person may attempt to alter or cognitively distort the other party's inputs and outcomes, or try to force the other party to leave the field.

6. Another alternative is the person perceiving injustice may change the party with whom he or she makes a comparison, particularly when there is a third party involved in the relationship.

Reciprocal Theory and Customer Relationships

Applying Adams's hypothesis, instead of trying to maximize their own personal outcomes in an interactive, networked marketplace with a wide range of alternatives, customers will seek a reciprocal relationship with a select group of sellers from whom they will purchase products and services. Customers expect to pay for value, but customer loyalty can only occur when the two parties perceive that the value exchange between them is equal, that is, each party gets as much out of the relationship as they believe they have put in. Thus, the IMC approach is to refer to *brand relationships*, which are defined as "the relationships that exist between buyers and sellers through the exchange of value for products or services over time." It is this reciprocity that will define buyer-seller relationships, particularly in interactive space. Both the buyer and the seller are seeking reciprocity, and it is this shared value that creates ongoing relationships.

Since relationship value can be determined quickly and easily in an interactive and networked marketplace, it provides the basis for what marketers will likely see develop—that is, brands, firms, and products that revolve around customer interactions and shared value. Both parties are, as Adams suggests, seeking "justice" and that justice is perceived to exist when all individuals in the relationship receive a return that is proportional to their investment. In the converging IMC marketplace,

WIN-WIN SHOPPING AT NORDSTROM

When talking about reciprocity, it seems difficult to find examples of an equal relationship in the marketplace. In a typical retail environment, for example, the consumer does the majority of the work, sifting through merchandise, making a selection, and often having to wait in line to pay. Nordstrom's personal shopper service, however, aims to shift some of the burden away from the customer. The services of a Nordstrom's Personal Touch shopper are complimentary. The shopper will fill almost any request for apparel, shoes, or accessories. If a customer sees an item of interest in Nordstrom's magazine ads, newspaper ads, or mailers, the shopper will help find it. If an item is not available in the store, the shopper can help find it online.

Note that the buyer-seller relationship is reciprocal: the buyer wants to purchase and Nordstrom's employees do the work to find the desired merchandise. The same relationship exists online. At nordstrom.com, a consumer can chat live with a customer service representative, and the representative will answer any questions and help locate any item.

that reciprocity will be determined and continually redefined based on every brand contact and every communication delivered and received by both marketer and customer.

Note that Adams points out that inputs to and outcomes from a relationship are generally highly subjective. Depending on the relation of outcomes to inputs, one party in the relationship may deem it equitable, while the other may view it as inequitable or out of balance. In other words, it is the *perceived relationship* that is important and that becomes highly relevant in an interactive marketplace where many alternatives exist for both parties. Recall, too, that perceptions are generally created by communication, making IMC a critical element in the marketer's set of strategic resources.

Adams further suggests that perceived inequity leads to tensions in the relationship. There are several alternatives for resolving such tensions. If, for example, individual A feels his or her outcomes are too low relative to those of individual B, individual A can choose to do one of the following:

- **Reduce his or her inputs.** A customer might only buy the brand when it is on sale or buy competing brands from time to time; a marketer might slightly reduce quality or begin charging for what had previously been "free services."
- **Increase his or her outcomes.** A customer might attempt to enhance his or her returns by negotiating the price of the product or service or by asking for additional services to accompany the price paid; a marketer might refuse to take certain credit cards or justify the loss of income from a present customer by considering lifetime value rather than immediate financial returns.
- **Leave the relationship.** A customer may permanently switch to other brands, products, or services; a marketer might "fire" customers who demand substantial service, do not purchase enough to support the relationship, or are otherwise not profitable.

A Practical Application of the Reciprocal Model

Having made a case for a reciprocal marketplace in which buyers and sellers share equal value, the next question is how to put the concept into practice in today's marketing environment. A paper delivered at a National Center for Database Marketing Conference suggests a model of how reciprocity can be adapted and applied as a practical planning tool for marketers.[6]

The model shown in Exhibit 6.1 balances the behavior-derived estimate of a customer's financial value to the brand against an attitude-derived value that the brand represents in the customer's mind. In step 2 of the IMC process (see Chapter 5), we calculated customer brand value as follows:

Exhibit 6.1 Relationship Framework

Value of the customer
to the brand
(Behavioral:
Penetration × Category
Buying rate × Share of purchase)

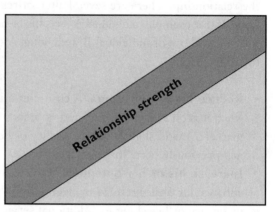

Value of the brand to the customer
(Attitudinal: Compatibility with needs, mind-set, environment)

From Don E. Schultz and Dana Hayman, "Fully Understand Consumer Behavior Using Your Database" (National Center for Database Marketing Conference, Chicago, July 30, 1999). Used with permission from Targetbase, Inc.

$$\textbf{Penetration (P)} \times \textbf{Buying rate (BR)} \times$$
$$\textbf{Share of purchase (SOP)} \times \textbf{Contribution margin (CM)}$$

In Exhibit 6.1, the vertical axis (value of the customer to the brand) is determined through a calculation of income flows and gross contribution margin that the brand receives from its customers over time. The horizontal axis represents the value of the brand to the customer, that is, the customer's view of the brand and the value it offers. Much of this customer value is attitudinal, consisting of compatibility with the needs, market, and environment in which he or she operates. Yet a great deal of it must be financial as well, since this is where the brand creates value for the customer. This combination makes brand value one of the most difficult metrics for the marketer to define.

In the IMC approach, the value of the brand to the customer is determined by taking into account three primary factors:

- Customer needs (What benefits are they looking for in the category?)
- Customer mind-set (What are their attitudes, motivations, and feelings about the product, the marketer, and the brand's value proposition?)
- The environment (What constraints and influences determine the boundaries of various types of purchase behavior?)

The broad diagonal bar across the center of Exhibit 6.1 defines the level of relationship strength that can or does exist between the marketer and the customer. The stronger the relationship, the greater the shared values between the two. Thus, when both the value of the customer to the brand and the value of the brand to the customer are high, the relationship will be strong and ongoing. Above or below this line, the relationship between the brand and the customer is out of balance, meaning one side is experiencing either actual or perceptual value to a greater or lesser degree than the other. Only when the two are in reasonable equilibrium is the relationship mutually beneficial and sustainable.

In an interactive, networked marketplace, this identification of customer value becomes the norm, not the exception. For example, almost any type of direct or online marketer can quickly and easily determine the value of each and every customer simply by knowing his or her purchase rate, frequency of purchase, and product margin and by subtracting the cost of acquisition and of incidental and ongoing service required by the customer from the customer's expenditures. The challenge, of course, is that the marketer knows what the customer purchased, but typically doesn't know why. That is where the concept of reciprocal relationships comes into play.

From the customer's view, the measure of brand value is generally attitudinal, although there may be some visual or actual value differentials apparent. Since so many products or services are similar today, the consumer commonly develops some type of internal calculus by which brand value alternatives are evaluated, and purchasing decisions are made based on that evaluation. From the three factors discussed earlier (needs, mind-set, and environment), the strength of the relationship between the customer and the brand can be identified and determined.

The beauty of the interactive, networked, and dialogue-driven marketplace is, of course, the marketer's continuous ability to gauge the strength of the ongoing brand relationship and to adapt his or her marketing activities to fit individual customer requirements. For example, by simply asking a few questions at the end of each brand contact, the marketer can identify the customer's attitudes toward the brand and the brand relationship. This instant feedback, as practiced by a number of online and direct marketing catalog organizations such as Lands' End, L.L. Bean, USAA, and others, radically changes the time frame in which marketer and customer interact. Rather than relying on traditional consumer survey research, marketers can have an almost instant read on their relationships with not just their most important customers but all of them.

Referring again to Exhibit 6.1, by knowing the value of the customer and understanding the nature of the relationship, it also becomes possible and practical for the marketer to categorize customers based on their value to the brand and the value of the brand to the customer. Thus, the actual strength of the brand relationship can be understood and managed. Where moderate relationships exist, they might be strengthened. Where they are strong, they can be reinforced. The marketer can become proactive in developing lasting relationships with desirable customers and prospects by understanding the reciprocity that must exist between the two.

The Reciprocal Model in the Interactive Marketplace

The proof of any model is its performance in the marketplace. The reciprocal approach discussed here can best be illustrated by the case history of a U.S.-based educational services provider.[7]

The company in question sought and acquired new customers through a broad variety of promotional approaches ranging from traditional advertising and direct marketing to websites and Internet home pages. Educational services were provided through traditional classroom instruction and Internet-based distance learning programs. Thus, one can immediately see the interactive and networked nature of both the organization and its products and services.

Using the reciprocal approach, the company was able to determine the three primary components of its revenue stream:

- **The number of enrollees.** This was approximately 63,800 per year.
- **The length of time students were enrolled.** Twenty-four percent left after the first two months, 60 percent after the first six months, and 77 percent after the first twelve months.
- **The revenue and profit per month (on average) for each student enrolled.** Each student represented, on average, $381 in revenue per month and a $39 monthly profit or earnings before income tax (EBIT).

The students were divided into seven segments according to revenue and profitability (earnings before income tax). The company determined that high revenue was not always associated with high profits and vice versa. The key was the compatibility between the students and the offerings. Thus, some students were willing to invest a significant sum toward their education, but defected when the course work did not meet their expectations. On the other hand, students who were compatible with the school's offerings could be profitable even at lower levels of financial commitment because there was less defection, greater continuity of enrollment, and, hence, ongoing income flows. Using these data, the educational center was able to evaluate in more detail the value of its programs to its various customer groups. Exhibit 6.2 shows the results.

The center had an excellent enrollment record, with over 7,600 enrollees per month, or over 91,000 per year. Customer retention was not nearly as impressive, however. The firm was losing, on average, approximately 7,700 students per month, or 92,400 per year. In short, the actual year-to-year enrollment was declining since more customers were leaving after one year than were being gained during that same

Exhibit 6.2 Revenue Stream Statistics

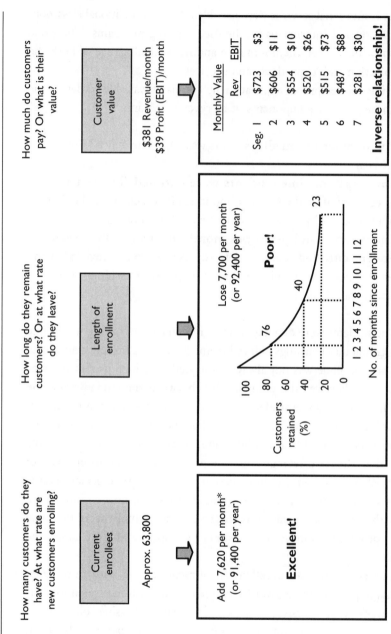

Note: EBIT = earnings before income tax; Rev = average revenue per segment.

From Don E. Schultz and Scott Bailey, "Building a Viable Model for Customer/Brand Loyalty" (ARF Week of Workshops, New York, NY, October 7, 1999). Used with permission from Targetbase, Inc.

period. And while the average revenue per student was impressive, on further analysis, it became clear that a small number of students were quite profitable while others provided almost no profit at all. In other words, there was an inverse relationship between length of enrollment and returns to the educational center. Thus, customer loyalty was working against the best interests of the company.

Turning to the other side of the equation, the value of the education center to the customer, some interesting results were found.

Further research identified two classifications of students. First, "nonbrand" types were those who had a low compatibility with the educational center activities and who were not satisfied with their experience. Second, "brand" types were those whose views of education and their educational needs were compatible with what the educational center was offering and who were generally satisfied with the services provided.

The two groups were then classified according to their financial value to the educational center. This analysis enabled the company to identify those students who were most likely "vulnerable," that is, most likely to terminate their enrollment by either dropping out or moving to another educational institution. As shown in Exhibit 6.3, the educational center brand was lagging behind competitors in terms of customer satisfaction.

By using the reciprocal evaluation model, the center was able to understand *why* students were leaving. Forty percent based their decision to leave on some type of dissatisfaction with the educational center, that is, the center was not meeting their needs or requirements. Fifteen different reasons were given for this dissatisfaction, with only five reasons accounting for about half of all defections. The question for the center, of course, became "Could those reasons for dissatisfaction be addressed with marketing and marketing communication so that the vulnerable students would be identified and the expected attrition of other students prevented?" In other words, if the center could address issues that caused students to leave, then dissatisfaction should be reduced and the loss of students stemmed.

Exhibit 6.3 Value of Brand to Customer

Brand lags its competitors in customer satisfaction.
Vulnerable customers are disproportionately "high value."

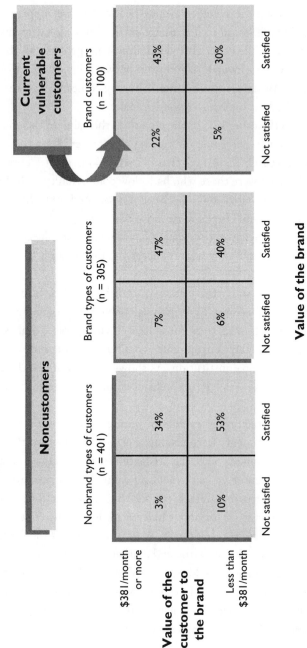

From Don E. Schultz and Scott Bailey, "Building a Viable Model for Customer/Brand Loyalty" (ARF Week of Workshops, New York, NY, October 7, 1999). Used with permission from Targetbase, Inc.

Further analysis of the fifteen major reasons for student dissatisfaction revealed that eight of them could potentially be resolved through marketing or marcom actions. Others were generally organizational (essentially inherent in the structure of the educational programs being offered) and thus beyond the scope of the marketing communication managers. Three key solutions were then identified: improvements in communication, provision for improvements in the operating systems, and development of direct systems solutions that could be implemented by local managers.

The final steps in the analysis came from an estimate of "recovered value" that was potentially available to the educational center if the necessary changes were made. Exhibit 6.4 illustrates that analysis.

While the dissatisfaction elements that were driving students out of the educational programs could be identified and their importance determined, simply removing the dissatisfaction factor did not guarantee that students would immediately become satisfied and regain their full value for the educational provider. Thus, an additional analysis was conducted. In this exercise, potential loss recovery was determined for each of the three available marketing-related fixes. This analysis was done on each of the seven customer segments shown in Exhibit 6.2, thus allowing the company to determine the potential impact on both revenue and profitability by segment. As a result, the company was able to concentrate its efforts on those marketing activities that would have the greatest financial impact.

As shown, substantial improvements could be expected in both revenue and profit if the marketing fixes were employed. Thus, the educational center managers had their answer: make the changes and student loss would likely be substantially reduced.

Exhibit 6.5 summarizes the concept of balancing the value of the brand to the customer with the value of the customer to the brand. The seven customer segments have been grouped according to the customers' compatibility with the school and its offerings (on the horizontal axis) and their financial value to the company as measured by EBIT (on the vertical axis). This provides a four-box matrix with the following groups:

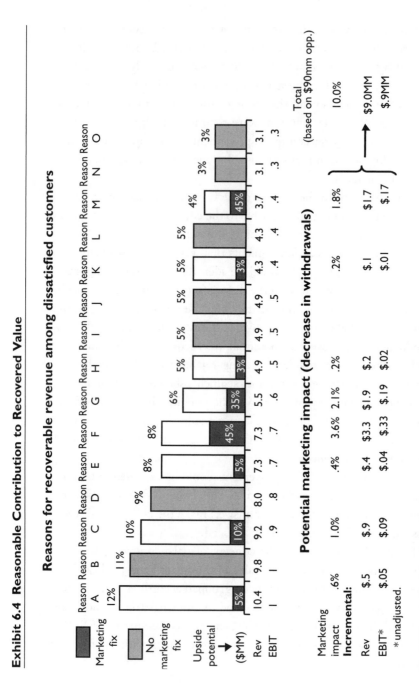

Exhibit 6.4 Reasonable Contribution to Recovered Value

Note: EBIT = earnings before income tax; Rev = average revenue per segment.

From Don E. Schultz and Scott Bailey, "Building a Viable Model for Customer/Brand Loyalty" (ARF Week of Workshops, New York, NY, October 7, 1999). Used with permission from Targetbase, Inc.

Exhibit 6.5 Managing Customer Brand Value

Focus on customer profitability (value to brand) and compatibility with brand positioning (value to the customer)

	Segment 7 59% of customers 43% of revenue 46% of EBIT	**Segment 5–6** 22% of customers 29% of revenue 46% of EBIT
Value of the customer to brand **(EBIT)**	**Segments 1–3** 10% of customers 16% of revenue 2% of EBIT	**Segment 4** 9% of customers 12% of revenue 6% of EBIT

Value of brand to the customer (compatibility with positioning)

Note: EBIT = earnings before income tax.

From Don E. Schultz and Scott Bailey, "Building a Viable Model for Customer/Brand Loyalty" (ARF Week of Workshops, New York, NY, October 7, 1999). Used with permission from Targetbase, Inc.

- **Segments 1–3: Low compatibility, low financial value.** These customers are a poor fit for the organization. There is little that marketing can do to improve the situation.
- **Segment 4: High compatibility, low financial value.** These customers perceive value in the school's offerings, but are either unable or unwilling to spend sufficiently for their training.
- **Segments 5–6: High compatibility, high financial value.** These students are the most appropriate for the school's current offerings. They are willing to make the necessary investment of time and money to complete their training.
- **Segment 7: Low compatibility, high financial value.** This group was willing to pay a premium for their training, but found the course offerings below their skill levels and expectations.

From this analysis, it is clear that understanding the total customer is necessary to properly manage customer and brand relationships in the new customer-driven marketplace. Further, as the example shows, various combinations of messages and incentives are necessary, not just single activities. Obviously, those messages need to be integrated and aligned if they are to be effective in solving problems. While the marketers had one view of the value of the education center—that is, how much revenue and profit it could generate—those estimates are worthless unless the value of the experience to the customer was also recognized. In other words, knowing the level of reciprocity between the two groups was key. By identifying the points of dissatisfaction among students, the center could begin to create marketing solutions that hopefully would prevent defection by those identified as being vulnerable because of their dissatisfaction with the various areas of the educational center.

Moving On

While reciprocity analysis is critical in managing customer relationships in an interactive, networked, customer-driven marketplace, it raises some important questions about the ability of the firm to develop the necessary types of marketing and communication that can provide effective solutions to identified problems. This leads us directly to step 3 of the IMC planning process: developing and delivering marcom messages and incentives.

PART IV

STEP 3: PLANNING MESSAGES AND INCENTIVES

1. Identify customers and prospects

5. Budgeting, allocation, and evaluation

2. Valuation of customers/ prospects

IMC

4. Estimating return on customer investment

3. Creating and delivering messages and incentives

CHAPTER 7

PLANNING MARCOM DELIVERY

S tep 3 of the IMC process gets to the heart of any marcom activity: the creation and delivery of messages and incentives. Using the inputs from step 1 (customer identification) and step 2 (customer valuation), the marcom manager has all the necessary ingredients to begin developing a powerful and effective communication program. Much of the groundwork is already done: the marketer thoroughly understands the product or service for which the program is being developed, is aware of competitive offers, and understands the structure and operation of the marketplace in which the program will be delivered. For the creation of messages and incentives to begin, the manager must further understand how customers come into contact with the brand (*brand contacts*) and how that brand is perceived by them (*brand networks*). These are the topics of this chapter.

Brand Contacts

Traditionally, marcom managers began the communication process by determining the appropriate "creative" content of the message or incentive, then selecting a delivery system, such as advertising, before finally choosing specific delivery vehicles, such as broadcast television or magazine advertising. On the surface, this made sense. Since it was assumed that all customers were essentially the same, the use of mass media was the obvious way to reach them. And since it was further assumed that only a limited number of delivery vehicles existed (print, broadcast, direct mail, and so on) and that most consumers would avail themselves of those vehicles at some time or other, it was up to the creative elements of any communication effort to make the brand stand out. Media selection was naturally considered less important and was therefore downplayed.

Today, however, there has been a virtual explosion of delivery systems. New media forms pop up almost daily, ranging from events and sponsorships to mouse pads to satellite sky beams to various options available on the Internet. Almost everything consumers see or hear—hats, clothing, cell phone displays, bus shelters—has been turned into a communication medium. The end result is that today creative—or what marketers say—is less important than how and where they say it. Because of this turnaround, IMC reverses traditional planning processes. The first order of business is to understand where customers or prospects might hear, see, or learn about the product or service and then use those points of contact that offer the greatest opportunity for relevance, receptivity, and response. Only then does the marketer determine creative, or what the message will say.

Analyzing Brand Contacts

Once marketers accept, as seen in previous chapters, that consumers' purchase behavior results from the sum total of all contacts with a brand—elements like word of mouth as well as the communication activities sent out by the firm—they see why it is critical to know exactly where, when, and how people and brands come into contact.

The customer "meets" or is touched by the brand in many ways, including but not limited to direct experience (either through previous purchase or sampling), contact with front-line employees, use of the physical product and services, or various forms of marketing communication.[1]

A primary method marketers can use to understand such brand touch points is the *brand contact audit*. An audit helps identify how customers actually come in contact with the firm and its products or services, either through messages and incentives sent out by the marketing group or through other forms of contact—like word of mouth or product usage—that are outside the marketer's control.

For purposes of conducting a brand audit, we define a *brand contact* as any element of the customer's experience with the entire product or service offering that he or she attributes to the brand. The simple test of a brand contact consists of two questions:

- If a particular element of the customer's experience with the brand goes well, who gets the credit?
- If an element of the customer's experience with the brand goes poorly, who or what gets the blame?

If the answer to either of these questions is "our company" or "our brand," the experience is a brand contact. Exhibit 7.1 illustrates typical

Exhibit 7.1 The Whole Brand

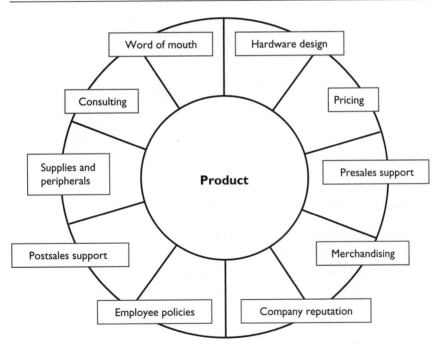

From Lisa Fortini-Campbell, "Communications Strategy: Managing Communications for the Changing Marketplace" (presented at Northwestern University, Evanston, IL, October 19, 1999). Used with permission from Lisa Fortini-Campbell.

brand contacts for a technology product.[2] As shown, the whole brand consists of much more than just traditional communication elements. It includes employees, word of mouth, merchandising, postsales support, and so on. In short, it is all the ways a customer or prospect might have contact with the product or service before purchase, during use, and after experiencing the product in action.

BRAND CONTACTS AT CIGNA

A program known as Aligning Performance with Promise at CIGNA Insurance is based on brand contacts. CIGNA believes that through its many communication systems it makes a series of promises to customers, prospects, employees, and other stakeholders. Those promises (contacts) are delivered wherever and whenever the company touches people or people touch the company, including advertising, employee communication, and so on. The touch points are summarized in Exhibit 7.2. Once CIGNA has identified all promises, it then tests how well it has met them. As shown, CIGNA analyzes its sales practices, its information systems, and even its employee recruitment practices in order to ascertain how effectively promises have been kept and how they can be kept in the future. All of these elements contribute to CIGNA's overall understanding of its brand contacts.[3]

Conducting a Brand Contact Audit

A brand contact audit enables the marketer to determine how and under what circumstances and conditions the customer or prospect comes in contact with the brand, product or service, or organization. Lisa Fortini-Campbell developed the following three-step process[4]:

1. Identify all brand contacts from the customer's or prospect's point of view, whether they are controllable or uncontrollable by the organization, and whether the marketer is directly responsible for them.

Exhibit 7.2 Aligning Promise and Performance

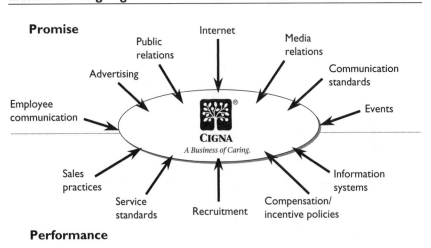

Used with permission from CIGNA Insurance.

In short, the marketer must develop a full inventory of the various forms of communication to which customers and prospects are exposed.

2. Organize and prioritize the brand contacts from the point of view of the customer or prospect. Fortini-Campbell identifies specific "moments of truth," decisive points that either spur the customer to embrace (because of a positive contact) or reject (because of a bad contact) the brand. This step involves identifying which contacts reinforce compelling brand impressions and which contribute to nonintegrated impressions that can drive customers away. The information is brought together in the chart shown in Exhibit 7.3.

   The first column is a comprehensive list of all points of contact described in the first step of this process. It naturally includes all forms of outbound marketing communication, such as advertisements, brochures, in-store displays, and so on. It also includes such points of contact as a call to the customer service desk; the bill sent from the accounting department; interaction with delivery personnel and technicians; and third-party contacts, such as stories in the press, word of mouth from other users, and so on.

Exhibit 7.3 Whole Brand Contact Inventory

Brand contact	Importance evaluation	Impression evaluation	Customer expectation	Customer experience	Message sent	Resources currently allocated

From Lisa Fortini-Campbell, "Communications Strategy: Managing Communications for the Changing Marketplace" (presented at Northwestern University, Evanston, IL, October 19, 1999). Used with permission from Lisa Fortini-Campbell.

In the second column, each point of contact is rated—high, medium, or low—to indicate its importance to the customer's evaluation of the brand. For example, product use or personal experience with the product or service is almost always more important than forms of media communication and thus would receive a higher rating.

The third column represents the impression left with the customer at the point of contact. That simply means identifying whether the impression left on the customer or prospect was positive (yes) or negative (no). Obviously, the IMC manager wants to generate more positive impressions than negative ones.

The information gathered in the first three columns is now plotted on a brand contact priority grid, shown in Exhibit 7.4. This is a simple way to identify which brand contacts are most important and should be managed first. The brand contacts in areas I and II, for instance, represent the first order of business for the marcom manager, while those in areas III and IV have lower priority.

Exhibit 7.4 Whole Brand Contact Priority Grid

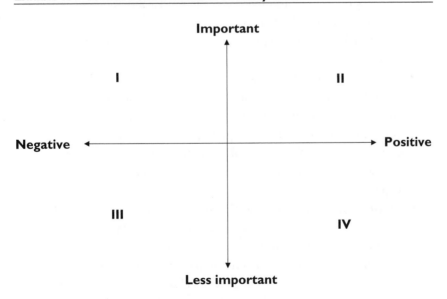

From Lisa Fortini-Campbell, "Communications Strategy: Managing Communications for the Changing Marketplace" (presented at Northwestern University, Evanston, IL, October 19, 1999). Used with permission from Lisa Fortini-Campbell.

For long-term brand communication success, it is important that the message or messages the customer or prospect receives at all points of contact are fully integrated and aligned. That means the easiest way to improve those brand contacts in areas I and III of the grid is to align and integrate them with the positive contacts in areas II and IV. This integration and alignment process is necessary even if the contacts are difficult to manage or control. To resolve some nonintegrated and negative contacts, it may even be necessary to move resources from one budget area to another, thereby ensuring success for the brand going forward.

3. Develop a better customer experience at each point of contact. To do so, actual customer experience must be analyzed in great detail. This involves completing the last four columns in Exhibit 7.3, which pose the following questions:

   • What do customers expect at each identified contact point? What level of quality or service do they associate with and expect from our brand? What level of knowledge and expertise do they expect? What image do they have of our brand and organization?

   • What is the actual customer experience at each point of contact? That is, are we living up to their expectations, or are we delivering a different experience than what they had anticipated?

   • What is the true message sent at the point of contact? That is, what does each contact point actually communicate about the brand, our company, and our commitment to the customer or prospect? Do we send a message of poor or slow service, in spite of our ad that promises fast and friendly service? Is the message consistent with what customers have been led to expect?

   • What resources are we allocating to each point of contact, and is resource allocation commensurate with the contact point's importance and relevance to customers? Are we overspending on communication that has little impact, while underinvesting in points that customers feel are critical to their experience? Is there an expensive brand contact that actually has a negative impact? (If so, the company is not only wasting money, but may be actually driving customers away by investing in this contact point.)

Once the inventory chart and priority grid have been completed, they can be used in a number of ways. Clearly, they are useful as the basis for deciding which points of contact will be most effective in delivering messages and incentives and in helping the marcom manager fashion the content of each communication. Beyond marcom applications, they are a useful starting point for developing a fairly sophisticated customer satisfaction measurement plan that identifies areas for reinforcement and improvement. For example, the inventory chart gives a broad understanding of the areas that should be included in a satisfaction initiative. Similarly, the priority grid provides guidance on how to weight each area or contact point. The analysis of customer expectations versus actual experience is a telling (and often painful) indication of critical gaps and misalignments within the organization's operations and communication efforts. Additionally, an examination of the priority grid can identify how well the firm's priorities line up with those of customers and prospects. Finally, the grid can help identify where resources are currently being allocated or distributed to customers and prospects and helps the manager identify areas of misallocation.

MATCHING EXPERIENCE TO EXPECTATION

Most companies are aware of gaps that exist between customer expectations and customer experience, yet few know how to close them. Brand Imprinting, a research group with branches in Detroit and Chicago, offers a methodology to remedy the situation. Through extensive interviews with customers, the firm seeks to determine not only how customers feel about a brand, but how they behave toward it. (Recall that it is behavior, not attitude, that is the basis for customer valuation.) Researchers are then able to deconstruct how demand occurred and map out the customer purchase process. The firm can then demonstrate to the client the gap between what the client wants its brand image to be and what that image *is* in the mind of specific customers and why it exists. This type of customer-information feedback allows the client company to modify its selling process based on customers' image of the brand.

Let's look at an example. In a study for Audi in Florida, Brand Imprinting was assigned the task of understanding how the customer discovers the Audi brand. Researchers learned that this occurred primarily through curiosity of what the brand and automobile were all about. It seemed that curiosity, rather than expectation of the kind of car it was, triggered demand. Brand Imprinting reasoned that if curiosity leads customers to discover the brand, then the dealership experience is the most important aspect of the selling process. Yet as researchers followed customers through the buying process, they discovered that most cars on the showroom floor were locked. The prospect could not experience the interior of an Audi without finding a salesperson, thus violating the first expectation of "curiosity." Researchers further discovered that the test-drive experience helped transform curiosity into demand. With this insight, Audi was able to adjust the showroom experience by having dealers unlock the car doors and urge more people to test-drive its vehicles.

In another study, this time for teenage clothing company Union Bay, Brand Imprinting sought to determine how the brand should be portrayed at the retail level. Through observation of teenage shoppers and one-on-one interviews, researchers discovered that most teens were not confident when shopping. They had trouble determining which separates went together well or looked "cool." Brand Imprinting concluded that stores were somehow failing to help nonconfident shoppers fit in. Union Bay seized the opportunity to close the gap between expectation and experience. They helped department stores increase sales by placing shirts together with pants so that teens could easily see which pieces worked together as outfits.[5]

Discovering How and When Customers Want to Be Contacted

Everything we have discussed so far about how customers interact with brands shows that brand contacts are not under the exclusive control of the marketer. This means that to find out about effective brand touch points, the marketer needs to stop talking and start listening! For this reason, the IMC approach to message or incentive creation is to start off by determining how customers want to receive brand information. This requires a new method of customer research that revolves not around the brand or the organization but around the requirements of the customer. Research questions focus on how prospects would like to receive information or material from the company or about the brand. These alternative brand contact points are ranked based on the individual customer's preferences. The results are then matched against the firm's current delivery investments. In almost all the companies we have researched, we have found that 50 percent to 60 percent of the message delivery systems used by the firm do not align with customer preferences or desires. This means that—regardless of the communication message itself—marcom managers can potentially increase consumer response and decrease communication costs simply by aligning their delivery systems with customer preferences. The message to marketers is elegant in its simplicity: talk to customers and prospects when and where they want to hear from you, not at your own convenience!

One final point to consider when determining brand contacts: we recommend that marcom managers always keep in mind that people generally feel more comfortable—and therefore more receptive—when they feel they have some control over a situation. A recent study, for instance, found that when blood donors were allowed to choose which arm blood would be drawn from, they showed significantly less discomfort.[6] Similarly, customers respond well to choice, whether they're deciding between an alarm clock and a wake-up call at a hotel or when to have their meal on an airplane. Not only does choice increase value in the eyes of the consumer, but it increases the value of the brand as well. Choice allows customers some control over brand contacts. If they can choose when and where they receive marketing communication, they typically are more active and involved in the process. When given the choice between E-mail, telephone calls, or direct mail as delivery vehicles for marketing materials, customers feel some control. When the communication arrives, it is not rejected out of hand as unsolicited junk mail, but merits—and typically receives—closer inspection.

Determining the Relevance of and Receptivity to Brand Contacts

A brand contact is meaningful to customers and prospects on two conditions: it must be relevant to them, and it must be delivered when it is wanted or needed—that is, when customers are receptive to it.

For a brand contact to be relevant, it must be available to the customer or prospect when he or she wants or needs it, not when the marketer wants to make it available. Because they ignore this simple tenet, traditional marketing efforts have rightly been perceived by consumers as intrusive or interruptive. Marketers interrupt television dramas to advertise products or slice up a football game to allow for commercial breaks. For the most part, the only relevance in current marcom delivery systems is relevance to the marketer.

Receptivity is directly related to relevance. When a brand contact is relevant and comes at a time that is convenient to the customer or prospect, he or she will generally be receptive to it. People are most receptive to brand contacts when they either have a current or latent need to solve a problem or make a marketplace choice. For example, when a couple get engaged, they suddenly become receptive to brand contacts related to married life, such as setting up a house, decorating, and so on. As the wedding approaches, they seek out information that will help them make the most of their special day. During a specific window of time, the prospective bride and groom are very receptive to specific types of information. The marketer who wishes to offer relevant brand contacts at a time when customers and prospects are likely to be most receptive to them has a duty to know, understand, and identify not just when that window is going to open and close, but the form and method through which specific customers would like to receive information. This kind of relevance and receptivity planning is a key element of the IMC process and is illustrated in Exhibit 7.5.

Exhibit 7.5 IMC Model of Brand Contact Delivery Systems

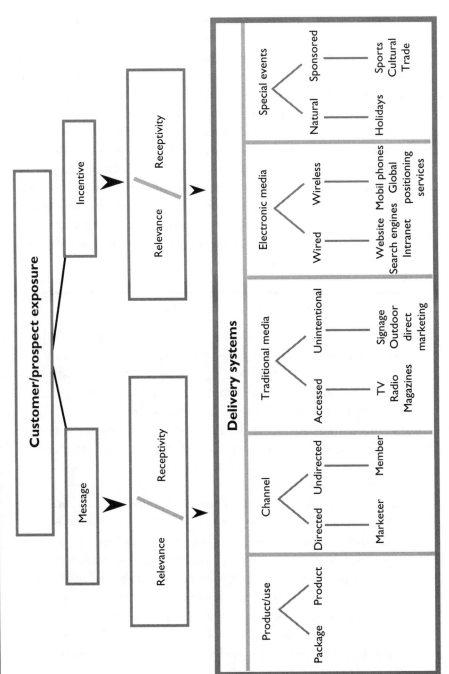

Brand contact information can provide clues as to what customers or prospects may consider relevant about a brand as well as when they might be most receptive to communication about it. This leads directly to the selection of delivery systems most likely to be relevant and to which customers are likely to be receptive. As noted before, the choice of vehicles is not driven, as is the case in traditional marketing, by how marketers want to distribute their messages or incentives, but how customers are most likely to want to receive them. Thus, in an IMC plan, delivery efficiency takes on a new meaning. Instead of measuring media efficiency in terms of the cost of reaching so many thousands of consumers, cost is directly related to outcomes or behaviors that occur. That is, for the first time marketers are able to measure what it costs to achieve the desired behavior on the part of the customer or prospect.

WHY MEDIA INTEGRATION IS SO DIFFICULT

While over the last fifteen years, companies have made significant progress in integrating their marketing and communication processes, media planning has lagged woefully behind. Though marketers have recognized that the communications world has changed, most still try to develop media plans with the traditional tools of reach, frequency, duplication, and exposure. The problem is that these methods are not just inadequate, they are downright wrong for the changed environment in which businesses now operate.

Today's media planning approaches were designed for a marketplace in which each and every media impression was a separate and unique event. Media planning assumes nothing else is going on in the target audience's world except the media exposure at the specific time it appears; nothing else is happening in a consumer's life during the time a radio commercial is broadcast, a newspaper is opened, or a direct mail piece is delivered.

However, a recent study that Don Schultz and Joe Pilotta conducted and presented (in conjunction with BIGResearch) to the Advertising Research Foundation clearly showed how wrong these assumptions are. Using a base of more than 7,500 individual responses gathered online and balanced demographically to reflect the U.S. census, consumers told Schultz and Pilotta the following:

- Those who simultaneously read magazines and listen to radio equal 50.7 percent.
- Those who read newspapers and watch TV at the same time equal 53.4 percent.
- Those who simultaneously watch TV and read magazines equal 50.4 percent.
- Those who watch TV (primary activity) while they are online equal 66.3 percent.
- Those who say they are online (primary activity) and watch TV simultaneously equal 75.2 percent.

What marketers really need today is a new approach to media planning, one that recognizes consumers' increasing ability to multitask and make use of a number of media simultaneously. They also need a media planning system that is based on measuring outcomes and results rather than delivery.

Who is going to enter this brave new world of media planning? We suspect it won't be the media themselves; they have too much invested in existing media planning approaches. It won't be the advertising or media services agencies, for that would require them to start all over building new systems. Nor will it likely be research organizations, since they have built their entire business on traditional media concepts.

Our suspicion is that it will be a group of shiny-pants university professors, because by and large they are the ones who invented the current media planning systems some fifty years ago, as witnessed by media pioneers such as Broadbent, Agostini, Metheringham, and Sissors and Jones, among others. And they are one of the few groups that do not have a vested interest in seeing the systems remain the way they are.[7]

Reversing the Communication Flow

Historically, marketing communicators have relied on the outbound distribution of messages and incentives. That is, the organization decided what it wanted to say, developed messages or incentives, selected distribution forms and methods, and then sent those messages and incentives on their way. They then sat back and waited for customers and prospects to respond to or ignore their communication. Yes, there was "noise" in the process, caused by a wide variety of factors ranging from the receiver's inability to decode the message to clutter in the media channels to interruptions and message conflict. And there was generally some type of feedback loop where the sender tried to determine some type of response from the intended audience such as whether they would buy the product or service, visit the retail store, repeat a purchase, and so on. The basic model, however, was and continues to be much the same as it is shown in Exhibit 7.6.

The problem, as we have already discussed, is that in the new interactive marketplace, the communication process has changed. Instead of

Exhibit 7.6 Traditional Outbound Marketing Communication Model

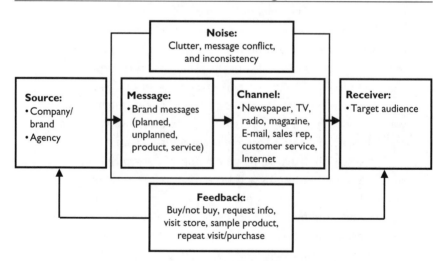

From Tom Duncan, *IMC: Using Advertising and Promotion to Build Brands*, 2002, McGraw-Hill. Reproduced with permission of The McGraw-Hill Companies.

the marketer being in control, power has shifted to the consumer. The customer or prospect becomes the message sender or message requester, and the organization is now the receiver and respondent. As an example, the customer or prospect can now access the marketer's website; ask questions online; or raise issues with customer service about the product, service, offer, warranty, and the like. In short, the communication flow is reversed, as illustrated in Exhibit 7.7.[8]

In this reverse-flow model, channels change, too. Rather than consisting of traditional media forms, channels are those to which the customer or prospect has access, including toll-free numbers, letters, salespeople, customer service, the Internet, and so on. Noise still exists in these channels, of course, but that noise is now a busy signal on the telephone, delays in response from the organization, incomplete information packages, and so forth. The feedback loop changes as well. It is now driven by how well the organization responds to the customer or prospect. It includes such factors as response time, the opportunity for recourse by the customer or prospect, or what kind of respect the marketer gives the customer.

Exhibit 7.7 Customer-Initiated Inbound Communication Model

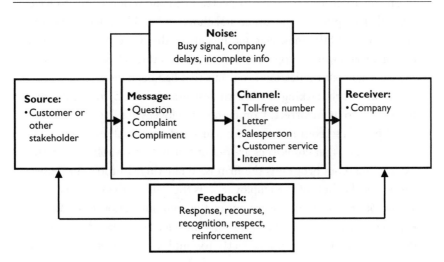

From Tom Duncan, *IMC: Using Advertising and Promotion to Build Brands*, 2002, McGraw-Hill. Reproduced with permission of The McGraw-Hill Companies.

Browsing through the Internet, on any given day, one can easily see that consumers can talk to companies. For example, Nordstrom has a live customer service representative who can answer questions over the Internet for inquiring customers. Ben & Jerry's invites comments, suggestions, and questions through its website. Toll-free numbers, websites, and mailing addresses are all mechanisms that offer customers a new freedom to talk with and to companies. These forms of inbound communication are a prerequisite for any company wishing to incorporate reverse communication into its marketing efforts. In short, the marketer must be prepared to *listen* as well as *talk* to respond to customers as well as communicate messages to or at them.

Recognizing Internal Brand Contacts

As noted in earlier chapters, IMC is an inclusive approach to marketing. This means that including every stakeholder involved in the brand—employees, channel partners, wholesalers, distributors, the financial community, shareholders, and other relevant stakeholders—is a crucial step in the overall success of an IMC program. Historically, most IMC programs have focused primarily on delivering external messages and incentives to customers and prospects. The assumption seems to have been that employees and other stakeholders would somehow "know about" or "get" the messages and incentives that were being delivered externally and would support and work to align their efforts to enhance the external communication programs that had been developed.

In our benchmarking work with best practice IMC companies, we found that to be incorrect. Commonly, employees are the last to know about marcom programs. Indeed, managers continually complain, as do customers, that employees are out of touch with or oblivious to the external marcom programs the firm is conducting. In too many cases, this is not the fault of the employee. It is the fault of the manager, who all too often leaves employees out of the communication loop. In our experience, unless specific programs and activities are designed to deliver the IMC programs directly to employees and other relevant stakeholders, they are often ignored. In some companies, human resources thinks that marketing is responsible for internal communication, while marketing thinks it's the other way around. The result is that internal communication falls through the cracks, and even those employees on the front line—who constantly interface with customers, fielding questions and answering complaints—are commonly unaware of communication initiatives.

For an IMC program to be successful, then, it is vital for the marketer to recognize that brand contacts can be internal as well as external. Unless employees and partners understand the promises made to customers and prospects, they have no hope of delivering against them. The next question, then, is who is responsible for making internal communication happen?

Part of the difficulty in getting employees and other stakeholders into the communication loop is organizational structure. That is, marketing and communication managers generally do not have direct responsibility for internal communication, which traditionally lies in some other functional area such as employee communication, human resources, investor relations, or even people management. Where this is the case, the first task of the IMC manager is clear: to convince senior management of the importance of employee involvement and then convince functional specialists of the importance of communicating the IMC program to appropriate employees and stakeholders.

Professor Christian Gronroos, Hanken School of Economics in Helsinki, one of the pioneers in relationship marketing, sums it up neatly:

> *Most of the firm's marketing is carried out by "part-time" marketers. That is, employees who are charged with making, processing, delivering, providing customer service, billing, and so on. They are the persons who really carry out the marketing and communication programs for the organization. Trained marketers are too busy "doing marketing" to spend face-time with customers. It is these part-time marketers who are the front-line troops in the marketing team. They put life and meaning into what the firm and the brand really is and does. Yet, they have not been trained in marketing or communication and too often*

don't know what the firm is promising customers or what they are sup-
posed to deliver.[9]

Juliet Williams, chief executive officer of Strategic Management
Resources in the United Kingdom, also puts the value of internal communication into perspective. Williams has developed over 150 case
studies on the importance of employees and other stakeholders in carrying the IMC message to customers and consumers. She says:

Based on research, we have found that up to 40 percent of an organi-
zation's marketing and communication dollars can be either wasted or
destroyed when the internal marketing and communication programs
don't support or align with the external marketing and communica-
tion programs.[10]

Brand Networks

As we stated earlier in this chapter, customers and prospects have an
easy and effective way of dealing with messages or incentives that are
irrelevant to them: they simply ignore or reject them. Thus, the oft-
stated challenge the marketer faces today is "Be relevant to customers
and prospects or be gone!"

So, what does the struggle to be relevant require of the marketer?
The answer lies in his or her ability to understand customers and prospects. This does not mean knowing who the customers and prospects
are; rather it means knowing *how they think*. The reason is simple: one
can only find out what is relevant to people and what they are likely to
be receptive to if one knows the thought processes that lead them to
ignore some messages while giving their attention to others.

Brand networks are the internal combinations of icons, thoughts,
ideas, and experiences in the customer's or prospect's mind that converge to form an overall image or definition of a particular brand for
that individual. Marketers might think of these interconnected elements
as forming a network because, in terms of human physiology, that is
what they are.

How Mental Brand Networks Operate

As a crude simplification, the human mind works through a set of inter-related series of neural networks in which individual nodes or neurons store bits and pieces of information. When two or more neurons collide or connect, they form a loop in which a new memory or concept is stored.

When an individual is exposed to marketing communication containing new information about a product, service, or anything else, previously stored information from any existing network is called up and the new information is added to it. This is then held in memory until more new information is collected and added, creating another new node. Thus, every individual has a series of connected nodes, forming brand networks in their minds. Some of these nodes are good for brands, some are bad. Some are strong and some are weak. They are constantly changing and adapting as new information is acquired and processed.

Our minds contain myriad associated concepts, perceptions, and ideas that are related to brands. Some of these associations are in conscious memory and easily retrieved and explained; others may be more subtle, residing in the unconscious recesses of the mind, and may require probing to come to the surface. Giep Franzen and Margot Bouwman have noted that some associations are straightforward and linear, for instance, Shredded Wheat to cereal to breakfast. Other associations are connected in a more complex, chainlike fashion, such as Perrier to mineral water to France to stylish. Franzen and Bouwman provide an example based on interviews conducted in the Netherlands regarding associations with 7-Up. It is shown in Exhibit 7.8. Each associative network consists of a link of subnetworks, with the strength of the associations depicted by the weight of the connecting lines. The researchers concluded, "Each brand is usually associatively connected to one or more products, which in turn are represented in our memory in the form of associative networks."[11]

In reality, brand networks can become quite complex and understanding them requires extensive research. A complete discussion of brand network research is beyond the scope of this text, but we rec-

Exhibit 7.8 7-Up Brand Network

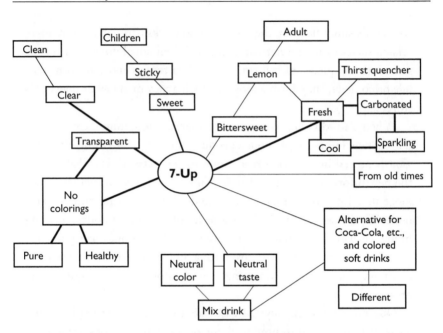

From Giep Franzen and Margot Bouwman, *The Mental World of Brand: Mind, Memory, and Brand Success*, World Advertising Research Center, 2001. Reprinted by permission of World Advertising Research Center.

ommend that marketers investigate brand associations along several distinct dimensions reflecting the brand's functionality, personality, symbolism, and supporting organizational culture. For our purposes, it is sufficient to state that brand networks are the basis for all brand and marketing communication storage in the human mind. If the customer or prospect has nothing stored away about the brand, product, or service, it is difficult to add new concepts or get new messages embedded. They simply have no relevance for there is no connection to be made in the mind. The same is true of marketing communication. For example, when customers or prospects are exposed to some type of brand communication, they immediately pull up the brand network for that product or service. They then mentally test the new information against what they already know. If it fits, they may add it to the network. If it does not, they will likely reject it.

How Brand Networks Create Relevance

By now, the connection between brand networks and the creation of relevance in the mind of the consumer is clear. Customers have certain needs, wants, and desires. They may actively seek to solve a problem by examining marketing communication as an information source. For example, when a couple decide to purchase a new washer and dryer, they typically review newspaper ads, ask friends and neighbors, look through *Consumer Reports*, or gather information in many other ways. They add all the information they find to their brand network for washers and dryers. Because it comes at a time when they are receptive to information about washers and dryers, any marketing communication about the appliances has increased relevance for them.

Consider what happens when the same couple are simultaneously bombarded with marcom materials from automobile manufacturers. Knowing they can't buy a new washer and dryer and a new car at the same time, the couple finds less relevance in the marketing communication from the automobile manufacturers. Yes, they may store some information away and refer to it at some later time, but for the present, automobile communication is simply not relevant for them. Washer and dryer information is. This example begins to show the connection between relevance and receptivity and how brand contacts and brand networks influence what people purchase or don't purchase, what they ignore and to what they pay attention. Most of all, it shows why it is so critically important for the marcom manager to understand the customers and prospects with whom she or he will be attempting to communicate.

A recent example is even more compelling. A study conducted by the University of Michigan looked at customer service in 175 companies. Researchers found that McDonald's was one of the poorest performers in customer service, costing the company up to $750 million per year.[12]

How can one of the world's most valuable brands be losing so much money? It's easy, according to the study. On any given day, 11 percent of McDonald's customers are dissatisfied. About 70 percent of dissatisfied customers are further dissatisfied with the way their complaint is handled. More than half of all dissatisfied customers visit McDonald's less frequently as a result and tell as many as ten other people about their unsatisfactory experience. If these dissatisfied consumers add up everything they know to be true about McDonald's in their minds, they start to realize that their brand network doesn't match McDonald's current communication: "We love to see you smile." This noted inconsistency resonates with consumers and the McDonald's brand is damaged. While the company is still a fast-food giant, it loses an estimated $750 million a year as a result of this marcom inconsistency. Even for McDonald's, that's a lot of money.

One final note on brand networks. It is clear that customers test the various communication or contact elements they encounter on a regular basis. If they have a certain brand network stored away and the company then presents conflicting information through its marcom program, the customer or prospect can make one of two choices:

- Accept the new information and change his or her brand network
- Ignore the new information and stick with what he or she knows and has stored away

Similarly, if the brand communicator presents two radically different messages through two types of marcom delivery systems (one message in mass media and a different message in a special event being held that weekend), which of the two should the customer believe? Which should be stored in the brand network? Maybe the best choice is for the customer or prospect to simply ignore both messages since they have no alignment or integration. This is a simple but very powerful argument for integration of marketing communication at all levels and by all groups that are attempting to communicate with customers and prospects.

How Brand Contacts Relate to Brand Networks and Vice Versa

Earlier in the chapter, we defined brand contacts as the touch points at which the customer or prospect comes in contact with the brand. Brand networks are the ideas and associations the customer takes away as a result of those points of contact. Brand contacts and brand networks thus combine to determine the customer's or prospect's knowledge, feelings, and perceptions about the brand.

Brand networks exist for any brand in any category. Without a network of ideas related to the brand, there simply is no brand image in the minds of customers or prospects. Brand contacts can add to, reinforce, change, or even diminish those brand networks. Thus, one of the key skills for the marcom manager developing an IMC program is the ability to uncover, understand, and influence the brand networks of customers and prospects through the careful management of brand contacts.

Moving On

Our discussion of brand contacts and brand networks moves us toward completing step 3 of the IMC process, for without knowing how people receive and accept information about brands and how they absorb that information, marketers cannot hope to deliver messages and incentives that influence their behavior. The next chapter takes us further along the same path—using identified consumer insights to begin creating effective messages and incentives.

CHAPTER 8

PLANNING MARCOM CONTENT

Now that we have established an understanding of how the customer comes in contact with the brand and how brand networks influence behavior, it is time to apply these concepts as the building blocks for creating messages and incentives. Professor Lisa Fortini-Campbell, Northwestern University, coined the term *creating customer insights* to describe how the marcom planner uses an understanding of brand contacts and brand networks to develop marcom programs. This chapter explains how the planner progresses from customer insights to planning IMC messages and incentives.

Defining Customer Insight

Lisa Fortini-Campbell has suggested that customer insight contains three primary elements[1]:

- Customer insight involves identifying the strongest motivational force in the mind of the customer or prospect.
- Customer insight is the identification of the psychological opportunity that offers the greatest opportunity for the marketer and the customer to intersect and connect.
- Customer insight is the "sweet spot," that is, the perfect connection between the marketer and the customer in terms of

what the marketer wants to deliver and what the customer or prospect wants to acquire.

Finding customer insight allows the marketer to develop a relevant "whole-brand" framework that is then developed, delivered, and reinforced with every brand contact. (Recall the discussion of the whole-brand concept in Chapter 7.) Brands that achieve customer insight leave customers feeling that the firm knows them, respects them, and can anticipate their needs.

This type of understanding comes only from a respectful, empathic, comprehensive understanding of the customer as a person who has needs and requirements that the brand may be able to solve or who seeks benefits the brand may provide. That information comes from an insight into customers' lives, that is, how the category fits in with the way they live and what distinguishes the brand from competition in terms of that fit. Most of all, customer insight is not a simple demographic description of a person or group of people nor is it an understanding based only on previous behavior. Instead, it is a deep, meaningful understanding of customers; their lives or businesses; their needs, wants, and desires; their history and background; their ambitions; and many other present-day and future factors. History and experience can help a great deal in developing customer insights, but it is the skill of the marcom manager in projecting that knowledge and information into the present and future that really distinguishes customer insight from traditional segmentation schemes, positioning approaches, or simple gut feelings.

Developing and Testing Customer Insights

The question, of course, is how do marketers know when they have captured the insight that will help gain a new customer or bond an existing customer to the organization? One of the best methods we have found is the simple test outlined here. If the marketer can complete the parts of the following statement easily and completely, he or she is well on the way to developing effective messages or incentives using the IMC process.

- *For* (Who is the behavioral target our communication program is to impact?)
- *Who* (What is the customer insight that has been identified, and what is the category motivation that drives that customer or prospect?)
- *Our product is a* . . . (What is our product or service in the eyes of the customer or prospect, that is, what is our whole product or whole brand?)
- *That provides* . . . (What is the key benefit or value the customer wants and our brand or product can deliver based on our insight or insights?)
- *Unlike* . . . (Who is the relevant competitor or competitors?)
- *Our product* . . . (What is our key point of differentiating relevance?)

Look again at the example of a business airline traveler in the sidebar. Fortini-Campbell illustrates how the customer insight for this person can be put to the customer insight test:

- *For* businesspeople who travel 100,000 full fare miles per year
- *Who* take pride in the personal sacrifices they make for the business
- *Our product is* a "business preparation and recovery service"
- *That* sacrifices itself to make you more productive
- *Unlike* any other business travel experience
- *Our airline* will gladly adapt itself to create the travel you decide you want

Clearly, this description of what the customer wants the airline to deliver would be difficult for any airline to match. Yet the insight is important, because if this type of service could be delivered to customers and prospects on a regular basis by an airline and its personnel through practice and performance, one can imagine how easy it would be for that airline to maintain its customer base and how easy it would be to get other business travelers to switch preferred carriers.

CUSTOMER INSIGHT IN ACTION

This example illustrates exactly what Fortini-Campbell means by a true customer insight. Based on research and experience, here is her description of a business traveler, an airline's key customer:

I'm the person at my company who sacrifices herself to make revenue happen. I do whatever needs to be done, wherever it needs to be done. When a customer needs me, I go. When there's a problem with a supplier relationship, I'm on it. If we're having trouble internally working together, I'm there to mediate. I do 120 percent every day. I'm one of those people who's willing to pay the personal price to see us all succeed. But there are great rewards, too. Helping make this company a success is one of my greatest achievements and a huge source of personal pride.

The insight continues:

If I'm going to put myself out for customers, suppliers, and the company, I need support. I need to focus myself on my objectives and I can't be accommodating myself to the people I'm paying to make life easier for me. An airline trip has everything to do with my success. It affects me personally. An airline trip can put me in a good mood or a bad one. It can make me feel rested and ready to go or exhausted. My airline is part of my support infrastructure, like my staff or my computer system.

With a description like this, most marcom managers can begin to understand and relate to the business traveler as a segment of the airline's customer base. Obviously, they should recognize that this is just one type of airline customer. Vacationers are quite different, as are overseas travelers and family groups. But this type of customer insight statement is tremendously helpful in developing relevant messages and incentives for these types of customers.[2]

At this point, it might be useful to ask whether this customer description and insight fit you or someone you know. How many airlines have this much customer insight? If an airline could deliver on this type of customer insight, how relevant would its marcom messages be? How much loyalty could the airline generate? How important would the ticket price be to the customers who chose that airline? Or how important would the price of the ticket be to those flying competitive airlines? How many advocates would the airline likely generate? By addressing each of these questions, one can see that insights help build brand relationships and help develop effective marcom programs.

With a firm understanding of the concept of customer insights, we are ready to begin applying this knowledge to the development of IMC messages and incentives. Since, as guiding principle 4 says, IMC goals must always align with overall corporate goals in order to be effective, the first step is to make sure that the customer insights the marketer has developed are in line with what the organization wants to and is able to deliver. That is the topic of the next section.

Matching Organizational Capability with Consumer Insights

A harsh criticism of marketers delivered by today's customers is this: "Marketers don't do what they say they will do!" As we discussed in the previous chapter, marketing communication typically makes promises to customers and prospects. Ads woo them with promises like "quick return policy," "friendly tellers," "easy to assemble," "no-hassle guarantee," and hundreds of similar statements. The trouble is that the customer experience is often quite different from the promises made. Returns are not just difficult; they are baffling and often impossible. And they take time—lots of time. Tellers and salesclerks could care less about customer problems or providing customer assistance. Salespeople don't return telephone calls. And products come with undecipherable instructions and inaccurate directions. In short, too many organizations don't deliver on what they promise customers and prospects in their marketing and communication programs.

Tackling the problem of unmet promises involves what we call *internal integration*. Quite simply, this is the internal alignment of external promises with internal capability.

Recall from guiding principle 1 in Chapter 3 that for IMC programs to work, the company must become customer centric. We suggested that it is critical for each and every part of the organization—external suppliers as well as internal employees—to focus on customers and be dedicated to helping customers meet their goals. This means that when developing and using customer insights, the goals of the organization must sometimes be subordinated to the goals of the customer. Customer insights help marketers understand the customer's goals and align organizational goals with what the customer is trying to achieve. Where there is conflict or a difference in corporate and customer goals, customer insights can often help bring the two objectives together so that each side finds satisfaction with the product, service, and marketing activities they share.

Developing a Message and Incentive Strategy

Exhibit 8.1 recaps the concept of messages and incentives first introduced in Chapter 3, where we reviewed guiding principle 7. Simply stated, IMC streamlines the many elements that marcom managers have created over the years as separate functions (advertising, public relations, and so on) into two groups:

- Those that deliver brand messages (brand concepts, ideas, associations, values, and other perceptions the firm wants customers to store away in memory for the long term)
- Those that deliver brand incentives (short-term offers or rewards for doing something the marketer believes will be of value to both the organization and the customer)

Exhibit 8.1 acts as a useful starting point for developing communication strategies around specific messages and incentives. The illustration looks at strategy development from the perspective of overall

Exhibit 8.1 Typical Goals/Tools of Messages and Incentives

◄ Brand messages	Brand incentives ►
Typical goals	**Typical goals**
Enhance brand	Gain trial
Outline benefits	Increase usage
Build preference	Encourage stockpiling
Differentiate from competitors	Promote cross purchase
Typical tools	**Typical tools**
Media press coverage	Price reductions
Events	Coupons
Literature	Sampling
Website	Contests/sweepstakes
	Gifts and free offers

program goals. Typical goals for brand messages are to enhance the brand, to outline specific benefits the customer or prospect might obtain from using the brand, to build preference for the brand, to clearly differentiate the brand from competitors, and so on. The tools the marcom manager can use to deliver messages include paid messages in various forms of media, public relations, events, sponsorships, product placements, and so forth. Messages can be delivered in almost any form and through almost any medium, but the goal is always the same: to leave some type of imprint or impression for the brand or product or organization in the mind of the customer or prospect.

For brand incentives, typical goals might be to generate trial of the product or service among nonusers, to increase usage among present users, or to get the customer or prospect to stockpile the product for future use. An offer might, for example, combine the brand with another product to encourage cross purchase or cross usage. In terms of tools, brand incentives might include price reductions for a limited time; coupons in all different sizes, forms, and values; or various free offers where the marketer provides additional volume or content or even gives free goods to the purchaser as a reward. Electronic media offer a wide variety of new incentives such as white papers, chat rooms, electronic coupons, and other E-mail offers.

It should be noted here that, while we have combined all the traditional marcom specialty functions such as advertising, sales promotion, public relations, and the like into just two basic communication tools (messages and incentives), it is understood that the line distinguishing them is not always clear-cut. In fact, that line often blurs in practice. Thus, while the primary focus of the IMC activity may be to deliver a message, that does not prevent the marketer from including an incentive as well. For instance, a cents-off coupon might be added to a message-dominated print ad to generate first-time trial by a new customer or to reward a present customer for past behavior. Similarly, high-impact promotional events often have a residual effect that may add to a long-term brand memory. Nevertheless, in spite of this modest overlapping of outcomes, we believe the IMC manager can, with some discipline and judgment about the primary objective of a communication effort, reasonably categorize almost any activity as predominantly focused on one purpose or the other.

Another complicating factor is the period in which market response is anticipated. Some programs are very short term in nature, while others seek to establish long-term brand identity and preference. The issue of time frame is critical to IMC planning and is addressed in future chapters.

Exhibit 8.1 makes it clear that the type of messages or incentives that can be used are limited only by the imagination of the marcom manager. How those messages and incentives are developed is discussed next.

Strategy Development: A New Methodology

The best way to understand any methodology is to look at an example of how it works. With this in mind, this section is based on a case developed by Stanley Tannenbaum,[3] a long-time ad agency executive, who enjoyed a distinguished second career in academia at Northwestern University. The strategy development form that follows the example also originated with Tannenbaum. Here's how the example begins.

It's a cold winter evening in Philadelphia. You're on Calumet Street between 13th and 14th. There are eight houses on the block. You're a door-to-door salesman. Your job? Knock on each door and sell each homeowner a bottle of aspirin. *You need a communication strategy.*

To be successful today, you obviously can't write the same strategy for all eight homeowners. A single strategy might lead you to say something like this: "Hey there, person, if you have stress, I have relief. And my product relieves stress faster." Of course, you would need a visual to accompany these words, so you would stand there with a pained look on your face, perhaps tightly twisting a rope to dramatize "stress."

One strategy for all eight homeowners? Of course not. But that's the kind of thinking taking place for many products and services. One strategy—and one commercial spun off that strategy—aimed at 100 million people.

This "massification" of the consumer has led to communication that is—like the aspirin salesman's pitch—vague, meaningless, and irrelevant. Marketers spend most of their time communicating about themselves and spend very little time figuring out how their product can solve consumer problems. The dilemma is further compounded by the fact that most marketers unintentionally send out a communication hodgepodge to the consumer. Mass market advertising might say one thing, while a price promotion creates a different signal. A product label creates still another message; sales literature uses an entirely different vocabulary; and the sales force does nothing but pitch price, price, price to the retailer. Mixed-up, mass-directed, incompatible communication stems from the manufacturer's wishes rather than from customer needs. This is why IMC is so necessary in a marketplace where the consumer calls the shots and the marketer listens.

A Different Way of Thinking

Good communication, like good selling, is personal. An effective salesperson would never ever use the same strategy to sell all eight people on that block in Philadelphia. A good salesperson would find out all he or she could about each customer and custom-tailor the communication strategy to that individual. In other words, the salesperson would get to know the customer! The better the marketer knows the customer, the sharper the selling message. Find out, for instance, how the people on the block experience stress. When? Is the stress job-related? Lifestyle-related? Is it real? Imaginary? Which products does the customer use to solve the problem? Is he or she satisfied? Does the customer enjoy using the products? Why? Would he or she recommend them to friends?

Think how much easier it would be to communicate with potential customers if you knew them as individuals rather than as merely other guys on the block. Today's technologies, as described in steps 1 and 2 of the IMC process, have the capability to make the marketer intimate with each and every customer. It's possible to get to know each customer's needs, behavior, and requirements so thoroughly that one can address each individual on a more personal basis than ever before.

This new way of thinking requires an almost evangelical dedication to the creation of a disciplined communication strategy. If marketers do their homework properly in the development of that strategy, the result will be a sharper, more persuasive, and fully integrated message or incentive directed to the most likely prospect. This, in turn, will result in the creation of a unique brand or service personality, one that separates their product or service from its competition. When done correctly, the use of an integrated selling message leads to personal communication, the kind of communication people want to listen to and act on.

The strategy form in Exhibit 8.2 is specifically created for IMC programs. It can be used by blue-chip marketers or small entrepreneurs. It doesn't matter whether the organization is selling packaged goods, services, or business-to-business products; whether it is in retailing; whether it is developing a corporate image program or selling aspirin door-to-door.

While at first glance, the strategy form may seem daunting, a closer look shows that all it does is bring together the material the marketer has already gathered and thought through during the first three steps of the IMC process. The greatest benefit of the form is that working through it forces the marcom manager into a disciplined thinking process that will result in a workable communication strategy. The strategy form brings all stakeholders together, since it forces everyone to sign off on who the customer is, what the customer wants, and how the

Exhibit 8.2 Communication Strategy Development Form

I. Who is the consumer?
   A. What is the customer's target buying incentive?
      What is the general product category: _____
      1. How do members of this group perceive the products or services in this category?
      2. What do they buy now? How do they buy and use the product(s)?
      3. What are their lifestyles, psychographics, and attitudes toward the category?
   B. What is the key customer insight?
   C. What do these customers want from the product category that they are not now getting?
      Target buying incentive: "I will buy a product that _____ than any other product in the category."
   D. Which would best achieve the IMC goal: message, incentive, or combination of the two?
II. Does the product or service fit the group?
   A. What is the reality of the product or service?
      1. What's in it?
      2. What does it do?
      3. Why is it different?
   B. How does the customer perceive the product or service?
   C. How does it look, feel, taste, work, and so on?
   D. How does the customer perceive the company behind the product?
   E. What is the "naked truth"?
   F. Does the product or service fit the group?
      Recommendation: _____
III. How will the competition affect our objectives?
   A. What is the brand network, the competitive frame? Why?
   B. What do competitors now communicate to customers or prospects?
   C. How will the competition retaliate against our program?
   D. How vulnerable is the competition? From whom will we take business?
IV. What is the competitive consumer benefit?
   • Must be a true benefit (solve a consumer problem, better the consumer's way of life, etc.)
   • Must focus on one benefit for each group
   • Must be competitive (that is, "better than" the competitive frame)
   • Must not be a slogan or an ad phrase
   • Must be one sentence (e.g., "Sanka tastes better than any other instant coffee." "Holiday Inn gives you a better night's sleep than any other hotel.")
V. How will marketing communication pertaining to each of the following make the benefit believable to the customer or prospect?
   A. Product or service itself: _____
   B. Perceptual support: _____
   C. Communication support: _____
VI. What should the personality of the brand, company, or product be? What unique personality will help further define the product or service and discretely differentiate it from the competitive frame?

(continued)

Exhibit 8.2 Communication Strategy Development Form *(continued)*

VII. What main message do we want the consumer to take away from the communication?
    A. What main incentive will be offered?
    B. What action do we want the consumer to take as a result of the communication:
       • Try the product or service
       • Send for more information
       • Use the product more often
       • Try other products in the line
       • Other: _____

VIII. What will the perceptual or promotional effect of the communication be?
    A. If the communication is successful, how will the customer perceive the product as compared to the competition in (months/years)?
    B. If the incentive is successful, what customer or prospect action will occur?

IX. What are the consumer brand contact points? To most effectively reach the consumer with a believable persuasive message or incentive, what consumer contact points should be considered? Why?

X. How will we handle future research? (List the types of future research needed to further develop the IMC strategy and your reasons for each.)

---

brand or product will meet those expectations. The strategy defines the position of the product, its personality, its competitive reason for being, and the benefits the consumer will derive from it. The form also captures how the marketer thinks customers will be influenced by competitive forces. Importantly, it provides behavioral criteria for which the marketing department will be held accountable. The strategy includes the best media contact points where the customer can be reached. It also answers the need for future research to further refine and update the strategy.

In this new IMC approach, the communication strategy is a critically important element in the communication process for all departments within the organization. It forces every aspect of the communication process to reach the consumer clearly and consistently. Every communication tactic that flows from an integrated strategy reinforces the reason why the consumer should believe in the product or service.

If you are selling aspirin, for example, all communication for the aspirin should be driven by the basic consumer need and should lead to the creation of one unified personality for the brand. The overall strategy can be broken down to allow the marketer to reach subgroups of consumers, such as loyal users, occasional users, and so on. Also there can be specific strategies against wholesalers, distributors, retailers, trade groups, and all other peripheral stakeholders that can affect the sale. Each of these segments has their own buying incentive, and as a result, the communication strategy offers each group a distinct competitive benefit. This is true integration because your analysis of the customers leads to well-founded conclusions regarding which group to target and how to reach each group.

It is easy to see the importance of the strategy. It is the key to integrating all communication about the product—elements that affect everybody and everything that has to do with the sale and repeat sale of the product. When done correctly, the development of a communication strategy creates a bond within a company and a stronger bond between the company and the various communication agents that serve it.

Strategy Development: An Example

To illustrate the strategy development form at work, let's revisit the Philadelphia aspirin salesperson and show how a strategy might be developed to reach each distinct customer.

Who Is the Consumer?

To create a powerful IMC strategy, each of the eight aspirin prospects must be investigated. The target buying incentive (TBI) statement tells the marketer what people think about a product category and why they think that way. It shows what problems they have with the category (or brand) and what it would take for a product to overcome those problems and thus make a sale. The TBI analysis provides insights into the consumer's behavior and thought process. How does the consumer define the quality of aspirin? How does the consumer evaluate brand names? What does the consumer define as "value" in the aspirin category? Why does one group only buy a certain brand occasionally?

The TBI analysis further forces the marketer to develop key insights into the way the consumer lives, works, and plays; the stress the consumer is under at work, in social situations, or at home with children. Does the consumer get uptight when going to a dinner party? When making a business presentation? When going shopping at a fancy store? Is the consumer in management at work? Does her boss put her under extreme pressure? Does her husband? Does her mother-in-law? How does she use aspirin? How many does she take at one time? How often? What brand does she take? Does she switch brands? Does she have confidence in her doctor? In prescription drugs? Does she buy generic brands? Is she an educated consumer? Does she buy on evaluation rather than on reputation? Which does the consumer have more confidence in, the product itself, where he or she buys the product, or the person who sells the product? How is the consumer affected by news stories? By word of mouth? By parents? By price of products?

This investigation of the consumer should result in a one-sentence summary that succinctly states the TBI. It will say clearly what incentive or product benefit will get this particular customer to consider switching from the brand he or she is currently using or reconfirm why he or she should continue buying your brand.

In the case of the eight people in Philadelphia, you may have found that the members of the group buying generic aspirin are terribly insecure about the entire category. They may think aspirin is aspirin and, with great trepidation, choose the lower price, no-name brand. They may be uncertain of this decision and really wish there was a brand they could have confidence in—even if they had to pay a little more for it. This group's buying incentive would be simply, "I would buy another brand of aspirin if it gave me more confidence it was working better than the brand I am now using."

Of course, TBI sheets should be developed for each similar consumer group in the marketplace. The information to construct the profiles could come from behavioral data; primary research; or hypotheses based on the marketer's personal interviews, observations, or experiences. After a TBI sheet is made up for each discrete consumer group, a decision must be made on which group or groups would be most profitable for the aspirin manufacturer to pursue.

To properly plan the communication strategy, each group that can affect the sale of the product must be considered a potential opportunity. It is likely that separate TBI sheets would be constructed for retailers, medical professionals, the company sales force, corporate health offices, and so on.

For the purposes of this example, let's assume the company has decided to develop a communication campaign directed at people who are now buying generic aspirin but are looking for a brand in which they could have more confidence. This brings up a key question: Can your product—real or perceived—satisfy the needs and wants of the selected TBI group? This raises two issues.

- Is the current reality of the product good enough to satisfy the confidence needs of the consumers? Is there "news" in the product itself—facts never heard before—that would convince the targeted consumers that this brand is one about which they can feel more confident? Even pay more money for?
- What are the current perceptions of the product by the consumer group? Do they inspire confidence? If not, can new perceptions be created through communication in order to build a strong, unique, positive perception of confidence in the minds of the consumers? Or are the existing perceptions of the product so ingrained in the minds of the consumers that they are impossible to change?

These issues can only be answered by conducting objective examinations of both the reality of the product and the potential consumer's current perceptions of the product. This leads directly to the second section of the communication strategy form.

Does the Product or Service Fit the Group?
Too often communication people are satisfied with the superficial ingredients of the product. They rarely dig for news and find the surprises that exist in every product. Sure, all types of aspirin have common ingredients. But this thinking leads to complacency. Look for information beyond ingredients, for surprises about the product that can affect perception. That is the purpose of this section of the strategy form

Consider, for instance, how the product is made. Who invented it? Why? How? In how many seconds does it dissolve? How does it actually work? Does it work faster on smaller people? Does it work faster if the user thinks it's going to work? Why does it work? Why are most aspirin bottles colored? How long can bottles safely remain in the medicine chest? What happens if the user takes aspirin with orange juice? How about in a space capsule or gulping them down with a Pepsi? Where are the aspirin tablets made? Does the manufacturing process need certain light or heat conditions? Who are the people on the production line? Do they care about the user? Is the manufacturing process supervised by doctors, nurses, or epidemiologists? Who is president of the company? Who does the research on effectiveness? Do aspirins work differently on different symptoms? Why? Can consumers determine how many aspirins should be taken in a given situation? Should they be able to? Should aspirin be taken prior to stressful situations?

All these questions—and scores more about the reality of the product—must be answered. Everyone in the marcom department should contribute questions. What you are looking for are insights that deliver facts that are instrumental in affecting consumer perceptions, facts that could conceivably dispel the perception that all aspirin brands are alike.

As important as the issue of product reality is the issue of how the product and product category are perceived by the consumer. Although you have gotten information about this in the TBI section, more detail is needed here because perception is a vital part of the product. It is what creates the real value of the product. How does the prospect perceive the quality of the product? Does it do a good job for its cost? Does the brand name offer confidence? What does the consumer think of competitive brands? How is the consumer affected by news stories in the papers? By word of mouth? By retailer recommendation? By price points? Is the brand seemingly always on sale? Is it old-looking? Does the prospect trust the retailer? How close is the brand to what is perceived as the category generic? What does the label say about the user? Most importantly, has the potential customer positioned the brand so definitely as a "me-too" parity product that he or she is unable to accept new information and thus make a change?

Now back to the strategic issues that were stated earlier: Is the reality of the product good enough to inspire confidence? Can this sense of confidence be persuasively communicated to the potential customer? If research and good judgment determine that the consumer's perceptions of the product will never allow it to be accepted on the basis of confidence, then most likely other promotional tactics should be considered, such as price promotions or incentive purchases. If, however, it seems that the consumer's judgment system can accept the brand's confidence stance, a repositioning of communication strategy may be called for. Of course, there are other consumer segments to which marketing could appeal profitably. These also must be investigated to determine which type of communication will be most effective.

In the aspirin example, let's say research has truly uncovered a group of people whose needs are not being fully satisfied with products on the market. These people have stressful jobs—office managers, TV repairmen, door-to-door salespeople, purchasing agents, bus drivers. They get bad headaches and dread the thought of getting them. They buy generic aspirin but they wish there were something better, different— something they could have confidence in and enjoy the secure feeling of knowing it would work. They would be willing to pay a premium price, as they do when they choose brand name prescription drugs over generic. These customers rely on their doctors' and pharmacists' recommendations. They think their headaches are special and they need something special to relieve them.

If you are successful in directing your brand to this group of consumers, your product is no longer mere aspirin. It is a unique solution to a unique problem. If this solution is communicated effectively, it will add to the perceived value of the brand in the mind of the user. It will separate your brand from all others. It will allow you to establish a long-term, profitable relationship with the customer.

How Will the Competition Affect
Our Objectives?

Knowing the competition means a lot more than merely knowing about competitive market share and ad spending. First of all, the company must determine against whom it is competing. What network of brands and brand alternatives are in the consumer's mind? Are Hallmark greeting cards competing against American or Gibson? Or, in the mind of the consumer, are they competing against the telephone, fax machines, E-mail, or the U.S. Postal Service? Or are Hallmark cards competing against short bus or automobile trips to Mom's house on Mother's Day?

Returning to the aspirin example, consider whether you are competing only against other brands. Might you, perhaps, also be competing against tranquilizers? Alcohol? Cigarettes? Vacations? Or special kinds of analgesics such as aspirin with antacid, baby aspirin, acetaminophen, and ibuprofen?

Remember that the determination of the competitive frame must come from the consumer's mind. What do consumers think about the various pain relievers on the market? What do they consider a pain reliever? What are the alternatives to aspirin, as well as their pluses and minuses? Where are the consumers' loyalties? How are consumers affected by messages? The conclusion of the competitive analysis should lead to the determination of which brand is most vulnerable in the marketplace, from which company your brand will most likely take business, and the new customers who can most likely be acquired.

What Is the Competitive Consumer Benefit?

You know your customer, your product, and your competition. Now, what is the one key benefit that can motivate the customer to buy your product rather than a competitor's?

In the aspirin example, the TBI group has given their buying incentive: "I would buy another brand of aspirin if it gave me more confidence it was working better than the brand I am now using." At this point in the strategy, the competitive consumer benefit should reflect the TBI's buying incentive. In other words, the competitive benefit should read, "Brand A aspirin gives you more confidence it's working than any other brand of aspirin."

This statement of benefit—or promise—is what consumers have told you they want from a brand. The statement is directional. It is in no way intended to be the words in a communication message. The determination of the benefit must stem from the consumer. Is this what the consumer needs and wants? It is vital to remember that the key to effective IMC strategy is the solution of consumer problems—a consumer benefit that's presented in every brand contact in a way that's unique to your brand.

How Will Marketing Communication Make the Benefit Believable?

Once marketing managers have come up with a viable consumer benefit, how do they give the consumer a reason to believe that their brand can be trusted to deliver on its promise? This is the point where mere communication is insufficient. What is needed is persuasive communication integrated into every piece of marketing; persuasive communication that gently, subtly, credibly convinces the consumer that the marketer's product is superior to every other product in the field. This necessitates building a rapport with the consumer that is the result of a deep understanding and a communication that reflects such understanding. In other words, the marketer must convince the customer that the product will produce the benefit paid for. The real genius in communication is to figure out how best to persuade the selected group that a product will solve a specific problem. Should a traditional demonstration message be used? What about a money-back guarantee incentive? Can the way communication reaches the target—the contact—create the reason to believe? Will the persuasion be greater if the message comes through a personal letter from the president of the company rather than a generic radio commercial? Would the persuasion be greater if marketing talked about specific solutions to specific problems rather than vague solutions to general problems? Would the persuasion be more powerful if the communication offered "news" about the product in a way the consumer has never heard before?

Whatever method is used to persuade—to present the reason to believe—it must be consistent in every type of communication used. The thinking behind IMC is that every communication—price, label, logo, promotion, distribution—should be created to help persuade the selected group of the competitive benefit. The greater the consistency, the greater the impact and the greater the persuasion.

What Should the Personality of the Brand, Company, or Product Be?

The meat of the message and the language—verbal and visual—with which it's delivered are important in building the reason to believe. However, the tone and personality that are created for the brand are equally important.

Devising a brand personality is not, as some critics believe, a creative exercise for creativity's sake. It is a process that gives the brand a life and soul with which the consumer can easily identify. It differentiates the brand from competition. It gives the consumer a feeling of familiarity and kinship. The personality created must fit the brand's competitive positioning. It must fit the consumer's perception and expectation of the brand. It must be credible. For example, if you are trying to build confidence in your brand of aspirin, the tone of every type of communication must exude confidence in its look, words, and attitude.

What Main Message Do We Want the Consumer to Take Away?

An IMC strategy sets out goals for which the marcom manager will be held accountable. But what goals should be set, and what goals are truly measurable? One element that must be evaluated is the main message or the primary incentive the customer takes away. Goals should be clearly spelled out and agreed to by all the participants in the strategy. They should be monitored constantly. Obviously, if the goals are not attained, the content of the strategy and the various tactical components should be reviewed and, perhaps, revised. It could be that the marketer is not in touch with the consumer.

What Will the Perceptual or Promotional Effect Be?

A key evaluation of the strategy and its implementation is the competitive perceptual value it creates for the product in the minds of prospects. In this section of the strategy form, it is necessary to state the desired perceptual value, along with a time frame for establishing that value. The desired perceptual effect should be measured over specific intervals with the target consumer. This is a practical way of telling if the strategy is working or should be amended.

In the case of your aspirin brand, the desired perceptual effect should be to have the consumer think of the brand as a more dependable form of relief because it is closer to a prescription-strength drug.

What Are the Consumer Brand Contact Points?

Another key element of the communication strategy is how or through what contact points to reach the desired TBI group. The TBI definition at the start of the strategy gives the marketer a lot of information about his or her audience. This type of information should be used as a brand contact plan to reach potential customers. Where are they when they need this product? Where are they when they are most likely to accept a "selling" message? Where are they when the communication can be of greatest benefit to them?

The beauty of the integrated strategy statement is that it leads to tactics that may not be traditional but are certainly more persuasive because they speak to individuals as individuals. It's almost back to personal selling—like a salesperson facing eight customers on that lonely block in Philadelphia.

How Will We Handle Future Research?

The strategy should end up planning for the future. What research should be conducted in the future in order to build a more perfect strategy? One year on, for instance, how have consumers reacted? Have they accepted the change in communication? Have they bought the promise of the product? Are they buying the product?

The answers to these types of questions will provide behavioral feedback that will aid in refining the strategy over the years. A sound IMC strategy is constantly being revised because the consumer is constantly changing. The marketer's communication, the competition's communication, noncommercial communication, new products, and changing lifestyles all make it imperative to continually update the strategy and tactics used to execute it. It cannot be overstated that the consumer drives the strategy. The marketer must establish a customer relationship—a friend rather than a conquest. As with the aspirin, always remember that you are not trying to sell a pill; you are trying to solve a problem.

Establishing a relationship, showing this knowledge of and caring for the customer, is the essence of what effective marketing is all about. Unlike traditional marketing, which paid lip service to terms like *customer-driven*, the core principle of IMC is that the strength of the product begins and endures with the confidence the consumer has in it. However, since the product is virtually the same as the competition's products, the marketer cannot depend on the product alone to build that confidence.

It's the rapport, the empathy, the dialogue, the relationship, the communication he or she establishes with customers and prospects that makes the difference. These separate the IMC marketer from the pack. Quite simply, one cannot set down an effective IMC strategy unless one starts and ends with the consumer's point of view.

Developing Message and Incentive Tactics

The challenge of developing effective messages and incentives that can influence customer behaviors flows directly from the customer insights the planner is able to identify. These are then matched up with the values, benefits, and solutions the product or service can provide and the organization can deliver. All of these are based on developing a sound IMC strategy as has just been explained. Effective messages and incentives are not bound up in clever slogans, brilliant illustrations, memorable music, or the myriad other tools available to the marcom department or its support agencies. While various tactics might enhance the message or incentive being developed, they are primarily elements that make a solid, value-based IMC strategy more effective. They do not replace the heart of the IMC proposition nor the customer insights. In short, effective messages and incentives come more from the mundane and often more difficult challenges of learning about customers and prospects. How do they think? How do they feel? What they are trying to accomplish? What do they enjoy? Messages and incentives derive from customer insights that help the marketer become more relevant to individual customers or prospects.

Alongside that customer insight must be an understanding of the organization's culture and capabilities. Unless the entire firm is in sync with the customer or prospect, there can be no ongoing relationship. Too often, in our experience, marketing organizations talk about what they know best. This leads them to focus not on customers and prospects, but on brands and products. And that focus typically has little or nothing to do with creating effective messages and incentives.

Moving On

By now, it should be clear that to develop effective messages and incentives, the IMC manager must start with the customer. The next step is to relate an understanding of the customer back to the marketing group and the company as a whole. For, discussed in the next chapter, it is that combination—value to both the customer and the company—that really makes the difference in the value-based IMC environment.

PART V

STEP 4: ESTIMATING RETURN ON CUSTOMER INVESTMENT

1. Identify customers and prospects

5. Budgeting, allocation, and evaluation

2. Valuation of customers/prospects

IMC

4. Estimating return on customer investment

3. Creating and delivering messages and incentives

CHAPTER 9

BASICS OF IMC MEASUREMENT

One of the critical elements in step 3 of the IMC planning process was to ensure that all messages and incentives were capable of measurement because step 4 focuses on calculating return on customer investment (ROCI). We look first at traditional marcom measures, which are attitude based. Because financial measures are becoming so important, this chapter then helps familiarize marcom managers with basic principles of accounting and finance that will make financial measurement easier.

The days when marketers could dismiss the financial people in the organization as "bean counters" who restrained creativity are long gone. As shown in Chapter 5, traditional marketing efforts, which focused on changing attitudes, have proven all but impossible to evaluate in financial terms. Because IMC treats customers as assets and is directly concerned with behavioral returns on investment rather than attitudinal change, it is now possible for marketing to answer core financial questions, namely the following:

- How much should be invested in marketing communication?
- What type or level of return will be achieved from that investment?
- Over what period of time will that return occur?

These three questions are nothing new. Senior management has always wanted to know the level of returns they could expect from their marcom investments. Yet because it was so difficult to link increases in sales directly to marcom efforts, finance executives have tended to view marketing as a "soft" function, lacking accountability. The rise in direct response marketing and E-commerce—which result directly in sales to an intended audience—has resolved some of the return on investment mysteries that confounded management. But in large part, communication—which often accounts for the highest levels of spending—is still a gray area. This chapter helps marketers understand why and provides a new model that overcomes the obstacles to proper measurement of the marcom function.

Why Marcom Measurement Has Proven So Difficult

There are four main reasons why the results of marketing communication have been difficult to measure in the past. This section first looks at each and then considers how an IMC approach helps overcome them.

- **"Black box" of communication.** As the children's game of Telephone illustrates, much is open to misinterpretation when any message is passed along from one person to the next. Everyone has taken down phone messages wrongly or added their own elaborations while retelling a story. This is because much of the effect of communication occurs inside the head of the person who receives it. As we discussed in Chapter 7, because of the way the brain processes information, people usually cannot explain what messages they have received, over what period of time, or what impact that communication had on their attitudes, much less on their behaviors. This is the "black box" of the communication process. Unless marketers can find a way to open the customer's mental black box, they are left with surrogate measures of the impact of marketing communication.

  The black box explains why many of the communication measurement techniques used in the past focused on factors that could be measured easily, such as the number or timing of media exposures, areas of coverage, distribution of literature, and the like. The focus has traditionally been on *outputs*, measuring the messages the marketer sends out, rather than on *outcomes*, identifying the results of those messages in terms of impact on the marketer's business. The IMC process reverses this situation by focusing on outcomes—changed behaviors that result from marcom activities—rather than outputs.

- **Time and timing.** Time is a major factor in communication measurement. Not every marcom message received by a customer or prospect, or even those that impact the customer's or prospect's behavior, results in an immediate response. That's why in IMC, marketers separate communication types into messages and incentives. Messages work over time; incentives generally work quickly. Additionally, some marketers believe multiple exposures to the message or incentive are needed for the prospect to learn or understand the value of the product or service and thus make a favorable purchasing decision. In the IMC approach, the goal is to be in front of customers and prospects when they need and want marketing communication. That's why the process starts with message delivery and then moves on to message content.

- **Source of message or incentive.** Customers and prospects are exposed to a large assortment of commercial messages from a wide variety of sources, ranging from television commercials to packaging to simple word of mouth. Untangling the source of messages and incentives is a major issue in determining the impact of marketing communication. Certainly, that is true when the marketer is attempting to determine which delivery system worked and which didn't. Fortunately, new statistical techniques, such as marketing mix modeling (described in the next chapter), provide the ability to break out which communication tactic worked and which didn't. These hold great promise for the future.

- **Those bothersome intervening variables.** Let's assume a prospect sees a newspaper ad or television commercial and is influenced to seek out a particular product for purchase. To go through with the purchase, the prospect must first identify the local dealer or distributor for the product, then go to the outlet. Assume the convinced prospect (a) cannot find a parking place, abandons the search, and buys another brand at another store; (b) goes to the retail outlet, but the desired model is out of stock—no sale; (c) finds the product in the store with a retail price much higher than that suggested by the manufacturer and purchases a competitive product at a perceived value price; (d) enters the retail outlet but finds the retail clerk unknowledgeable and unable to answer questions about the product—again, no sale; or (e) tries to navigate the company's website to place an order and finds the input system is so complicated that he or she abandons the shopping cart midstream. In cases like these, where the marketing communication obviously had a positive impact, can one really say it worked? Many marcom managers would argue that it did, even though no sale resulted. They would claim "success" based on effective communication. They would suggest that *intervening variables* entered the purchasing process and hampered what would otherwise have been a successful sale. While this argument has been used by marcom managers since the early 1960s, it is becoming less and less relevant today. If one agrees that marketing communication is the successful result of a combination of marketing and communication variables, the marcom manager must find ways to overcome these intervening variables. That commonly requires working with their internal sales, operations, logistics, and other departments to find ways to ensure the future success of marcom investments. Marcom managers can no longer walk away from the situation by claiming intervening variables. They simply must find ways to deal with them.

These four issues explain why marcom has, in the past, eluded effective measurement. Over the years, marketers have tried again and again to put measurement techniques in place. The section that follows describes some of these efforts while explaining why they are no longer appropriate.

Traditional Attempts to Measure Marcom Returns

In the mid-1950s, as mass media developed and mass distribution grew, marketers and their ad agencies began to seek ways to measure the returns on the ever-larger investments they made in broadscale advertising. Since products were sold through multiple channels, marketers became increasingly distanced from their actual purchasers. They needed an acceptable method of measuring the impact of mass advertising on their far-removed customers.

In 1961, two major approaches came to the fore. The first was the hierarchy of effects, which was explored in Exhibit 4.2. The second, developed by marketing consultant Russell Colley for the Association of National Advertisers (ANA), came to be known as DAGMAR, an acronym for defining advertising goals for measured advertising response.[1] Both models are based on the concept that consumers or prospects go through some sort of measurable, structured, and linear "attitudinal change process" on the way to making a product or service purchase. In short, they make the assumption that attitude change leads to behavioral change. As seen in Chapter 4, the hierarchy of effects took consumers from awareness to knowledge to hoped-for purchasing behavior. Similarly, DAGMAR moved customers and prospects through a hierarchical change in attitudes that were affected primarily as a result of advertising.

Thus, the hierarchy of effects and DAGMAR models both assume that advertising or marketing communication works to change customer awareness and attitudes over time as the consumer goes through a learning process. In other words, advertising is thought to inform or instruct, while customers, in turn, "learn" the marketer's message. Both models further assume that multiple advertising exposures are required for the advertising to "work," that is, for there to be behavioral change.

As a result, advertisers have generally subscribed to the premise of an *S-curve*, shown in Exhibit 9.1, as the basis of advertising response. Here, the number of advertising exposures are plotted on the x-axis, and the consumers' response to the advertising, however defined, is plotted on the y-axis. The S-curve theory says, in effect, that there is little impact on the consumer in the first one or two exposures. At the third exposure, the advertising message is learned and the advertising impact occurs, whether the latter is defined as "preference" or "conviction" or even the elusive "purchase behavior." Most advertising media planning and purchasing relies on S-curve assumptions, which are based on the hierarchy of effects and DAGMAR models.

Exhibit 9.1 S-Curve of Advertising Response

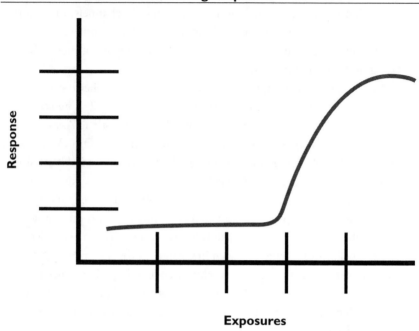

In recent years, however, new analysis of existing data, primarily developed by John Paul Jones and Erwin Ephron, has suggested that advertising may work in a different way.[2] The premise is that advertising can have short-term, immediate effects in addition to the long-term, brand-enhancing value traditionally ascribed to it. Jones and Ephron suggest that advertising works on the basis of *recency*. By that, they simply mean that advertising often has short-term effects in terms of influencing consumer behaviors, providing some support for the hierarchy of effects model. Thus, they subscribe to the recency model based on a convex curve—shown in Exhibit 9.2—in which the first exposure is the most important. So, the argument still rages on how advertising works, but progress is being made.

In support of this convex curve of advertising response, Jones and Ephron have used grocery store scanner data showing that consumers

Exhibit 9.2 Convex Curve of Advertising Response

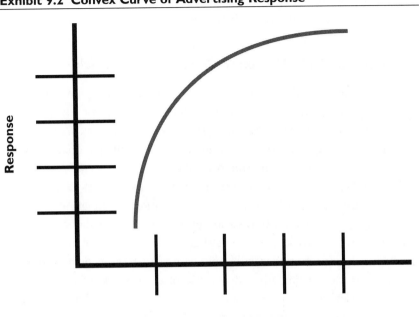

who were exposed to—or had an opportunity to see—a television commercial for a particular brand during the preceding week were much more likely to purchase that brand than those who were not exposed to the commercial. In other words, recency—or the nearer the advertising exposure is to the point of purchase—may be of as much or more importance in generating actual sales than the frequency of advertising exposures.

Whether one subscribes to the recency approach to advertising impact or the more traditional frequency approach, there are inherent assumptions about the long-term impact of advertising exposures. As noted earlier, the real challenge in measurement is the time factor. During what period of time should one measure the results of marketing communication? The time factor is critical, since it is directly connected with how quickly the firm gets a return on its marcom investment. After all, that is what management is concerned with: "How much did we spend? How much did we get back? How soon did we get it back?"

A Step in the Right Direction: Measuring Ad Stock

As a precursor to the emergence of value-based IMC planning and measurement, Simon Broadbent introduced a concept of advertising measurement that moves beyond just exposure or *opportunities to see.* Terming it "the measurement of ad stock," Broadbent's goal was to measure response to advertising over time.

Broadbent, a long-time researcher at the Leo Burnett advertising agency, defined *ad stock* as the combination of good feelings, attitudes, and experiences that customers and prospects build up about a brand over time.[3] Ad stock, Broadbent suggested, has a major impact on whether or not a customer will repurchase a brand or become an advocate for it. By viewing a brand in terms of its ad stock, marketers are able to understand the long-term effects of advertising and other forms of marketing communication on purchase behavior. Over time, ad effects deteriorate, possibly through memory loss, exposure to competitive products and competitive advertising, and personal experiences. Thus, the goal of marketing communication becomes to maintain the ad stock or customer reservoir of good feelings, enabling the brand to remain a contender for future purchases.

Inherent in Broadbent's concept is the idea of some type of lead and lag in advertising and marcom effects. In other words, some advertising likely works in the short term to generate immediate sales, and some is stored away and works over time—that is, from the ad stock base— by creating long-term behavioral effects.

While Broadbent and other researchers have focused almost entirely on the attitudinal changes that occur as a result of advertising exposure, IMC takes these concepts to a new level, arguing that there are surely both short-term and long-term behavioral effects of marketing communication. We refine the equation so that those effects can be measured in terms of financial returns to the organization, not just in terms of attitude change on the part of the consumer.

The Advent of Interactivity

Beginning in the early 1980s, direct marketing became a core element of marcom programs, particularly in the United States. Growing out of the areas of direct mail and catalog marketing, new technologies such as large-scale storage systems, databases, and statistical software brought a new level of expertise to the entire marketing field. With their aid, marcom managers could individually select the recipients for marcom messages and incentives. And, if successful, they would receive individual responses. But the big change was they were able to do both types of communication on a broad scale. Thus, many marketers began to precisely target their communication rather than simply using mass-media distribution systems in the hope of reaching appropriate customers and prospects.

Closing the Loop

For the first time in modern marketing, direct techniques enabled communication managers to "close the loop" on marcom investments and returns. As explained under guiding principle 6 in Chapter 3, the concept was simple. First, the marketer could individually select those persons he or she believed to be the best prospects for the marcom messages. In many cases, they proved to be present customers or those who had dealt with the organization before. The marketer first had to value the customer to enable some sort of intelligent investment decision. He or she commonly knew the cost of goods and the margins that would be available if a sale were made. The marketer could therefore calculate the cost to direct a specific communication program to the selected individual. Knowing the communication cost and the product margin, and estimating the delivery and service requirements, it was possible to determine the return on communication investment. This was done by knowing how many customers or prospects were contacted and how many responded with a purchase with what profit margin. In short, return on communication investment could be calculated following the completion of the marketing program, or with sufficient historical data, estimates of future results could be determined equally well. In either case, the marketer could directly connect expenditures to returns. While there were still unknown factors such as uncontrollable competitive messages, economic changes, and the like that complicated the measurement process, for all intents and purposes, the investment and return loop could now be closed.

Also important was that if the customer response rate to marcom programs could be calculated based on numerous contacts and responses over time, historical and predictive models could be developed. Those models would then enable the marketer to determine the current response value of a customer and also make it possible to develop a series of hypotheses and models that could predict those returns in the future. Thus, the *lifetime customer value* (LTV) calculation was developed and still drives many direct marketing programs today. The LTV approach could be used to indicate how much a customer might be worth to an organization over a specific time frame.

Developing New Models

These newfound predictive capabilities enabled marketers to develop financial models that simply hadn't been available earlier. Today, marketers can estimate how much they would be willing to invest either to gain a new customer, retain or grow a present one, or get a customer to "trade up" from one product line to another using a portfolio migration approach. All of these calculations rely, of course, on a sound estimate of a customer's present value and potential future returns to the firm. Thus, it is easy to see the value of step 2 of the IMC process, in which such an estimate is made. This is key, for to plan effectively, the marcom manager must first know how much of the firm's finite resources to invest in various customers and then be able to estimate some type of return on those investments. Thus, organizations such as FedEx, USAA, Dow Chemical, Fidelity Investments, and Williams Sonoma can now actually operate on the basis of "marcom investments out" and rely on fairly accurate estimates or calculations of returns on marcom investments coming back in.

By now, the value of financial marcom models is clear. They give marketers the ability to move from relying on simple attitudinal measures of awareness, preference, liking, and the other steps in the hierarchy of effects to using reliable financial measures that show what the firm got back or is likely to get back from its marcom investments.

The ability to switch from attitudinal measures to behavioral measures and to deal with the lead and lag times that characterized traditional marcom methods sets IMC apart. More importantly, however, IMC clearly goes beyond traditional methods by recognizing the need for financial measures of marcom effects. The section that follows explains how IMC puts those measures in place.

Key IMC Financial Concepts

Step 3 of the IMC planning process introduced a communication planning framework built around messages and incentives. The next layer to that concept is added by considering the time frame in which communication responses are expected to occur. The matrix in Exhibit 9.3 separates the returns from the two core communication outputs—mes-

Exhibit 9.3 IMC Planning Matrix

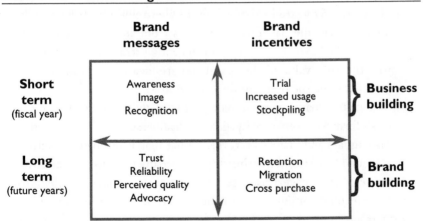

sages and incentives—into those that are short term and those that are long term. Short-term returns come from those *business-building* activities that will generate revenues during the current fiscal year. Long-term returns are those that will accrue over more than one financial accounting period or fiscal year thanks to *brand-building* activities.

Each quadrant of the matrix contains examples of the types of marcom programs that generate each form of return. Brand message efforts that are expected to generate a short-term return include the kinds of activities typically associated with new products or rebranding efforts (increase brand awareness, establish a clear brand image, build recognition and preference). These efforts are supplemented with short-term incentive activities (gain trial, increase usage, get consumers to stockpile). All these message and incentive efforts work together to build sales volume and business during the current fiscal year and are measured against short-term criteria.

Messages and incentives have a role in generating long-term returns as well. For example, incentive programs frequently encourage long-standing customers to behave in a certain way. They are geared to increase retention, loyalty, upgrades (migration), or cross purchases. Airline loyalty programs are one of the best examples of long-term incentive programs that help build and enhance brands. Long-term brand messages address the timeless and enduring qualities of the brand, with an emphasis on the trust, reliability, or quality it represents. They are less strongly geared to attracting new customers and are heavily focused on creating passionate advocates from an existing customer base. These long-term message and incentive strategies combine to impact the asset value of the brand and are measured through techniques that value the brand in financial terms.

The matrix helps marcom managers treat marketing communication as a financial investment by viewing that investment clearly in terms of cash outlays and financial returns. Rather than planning their activities around a finite marketing budget ordained from above, IMC advocates that managers use a set of financial tools that allow them to manage income, outputs, investments, and returns, just like any other asset group within the firm. Only with such tools can marcom stop using meaningless measures, such as communication effects, and begin to get a grip on the real value and returns its activities provide the organization.

Cash Flows and Shareholder Value

In today's global economy, most organizations operate on the basis of two primary values:

- Increasing or stabilizing the firm's cash flows that provide the resources to conduct ongoing operations and to provide the flexibility to react to marketplace changes quickly and easily
- Increasing or improving shareholder value that, hopefully, will attract greater investor interest and provide greater access to capital (In most cases today, shareholder value is primarily a reflection of the share price or dividend policy of publicly traded firms or the retained earnings of those that are privately held.)

Generally, little else matters to the senior management of the firm. If they can increase, accelerate, or stabilize cash flows or increase shareholder value, they consider the firm—and themselves—to be successful. Thus, in the twenty-first-century marketplace, every marcom manager must find ways to relate these clearly defined management goals to the development and implementation of marcom programs. In other words, the marcom investments the manager makes must somehow deliver one of four values[4]:

- **Increase cash flows.** The general focus of marketing communication here is to provide ways of acquiring new customers who can provide new cash flows or to improve the returns on those customers the firm already serves (that is, to grow purchases and cash flows from existing customers).
- **Accelerate cash flows.** Since most firms operate on the basis of some type of *net present value* (NPV)—that is, money in the hands of the firm today is worth more than money obtained in the future—the goal of marketing communication here must be to accelerate the customer cash flows. For example, if marketing communication can reduce the buying cycle for an automobile from four years to three, the cash flow of the car manufacturer has been accelerated. Future cash flows become available sooner, giving the firm more flexibility and leverage.

- **Stabilize cash flows.** This is a major challenge to any organization. By having a stable cash flow, borrowing can be reduced, planning can be more strategic, and the peaks and valleys of financial turbulence can be removed. One way to stabilize cash flows is to enhance customer loyalty and continuity. If marketing communication can build loyalty, the cash flows to the organization can often be regulated and the overall results of the organization improved.

- **Build or enhance shareholder value.** Traditionally, shareholder value has grown because the firm owned or controlled valuable tangible assets. As companies have moved into the intangible economy with the resulting emphasis on cash flows and short-term earnings, the importance of marketing communication to build shareholder value has naturally increased. These values can be created by building greater perceptual value for the organization among financial analysts and the investment community. Another way is by building the image of brands and other intangible assets so they are perceived to have greater value than in the past. While corporate communication is often the tool chosen to attempt to increase shareholder value, marketing communication has a vital role as well.

Investments and Returns on Finite Corporate Resources

All organizations have finite resources. The purchase and distribution of various forms of marketing communication use up a portion of those limited resources. Funds not invested in marketing communication can be allocated to another activity, invested in assets, used to pay dividends, or held as cash in order to enhance profits and the balance sheet. Thus, the investment by the firm in a marcom program must be viewed as any other use of finite resources. It must provide some return to the organization. If marcom cannot provide the same returns as other investments, its use becomes questionable.

Concurrent with that is the need for marcom managers to understand that the organization's resources are limited. There is no corporate well into which management can dip to come up with funds to support new communication programs. Marketing communication must be treated like any other investment and that means being able to justify the expenditure and having some idea of expected returns. Only in that way can senior management make intelligent decisions about marcom expenditures and investments.

Corporate Time Frames

Communication managers and communication activities work on a different time frame than does the financial system in the corporation. For example, commitments for advertising time or space may be made in the autumn of one year, but the advertising space or time is not used or billed to the firm until the spring of the following year. That may cross over two corporate fiscal years. The same is true for sponsorships that are made on the basis of multiyear contracts and even promotions that are initiated in one period but do not have an impact on the marketplace until they occur, resulting in cash flows in another financial time frame. Thus, communication is an almost continuous event or activity, whereas the corporation has clearly defined financial time frames.

Almost all organizations operate on the basis of a fiscal year, that is, 365 days of operation at the end of which the books are closed and the organization starts all over with a clean slate. True, financial commitments and obligations that cross over multiple financial periods are made, but these are unique situations and not the norm. It is this time factor, where communication is expensed in one period but the results are not obtained until a later period, that makes communication measurement and funding difficult. That's particularly true with brand-building investments.

From a financial standpoint, however, the organization has no choice. There are clear financial time frames, and marketing communication must be made to fit them. Thus, IMC takes a simple approach: use financial time frames and fit communication investments and returns to the accounting and financial standards on which the organization operates. It is simple but also challenging, given the impact and effect of marcom programs.

Net Present Value

The calculation of net present value has become a very important issue in the way organizations are operated and valued. Since organizations began focusing primarily on cash flows, or the net inflow and outflow of money, the focus of corporate management has shifted. Where once a firm was valued on the basis of tangible assets—that is, physical items or elements it possessed or could sell or that had marketplace value—today, this focus is clearly on how many "free" dollars or cash the firm generates that can be used in its operation.

Cash flows are interesting and unique elements. The theory that cash in hand today is worth more than cash promised at a future time drives many management decisions. Cash in hand today can be used to make investments, make purchases, or hire employees. Given the common assumptions of risk and inflation in the marketplace, estimates of future income flows are discounted at some rate to account for this current value of money versus its future value. Thus, organizations commonly value investments in terms of a *discounted cash flow* (DCF), or what the income or revenue might be worth in the future as a result of inflation, risk, and forgone interest or income over the time involved.

Since so many communication programs anticipate having an impact on future income flows to the organization, both in the short term and long term, NPV and DCF calculations become important elements in the IMC approach. They are explained in more detail in future chapters.

Brands as Assets and Investments

One of the key elements in the IMC process is the premise that the brands the firm owns are some of its most valuable assets. While it is true that brands are intangibles, they do have asset value. In truth, there are few things many companies control that have as much earning power or current marketplace value as their brands. Yet brands commonly are not managed as corporate assets. Instead they are too often treated as short-term investments in the hope that immediate returns will occur. Brand value builds over time. Brand returns come over time.

And brand marcom programs must be understood and measured as returns on investments over time as well. We discuss this concept of brands as assets and marketing communication as investments in more detail in Chapter 12.

Marginal Revenue/Incremental Returns

Marcom programs must provide a return to the organization. Ideally, that return will be greater than the cost. While there are some instances where the organization is willing to invest in communication in the hope of future returns, IMC must generally at least break even for senior management to consider it a viable investment. Thus, marketing communication, in the IMC approach, must generate greater returns than costs, certainly in the short term. We demonstrate this point in the next chapter.

Moving On

With this quick review of the principles of financial analysis in place, we are ready to apply these concepts to the measurement of returns from marcom investments. That is the goal of step 4 of the IMC process.

CHAPTER 10

ESTIMATING SHORT-TERM RETURN ON CUSTOMER INVESTMENT

S tep 4 of the IMC process begins with the estimation of the short-term returns that have been or can be achieved from marcom investment. Unlike traditional models based only on communication effects, the goal of IMC is to clearly determine the returns on the investments that have or will be made by customers and prospects as a result of marcom programs.

In this chapter, we describe a basic approach to calculating return on customer investment (ROCI). We first provide a framework that can be applied to any type of organization. The method is then illustrated in a detailed case history that demonstrates the actual steps one marketing manager took when estimating the potential returns from a proposed IMC program.

Marginal Analysis of Business-Building Marcom Investments

A tangible return on the marcom investment is critical if senior management is to be asked to compare that investment against other uses of finite corporate resources. For this reason, IMC offers a marginal analysis system through which to value marcom programs. The system is simple: dollars go out in the form of investments in various communication programs that impact customers and prospects immediately and in the long term; dollars come back in, in the form of increased or retained income flows from those same customers and prospects. With this marginal return approach, all current marcom investments, which have short-term measurable results, can be converted into *variable costs* to the organization. In other words, short-term, business-building marcom investments become variable costs rather than fixed expenses. The primary requirement to make this fundamental change is the ability of the firm to know the value of a customer or customer group and have some way to manage and measure changes in the value of that customer or group over time.

The justification for this variable-cost approach is simple: If marketers can determine the economic value of customers or prospects (either individually or as a group), they can determine how much they should invest against those individuals or groups. Recall from Chapter 5 that the value of customers must be calculated at the contribution margin line based on their income flows to the organization. If one adjusts the contribution figure slightly—that is, break out all costs and other charges so that the contribution margin figure includes only marcom expenditures and profits—one can quickly and easily determine the return on investment. This is now being done in many firms through activity-based costing methodologies. In these methodologies, with the contribution figure containing only marcom costs and profits, it becomes clear that money not spent on marketing communication becomes profit, and profits not taken can be used for marketing communication. Thus, marketing communication is converted into a variable organizational cost for accounting purposes. (This is illustrated further in the examples that follow.)

Likewise, other types of marcom investments in customers, such as customer retention, protection of existing customers from competition, and migration of customers through a product portfolio, can be accommodated in the same way. In fact, the marcom manager can estimate or determine the value of any type of marcom investment against any set of customers or prospects based on the marketing strategy being developed. This planned marcom expenditure against specific customers or groups of customers or prospects forms the core of the value-based IMC measurement system.

Let's illustrate the difference in how business-building marcom investments and returns are treated in IMC compared to traditional marketing budgeting and allocation processes. Table 10.1 illustrates a typical line item budget for a fast-moving consumer goods product. It shows advertising and sales promotion as fixed line expenses. The budget for this product has been based on an organizational budgeting model. In this case, it is a flat 6 percent of gross sales with a built-in inflation factor of 10 percent. That is, it assumes costs of communication activities will increase by 10 percent over last year. Thus, the budget for each of these functional marcom activities has been increased by that amount from the previous year. Using this annual fiscal budget spreadsheet, the brand manager can allocate marketing and communication programs over the coming year, keeping in mind the limits that senior management has established through the budgeting process.

Contrast this with the IMC model in Table 10.2. Note there are no functional communication budget lines. All marcom programs have

Table 10.1 Line Item Budget for Fast-Moving Consumer Good

	1995 (millions)	1996 (millions)	1997 (estimate) (millions)
Gross sales	$1,750.00	$1,897.50	$2,108.00
Units	500	550	620
Price per unit	$3.50	$3.45	$3.40
General and administration	$170.00	$166.60	$163.27
Advertising and promotion	$105.00	$115.50	$127.05
Total fixed expense	$275.00	$282.10	$290.32
GMBT and COGS	$1,475.00	$1,615.40	$1,817.68
	84%	85%	86%
COGS	$525.00	$550.28	$590.24
GMBT	$950.00	$1,065.13	$1,227.44
	54%	56%	58%

Note: COGS = cost of goods sold; GMBT = gross margin before tax.

From Don E. Schultz and Jeffrey Walters, *Measuring Brand Communication ROI*, New York: Association for National Advertisers, Inc., 1997. Used with permission from Association for National Advertisers, Inc.

been included as variable product expenses in the budget sheet. Since expenses will be included as cost of the product, the only requirement of the IMC manager is to reach his or her income flow goal for each customer group. Thus, all marcom investments will be recorded as part of product financials.

From these two spreadsheets, it is obvious that the business-building investment approach is a form of basic economic marginal analysis. Using marginal analysis, the organization could theoretically invest unlimited marcom funds against groups of customers or prospects as long as the return income flows were equal to or greater than the expenditures (and also covered the cost of capital), since marketing communication is being treated as a variable product cost.

How to Estimate Returns on Business-Building Marcom Programs

As discussed in the last chapter, a key element needed to effectively measure ROCI is the ability to separate short-term business-building marketing communication from brand-building communication. While

Table 10.2 Business-Building Spreadsheet

	1995 (millions)	1996 (millions)	1997 (estimate) (millions)
Gross sales	$1,750.00	$1,897.50	$2,108.00
Units	500	550	620
Price per unit	$3.50	$3.45	$3.40
General and administration	$170.00	$166.60	$163.27
Total fixed expense	$170.00	$166.60	$163.27
GMBT, COGS, and marketing communication	$1,580.00	$1,730.90	$1,944.73
	90%	91%	92%
COGS	$525.00	$550.28	$590.24
Marketing communication	$105.00	$115.50	$127.05
GMBT	$950.00	$1,065.13	$1,227.44
	54%	56%	58%

Note: COGS = cost of goods sold; GMBT = gross margin before tax

From Don E. Schultz and Jeffrey Walters, *Measuring Brand Communication ROI*, New York: Association for National Advertisers, Inc., 1997. Used with permission from Association for National Advertisers, Inc.

the line between the two will not always be distinct, the basic separation between short term (returns within the organization's fiscal year) and long term (returns over typically several fiscal years) is critical because of current accounting standards.

The ROCI measurement system proposed for IMC planning is based on the premise that all business-building marcom programs will contribute incremental returns to the organization. The planner must, in advance, estimate or account for additional revenue that is or should be expected to be generated by the marcom program. This is important, because almost all organizations have some form of income flow from present customers or expected income flow from prospects. Additional investments in marketing communication should therefore either enhance or protect those revenue streams or, in some cases, alter them to create more cash flows and hopefully a greater profitability.

This incremental revenue approach is possible because some measure of income flows from the customer or the value of a customer group is known prior to executing the marcom program. Thus, the calculation of incremental financial return is the goal, replacing the determination of total sales volume or total profit in traditional budgeting. Also, the incremental revenue approach works just as well for a customer retention strategy—the marketer can estimate what it costs or will cost to retain a customer's income flows, and from that, the level of investment and ROCI can be determined. Similarly, a marketing communication manager can estimate or calculate the cost to acquire a new customer from whom the initial income flow to the organization will be zero until a purchase has been made. Thus, the proposed process works equally well with most any type of customer or prospect marketing strategy. This is a critical element in the success of the IMC program.

A key element in the process, explained in more detail in the following examples, is that it is designed to work either with customer or prospect groups or with individuals. If the planner could estimate or calculate the return on every individual customer, that would be the ideal situation for most organizations. However, this is not always practical or possible. Therefore, the focus in this chapter is on customer groups, since that is what the majority of marketers will likely be using.

How the Incremental Revenue Method Works

The spreadsheets that follow demonstrate how the process works. The same method can be used to calculate either the actual return that has been achieved on a marcom investment program or to estimate potential returns using various "what-if" scenarios.

Table 10.3 provides a standardized overview of a typical ROCI analysis spreadsheet.

In the column headings across the top, customers are aggregated by their behavior. These groups can be as broad or as narrow, as many or as few as needed for the market being estimated or calculated. Along with each customer group, the marcom manager specifies the behavioral objective the plan aims to achieve during the measurement period (acquire new customers, retain existing customers, grow share of business, migrate customers through the product portfolio). Note that there may even be times when the marketer aims to divest high-maintenance, low-profit customers.

The spreadsheet itself is composed of rows divided into the five sections that provide the basic building blocks for the ROCI calculation. Let's look at each one in more detail.[1]

Category Requirement Assumptions
In this section, the customer's entire demand in the product category, spread across all vendors, is determined. (Note that for organizations that sell through channels, this estimate is based on sales at the factory level.)

Line 1: Estimated Category Demand This is based on historical or what-if data about customer purchase behavior and is expressed in dollars rather than units, shipments, or other nonfinancial measures.

Base Income Flow Assumptions
Basic assumptions are made about the brand's share-of-customer requirements and its cost dynamics. These are factors that are then applied under alternative scenarios calling for differing levels of communication spending.

Table 10.3 Building Blocks of ROCI Analysis

	Aggregated Customer Group:	Group A	Group B	Group C
	Behavioral Goal:			
	Category Requirement Assumptions			
1	Estimated category demand	Historical data/estimate	$	$	$
	Base Income Flow Assumptions			
2	Base share of requirement	Historical data/estimate	%	%	%
3	Base income flow to us	Line 1 × Line 2 =	$	$	$
4	Noncommunication costs (product, fixed, G&A, etc.)	Operating estimate	%	%	%
5	Contribution margin (%)	100% − Line 4 =	%	%	%
6	Contribution margin ($)	Line 3 × Line 5 =	$	$	$
	Scenario A: No Communication Investment			
7	Change in share of requirement	Estimate	+%	+%	+%
8	Resulting share of requirement	Line 2 + (Line 7 × Line 2) =	%	%	%
9	Resulting customer income flow to us	Line 8 × Line 1 =	$	$	$
10	Less noncommunication costs (product, fixed, G&A, etc.)	− (Line 9 × Line 4) =	−$	−$	−$
11	Less marketing communication costs	$0	—	—	—
12	Net contribution	Line 9 + (Line 10 + Line 11) =	$	$	$

(continued)

Table 10.3 Building Blocks of ROCI Analysis (continued)

	Aggregated Customer Group: Behavioral Goal:	Group A	Group B	Group C
Scenario B: Communication Investment				
13	Marketing communication efforts (Lines A–M)	Estimate	$	$	$
14	Total marketing communication investment	Total lines 13A–M	$	$	$
15	Change in share of requirement	Estimate	±%	±%	±%
16	Resulting share of requirement	Line 2 + (Line 15 × Line 2) =	%	%	%
17	Resulting customer income flow to us	Line 16 × Line 1 =	$	$	$
18	Less noncommunication costs (product, fixed, G&A, etc.)	− (Line 18 × Line 4) =	−$	−$	−$
19	Less marketing communication costs	− Line 14	—	—	—
20	Net contribution	Line 18 + (Line 19 + Line 20) =	$	$	$
ROCI Calculation				
21	Incremental gain/loss vs. "no investment" scenario	Line 20 − Line 12 =	$	$	$
22	Incremental ROCI	Line 22 / Line 14 =	$	$	$

Note: G&A = general and administration; ROCI = return on customer investment.

From Don E. Schultz and Jeffrey Walters, *Measuring Brand Communication ROI*, New York: Association for National Advertisers, Inc., 1997. Used with permission from Association for National Advertisers, Inc.

Line 2: Base Share of Requirement (SOR) This is the proportion of the customer's total category requirements that the marketer's brand currently enjoys, based on historical or what-if scenario data.

Line 3: Base Income Flow to Us The customer's total category demand is multiplied by the percentage of that demand that comes to the marketer's brand, meaning the dollar income flow to the brand that the customer group represents.

Line 4: Noncommunication Costs This line shows all fixed and variable costs of running the business *excluding* marcom costs. For the sake of simplicity, this is shown as a simple percentage of the income flow.

Line 5: Contribution Margin (%) This is equal to 100 percent less the percentage used in line 4 to account for nonmarcom costs.

Line 6: Contribution Margin ($) Contribution margin for the brand expressed in dollars is determined by multiplying line 3 by line 5.

Scenario A: No Communication Investment
This section establishes a base line of profitability. That is, if the brand made no further communication investment, how much business would it receive from each of its customer groups during the period of analysis? It is, of course, unlikely the brand would lose 100 percent of its customers without any marketing communication in the fiscal year, although one could imagine such a situation for a direct marketing firm. However, chances are some change in demand, share, or requirements would occur. This section of the spreadsheet defines certain assumptions about just what that impact might be. From there, the brand's income flow, costs, and net contribution based on the factors established in the previous section are reprojected.

Line 7: Change in Share of Requirement This represents the estimated change in the brand's SOR during the period if there were no marcom investments. In most cases, this will result in a negative number, such as a 15 percent decrease in the SOR.

The key question for many organizations is how to develop an accurate estimate of the change in requirements of their customers or prospects. Companies with a great deal of historical data can extrapolate from past experiences. Others may have done A/B market tests that could provide a starting point. In most cases, all firms have had to cancel, adjust, or redefine their marcom programs at one time or another. The same data provide the basis for this estimate or calculation. In other cases, this estimate may be based on nothing other than the manager's own best professional judgment and insight from experience. In truth, assumptions about what would happen if no communication were done are made by marcom managers every day, albeit they are often done indirectly. The key is that this process forces the manager to focus on the issue(s) to be resolved and to make viable and supportable decisions, not just maintain the status quo or continue the traditional spending patterns as they have been done in the past.

Line 8: Resulting Share of Requirement This is the result of adjusting the initial SOR in line 2 by the factor increase or decrease specified in line 7. For example, if the brand's initial SOR were 50 percent, but the manager felt that brand share would decrease by 25 percent without communication support, the resulting SOR would be $0.50 + (0.50 \times -0.25) = 37.5\%$.

Line 9: Resulting Customer Income Flow to Us The adjusted SOR from line 8 is multiplied by the customer total category demand in line 1. This line represents what would happen to the brand's income flow for the period if no marcom expenditures were made.

Line 10: Less Noncommunication Costs Line 4 (the percentage allocated to cover all noncommunication costs and profits) is multiplied by the adjusted income estimate in Line 9.

Line 11: Less Marketing Communication Costs In this scenario, this line is $0 since there will be no marcom expenditures during the period of analysis.

Line 12: Net Contribution This shows what remains after the costs associated with lines 10 and 11 are subtracted from the income flow estimate in Line 9 (meaning the brand's contribution level under a scenario where no funds are invested in marketing communication). It is this figure that is the basis for estimating the incremental gain, if any, to be achieved when the firm invests in an IMC program, as in Scenario B which follows.

Scenario B: Communication Investment
The next step is to estimate how the value of each customer group would change if a planned communication program were directed toward it.

Line 13: Marketing Communication Efforts This includes all identifiable expenditures for marcom programs the organization plans to direct to a specific group of customers or prospects.

Line 14: Total Marketing Communication Investment This is the firm's total investment in its IMC programs, indicated by all items under line 13.

Line 15: Change in Share of Requirement This line estimates what percentage increase (or decrease) can be expected in SOR for the brand as a result of the total communication program.

Lines 16, 17, and 18 These lines recalculate the revised SOR, income flows, and noncommunication costs based on the percentage obtained in line 16.

Line 19: Less Marketing Communication Costs This number is equal to the total IMC communication investment figure in line 14. It is repeated here as a negative so that it can be subtracted from the income flow along with the noncommunication costs.

Line 20: Net Contribution This indicates the net income after all communication and noncommunication expenses have been deducted.

Line 21: Incremental Gain/Loss Versus "No Communication Investment" Scenario This gives a comparison of the two net contribution estimates obtained in lines 12 and 20. Note that these are incremental gains (or losses) to the brand as a result of the IMC program or lack thereof.

Line 22: Incremental ROCI This is the total incremental gain/loss (line 21) divided by the investment made in line 14.

An Example of the Incremental Revenue Method in Action

Table 10.4 is a walk through the process of developing an actual ROCI analysis for a marcom program step-by-step, using a consumer product example. The example incorporates real-world situations and shows how they fit into the model.

The product illustrated is a consumer brand that is sold through retailers. It is generally purchased three to four times per year by a using household and has a high rate of market penetration. There is limited brand loyalty in the category, so substantial price promotion and discounting by competing brands generally occur. Thus, there is considerable brand switching in the category.

For this example, customers have been divided into four groups based on their relationship with the brand. From previous experience with these groups, the firm has specific behavioral objectives it wishes to achieve through its marcom efforts.

The first group, loyals, consists of long-term customers who give the brand most of their category purchases. Previous analysis has shown that demand from this group is not growing significantly, but the brand obviously needs to maintain the substantial income flow it generates from these customers. Thus, the goal of the brand manager is to retain these customers' income flows at the same level as in the past.

The second group, switchers, are people who switch quite often between the marketer's brand and various competitive brands. While switchers purchase the brand on occasion, this usually happens during a promotion or special offer period. The brand's managers believe they

Table 10.4 Business-Building ROCI Example

CONSUMER PRODUCT

Line #	Aggregated Customer Group:	Loyals	Switchers	New or Emerging Customers	Problem Customers	Total of All Customers Groups
	Behavioral Goal:	Retain	Grow Share	Acquire	Divest	
	Category Requirement Assumptions					
1	Projected category demand	$1,000.00	$1,000.00	$1,000.00	$1,000.00	$4,000.00
	Base Income Flow Assumptions					
2	Base share of requirement	75.0%	40.0%	10.0%	15.0%	35%
3	Base income flow to us	$750.00	$400.00	$100.00	$150.00	$1,400.00
4	Noncommunication costs (product, fixed, G&A, etc.)	75.0%	80.0%	80.0%	90.0%	78.4%
5	Gross contribution margin (%)	25.0%	20.0%	20.0%	10.0%	21.6%
6	Gross contribution margin ($)	$187.50	$80.00	$20.00	$15.00	$302.50
	Scenario A: No Communication Investment					
7	Change in share of requirement	−20.0%	−25.0%	−30.0%	−20.0%	−22.1%
8	Resulting share of requirement	60.0%	30.0%	7.0%	12.0%	27.3%
9	Resulting customer income flow to us	$600.00	$300.00	$70.00	$120.00	$1,090.00
10	Less noncommunication costs (product, fixed, G&A, etc.)	−$450.00	−$240.00	−$56.00	−$108.00	−$854.00
11	Less brand communication costs	$0.00	$0.00	$0.00	$0.00	—
12	Net contribution	$150.00	$60.00	$14.00	$12.00	$236.00

(continued)

Table 10.4 Business-Building ROCI Example (continued)
CONSUMER PRODUCT

Line #	Aggregated Customer Group: Behavioral Goal:	Loyals Retain	Switchers Grow Share	New or Emerging Customers Acquire	Problem Customers Divest	Total of All Customers Groups
	Scenario B: Brand Communication Investment					
13	TV advertising	$0.00	$5.00	$4.00	$0.00	$9.00
14	Radio advertising	$0.00	$2.00	$2.00	$0.00	$4.00
15	Consumer magazines	$0.00	$3.00	$2.00	$0.00	$5.00
16	Direct mail	$4.00	$1.00	$2.00	$0.00	$7.00
17	Sales promotion	$0.00	$5.00	$3.00	$1.00	$9.00
18	Public relations	$2.00	$2.00	$2.00	$1.00	$7.00
19	Special events/sponsorships	$2.00	$2.00	$2.00	$1.00	$7.00
20	Custom media	$4.00	$0.00	$0.00	$0.00	$4.00
21	Customer service improvements	$2.00	$0.00	$0.00	$1.00	$3.00
22	Total brand communication investment	$14.00	$20.00	$17.00	$4.00	$55.00
23	Change in share of requirement	0.0%	10.0%	40.0%	3.0%	6.0%
24	Resulting share of requirement	75.0%	44.0%	14.0%	15.5%	37.1%
25	Resulting customer income flow to us	$750.00	$440.00	$140.00	$154.50	$1,484.50
26	Less noncommunication costs (product, fixed, G&A, etc.)	−$562.50	−$352.00	−$112.00	−$139.05	−$1,165.55
27	Less brand communication cost	−$14.00	−$20.00	−$17.00	−$4.00	−$55.00
28	Net contribution	$173.50	$68.00	$11.00	$11.45	$263.95

Line #	Aggregated Customer Group: Behavioral Goal:	Loyals Retain	Switchers Grow Share	New or Emerging Customers Acquire	Problem Customers Divest	Total of All Customers Groups
	ROCI Calculation					
29	Net contribution scenario A	$150.00	$60.00	$14.00	$12.00	$236.00
30	Net contribution scenario B	$173.50	$68.00	$11.00	$11.45	$263.95
31	Incremental gain/loss vs. "no investment" scenario	$23.50	$8.00	–$3.00	–$0.55	$27.95
32	Incremental ROCI	168%	40%	–18%	–14%	51%

Note: G&A = general and administration; ROCI = return on customer investment.

From Don E. Schultz and Jeffrey Walters, *Measuring Brand Communication ROI*, New York: Association for National Advertisers, Inc., 1997. Used with permission from Association for National Advertisers, Inc.

can strengthen their relationship with these customers with marcom activities and capture a greater proportion of their SORs.

The third group, new or emerging customers, consists of those purchasers just coming into the market. This group is expected to expand rapidly, and even though the marketer's brand now only receives a small portion of the group's business, the goal is to acquire more of its income flows now and in the future.

The last group of customers is called the problem group. In some instances, these customers give the marketer's brand only a small percentage of their business. In others, their general requirements in the category are simply very low. In still other cases, such customers often require a great deal of service and support. Therefore, customer service costs to maintain them are quite high, and product margins for the marketer's brand are squeezed. Demand from this group is also expected to decline in the coming period because of members' changing lifestyles. As a result of this analysis, the marketer would like to reduce the firm's marcom investment to this group and perhaps even divest some of these customers. Note, however, that the marketer can't afford to alienate these customers because this could damage the firm's reputation with other, more valuable customers.

For purposes of this illustration, the projected category demand for each group has been set arbitrarily at the same rate ($1,000.00) for the measurement period. Most likely, this would never be the case in the real world, but it is done to show the dynamics of the process so that comparisons can be made. Thus, the real data on which this analysis is based have been adapted to fit this example.

With overall category demand established, the next step is to move on to determine the base value each customer group represents to the brand. Line 2 details the base share of requirements each group gives to the brand in question. In this case, the marketer has been receiving 75 percent of the income flows from loyals based on what they spent or will spend in the category. This results in a base income flow (line 3) of $750.00. Switchers give the brand 40 percent of their business, so the marketer receives $400.00. Emerging customers provide an income flow of 10 percent SOR, equal to $100.00. And the problem segment is using the brand for 15 percent of its members' requirements, resulting in $150.00.

Next, line 4 shows an estimate of all costs other than those for marketing communication. This is the allocation for all fixed and variable costs, such as those related to product manufacturing and distribution, staff salaries, general and administrative costs, and so on. Typically, there will be some justifiable variation in costs attributed to different groups. New customers, for example, generate greater administrative costs as accounts are established, credit checks are run, and so forth. Established customers, on the other hand, are often the easiest and most efficient to serve. They understand the product, require less hand-holding, are acquainted with the firm's staff, and can easily and quickly explain what they want or need.

In this example, 75 percent of the total customer income flow will be needed to cover all these noncommunication costs for loyals. As shown, they cost somewhat less to serve than switchers or the emerging group, both of which have more churn (i.e., temporary or permanent customer defection to a competitor) and therefore greater administrative expense. Lastly, the problem group requires a high level of customer service and support, and often high promotional and retention costs. Thus, a cost factor of 90 percent has been determined for this group.

When deducted from base income flows, these cost factors give the contribution margin percentage available for each customer group (line 5). This is obtained by subtracting each percentage factor in line 4 from 100 percent. Line 6 expresses the gross contribution margin in terms of dollars. (Recall that the contribution margin in this approach includes only funds available for marketing communication and profit.) In this case, the contribution margin ranges from $187.50 for loyals, to $80.00 for switchers, to $20.00 for the emerging group, to $15.00 for the problem group.

At this point, it is time to recap. So far, the marketer has determined the baseline financial value of each of the four groups of customers at the contribution margin line, based on their estimated income flows to the organization. If the organization could generate these income flows without investing any marcom funds, the communication manager might be able to justify serving each of them. Given some of the group's value based on the calculations, however, even if the firm were able to drive its share of their requirements up substantially—say, getting 80 percent to 85 percent of each group's future business—the company would still have limited funds available for an IMC program. This is the challenge that every communication manager faces when using this type of ROCI analysis. There are some customers against whom finite resources simply cannot be invested, or if the investment is made, it must be done through some type of very efficient, low-cost communication activity that commonly limits its power and impact. This is not to say that these types of IMC programs are not possible or useful, but it does suggest that targeting and focusing on best customers or at least those who provide the greatest opportunity for returning income flows to the firm should be the first requirement of any integrated marcom program.

With this analysis of customer value, it is time to take the next step in the process, which is to identify the incremental value that can likely be created through a marcom program. This is done by first estimating the impact on the brand's income flows if no marcom investment were made and then comparing these results with the results the marketer expects to achieve when various marcom programs are developed and implemented. The results are often surprising.

First, it is necessary to create a "no communication investment" scenario in lines 7 through 12. This is done by estimating or calculating how much the brand's share of customer requirements would fall if all marcom programs were suspended for some period of time. In our earlier example, the brand operated in a competitive category with low customer loyalty and a great deal of competitive marcom activity. Here, the manager has estimated on line 7 that the brand would see a 20 percent decline in its SOR from loyals if there were no promotional investments in this group. Among switchers and emerging customers, the drop is even more dramatic, with decreases of 25 percent and 30 percent, respectively. Even the problem group SOR is predicted to decrease by 20 percent if there are no messages or incentives to encourage its members.

In earlier discussions we stated that, in our experience, the customer's total demand or income flow in the category commonly does not change as a result of diminished brand communication activity in the short term. It is, instead, the proportion of total SOR the brand receives that is impacted. That is, the SOR for the marketer's brand will commonly decline without some marcom support, although customer purchases in the category might continue at the same rate.

Lines 8 through 12 show a recalculation of all the components that lead to the net contribution, which is so critical to the brand. Since the SOR among loyals falls by 20 percent, the resulting SOR declines from 75 percent to 60 percent. When this is multiplied by their base category demand of $1,000.00, it produces an income flow of $600.00 to the firm's brand. From this amount, $450.00 must be subtracted to cover the 75 percent provision for product, administrative, and other noncommunication costs. This results in a net contribution from the group of $150.00, down from the baseline in line 6 of $187.50.

The SOR among switchers, as previously stated, falls 25 percent as well. That means an adjusted share of 30 percent and a resulting income flow of $300.00. With 80 percent of this ($240.00) required to cover noncommunication expenses, the group thus has a net contribution of $60.00.

The emerging customer group was impacted even more by the lack of communication from the brand. Its members are newer to the category, have less experience with the various product alternatives, and in some cases are still experimenting with various marketplace alternatives. Without a compelling communication program, their share of requirement is expected to drop by 30 percent, leaving an SOR of only 7 percent and an income flow of $70.00. Subtracting allocated costs of $56.00 provides a net contribution of $14.00 to the marketer's brand from this group.

Finally, a 20 percent decrease in SOR is expected to occur among the problem group if marcom programs are suspended. Thus, the adjusted SOR for these customers becomes 12 percent. This produces an income flow of $120.00. When allocated noncommunication costs of $108.00 are deducted, a net contribution of $12.00 is the result.

The net contribution income flow shown for each group becomes the basis against which the marketer will measure the incremental gain or loss resulting from the brand's IMC program.

The next step in the analysis is to estimate or calculate the alternative scenario of developing and implementing one or more marcom efforts against each of the groups. In this example, nine marcom efforts are shown on lines 13 through 21. Some are targeted to each group, although the message, incentives, and delivery systems may be different. In some of the programs, only one or two of the communication elements are to be used.

As part of the manager's analysis, the cost of each of these marcom efforts must first be determined. It is not the total invested in each communication method that is important, as much as the determination of how these expenditures are to be allocated across the individual groups. For example, the advertising campaign that has been developed to run on TV, over radio, and in consumer magazines is geared to attract new customers. So, the entire cost of advertising is allocated to switchers and loyals. While it could be argued that even loyals are positively influenced by advertising, the manager has special communication efforts planned for this group, including direct mail, public relations, and custom media.

Line 22 is a summary of the total communication investment made against each customer group. So, a total of $14.00 was spent against loyals, $20.00 against switchers, $17.00 against emerging customers, and $4.00 against the problem group.

In the previous scenario, the following questions were raised: "What if no marcom investment whatsoever were made? What would happen to the brand's share of requirements? What would happen to its sales volume?" In this scenario, the question is reversed: "What happens to the brand's share of requirements and income flows if these marcom investments are made, through the various communication efforts, against customers and prospects? How much, if any, will the brand's business increase in terms of dollars? Will profits increase as well?"

Just as in the "no communication investment" scenario described earlier, the key is to estimate or calculate any change in SOR that would result from the brand's IMC efforts. This is commonly based on some estimate or analysis, often using historical behavioral data, of the responsiveness of customers and prospects to the brand's message and incentive delivery programs. The goal is not to attempt to value each individual, functionally specific communication effort and then sum them. Instead, in the IMC approach, the objective is to determine the synergistic effect produced by all the elements in the integrated marcom program.

Once a determination has been made or estimated of how much (or if) the brand's SOR will change as a direct result of the marcom program, all the brand's income, costs, and net contribution for each group can be recalculated. This is shown on line 23 of the spreadsheet.

At this point, a number of observations are possible. Even though the brand invested $14.00 in communicating with the loyals, there was no impact on their SOR; it stayed the same. However, since the manager's initial goal was to maintain the current SOR level, that objective appears to have been achieved. As shown, the income flow remains at $750.00, with 75 percent ($562.50) of this allocated to noncommunication costs. However, the $14.00 communication expenditure must be deducted to arrive at the net contribution of this group ($173.50).

The estimated SOR among switchers increased by 10 percent as a result of using the marcom programs shown. That gave the brand a total SOR of 44 percent, producing an income flow of $440.00. Although income increased, so did costs; 80 percent ($352.00) of the income was allocated to noncommunication costs. So, after subtracting the marcom investment of $20.00, a net contribution of $68.00 remained.

Emerging customers were very receptive to the brand's marcom programs. Thus, the firm was able to increase its SOR for this group by 40 percent, to 14 percent, and increase its income flow to $140.00. Of this, 80 percent ($112.00) is required for noncommunication expenses. When the $17.00 that was invested in the IMC is deducted, the firm will receive a net contribution of $11.00 from this group.

The problem segment, unfortunately, had a very slight change in SOR as a result of the IMC program. The manager did not want to make a significant investment in communication with the problem customers, but realized that they would be exposed to a certain number of the communication efforts regardless. Thus, a total expense of $4.00 was deemed to have been spent on this group, with the result that the SOR increased, although only by 3 percent, leaving an overall SOR of

15 percent. Based on this, the brand's income flow becomes $154.50, from which $139.05 in noncommunication costs and the $4.00 in communication investment must be deducted, leaving a net contribution of $11.45.

Following these calculations, it is now possible to develop the actual ROCI estimation among the four groups. Only three lines are required for that calculation:

- Line 12, net contribution, under the "no communication investment" scenario
- Line 22, total amount of brand communication spending, under the "brand communication investment" scenario
- Line 28, net contribution, under the "brand communication investment" scenario

For each group, the incremental gain or loss in net contribution under the two scenarios is shown (line 30 − line 29). Because a comparison is being made between net contribution value after all communication spending has been deducted, the objective is to look at the change in profitability that each group of customers or prospects contributes during the time of the communication program. To determine the ROCI, the incremental gain/loss (or the "return") in line 31 is divided by line 22, the total brand communication investment.

As a result of these calculations, the following conclusions can be drawn:

- Loyals received the second smallest portion of the brand's communication spending, $14.00. That investment created no impact on their SOR when compared to their historical level. However, the alternative was to suspend communication, and in that event the brand would likely have lost 20 percent of its SOR among this key group. By spending the $14.00, the brand maintained its share and added to the company's profitability in the amount of $23.50 ($173.50 versus $150.00). Thus, the calculated ROCI is 168 percent ($173.50 − $150.00/$14.00).

- Switchers increased their net contribution from $60.00 under the "no communication investment" scenario to $68.00. This is an incremental gain of $8.00 that, when divided by the communication investment of $20.00, produces an ROCI of 40 percent.
- Communication dollars invested against the emerging customer group did not have as great an impact. The net contribution actually fell from $14.00 to $11.00. While the brand was able to increase its SOR by 40 percent, the additional income was not sufficient to offset the communication costs. There was a loss of $3.00, and an ROCI of −18 percent. This illustrates why it is often true that new customers are expensive to acquire and their value often occurs over time, not immediately. In many cases, organizations are better off trying to nurture the business they have established from existing customer relationships before investing significant amounts to acquire new customers. The true value of customer acquisition usually cannot be reflected in a business-building model such as this because the time frame is simply too short. There is, however, long-term value in acquiring new customers. This is discussed in more detail in Chapter 12.
- Communication to the problem group also produced a negative ROCI. While the SOR had a modest increase, net contribution went from $12.00 to $11.45, an incremental loss of $0.55 and generated an ROCI of −14 percent.

While this example is based on a real-world experience, it has been adapted and simplified to illustrate the ROCI process. Thus, the estimates and calculations are for demonstration purposes only. Other firms using this same approach and process may receive greater or smaller returns from their marcom programs.

Good Versus Bad Return on Customer Investment

A question often raised in this type of calculation is how to determine what level of ROCI is acceptable and what level is not. Obviously, marketing and communication managers want some sort of comparison with similar organizations or competitors. Unfortunately, such yardsticks do not exist or if used are of little value. All organizations are different. All have different strategies. All have different sets of expectations from management and stockholders. So, the only "good" or "bad" ROCI number is the one that fits (or doesn't fit) the financial or financial expectation requirements of the organization.

We have worked with clients who have set a "hurdle rate," that is, a level of return they would like to achieve, in the range of 20 percent to 50 percent. This is the level of return they believe they can achieve by using their finite resources in other ways. Other firms are more modest in their expectations. They believe a return in the 10 percent to 25 percent range is appropriate. Still others fall in between these estimates.

The true determination of whether or not the ROCI is good or bad is what return could be expected from investing those same funds in other corporate activities. If research and development is expected to return 40 percent, then that is a relevant number for comparison. If a new plant investment will return 9 percent, that is the relevant return on investment to use in comparing a marcom ROCI. Again, it all depends on the organization and its other uses for corporate resources. It is within this framework that marketing communication must function now and in the future.

ROCI in Action: National American Bank

The example that follows demonstrates how ROCI analysis, as step 4 of an IMC program, assisted marcom planners at a major financial organization, National American Bank (name has been changed to protect confidentiality). The bank's newly appointed marketing and communication manager was asked to determine and justify a marcom budget and to estimate the expected returns for one of the bank's most mature categories, its credit card division. The example shows how he tackled the problem, particularly as it relates to short-term, business-building communication solutions.

Before the Marcom Effort: National American Bank's Credit Card Portfolio

When the new manager took over responsibility for the marketing and communication programs for the bank's credit card portfolio at the end of 2001, he found a troubled department. Marcom investments had been declining for the past five years. Because the previous manager had been unable to provide senior management with solid evidence that marcom investments could provide measurable returns to the organization, the executive committee had failed to approve that manager's budget requests. Thus, funding had declined and marketing communication had become a minor element in the operation of the unit.

Historically, National American's credit card operation had been highly profitable. Its revenue stemmed from two sources:

- **Interest charged to cardholders on outstanding balances in their accounts.** National American made over $2.4 billion in interest revenue annually, more than that of any of its primary competitors.
- **Interchange fees charged to merchants who accept credit card purchases.** National American estimated its net credit sales in 2002 would be in excess of $7.8 billion, placing it second among its major competitors.

In recent years, the bank had benefited from a growing economy and a positive economic outlook. Thus, consumers were willing to take on additional charge card debt. Revenues had grown as a result of the economic good times. In addition, bank management prided itself on having the best financial performance among its primary competitors as measured by such ratios as cost to income, return on assets, and so on.

As a result, management was highly reluctant to increase marketing expenditures. The concern was that a substantial change in spending would, at least in the short term, result in deterioration in the key financial ratios that were closely monitored by the investment community and could influence the bank's stock price.

However, after conducting an assessment of the bank's recent performance and position against half a dozen competitors, the marcom manager spotted several negative trends that, if not addressed, could result in slowed growth and less profitability. He was particularly concerned about the bank's position vis-à-vis its two largest competitors, Worchester Bank and Valley National, as well as one small but very aggressive competitor, Garden City Bank. Highlights of his analysis, including data for these three competitors, are shown in Table 10.5.

Among the issues he identified were the following:

- **Slower growth than competitors.** While the bank's credit card business was growing at about 3 percent, two of its primary competitors were growing at more than twice this rate.
- **Lower levels of marketing investment.** The slower growth seemed to be related, at least in part, to lower spending levels for marketing activities. The competing banks that were growing faster than National American were investing substantially more in marcom activities. In fact, of the four major banks in its area, National American spent the least on marketing communication. For example, National American invested only $207,000 in above-the-line marketing communication in 2001 compared to the nearly $535,000 spent by Worchester Bank, $1,250,000 spent by Valley National, and

Table 10.5 National American Bank and Its Competitors

	National American Bank	Worchester Bank	Garden City Bank	Valley National
No. of accounts	1,435,000	1,225,000	950,000	1,515,000
Outstanding balances	$2.4 billion	$1.9 billion	$531 million	$1.8 billion
Net credit sales	$7.8 billion	$6.75 billion	$1.1 billion	$11.2 billion
Annual growth	3.0%	2.3%	8.8%	6.3%
Spending on marketing communication	$207,000	$535,000	$4,725,000	$1,250,000
Spending per account	$0.14	$0.43	$4.97	$0.83
Share of market	21%	18%	3.3%	27.0%
Share of wallet	62%	79%	85%	71%

a whopping $4,725,000 spent by Garden City Bank. On the basis of communication investment per cardholder, National American was investing only about $0.14, substantially less than any of the other banks in the analysis.

- **Declining share of market.** National American's share of revenues from interest and interchange income had declined from 26 percent five years earlier to only 21 percent. The marcom manager estimated that this decline in market share represented over $45 million in lost interest and interchange revenue.

- **Declining share of wallet.** Among its own cardholders, National American had seen its share of requirement—or "share of wallet"— decline from 69 percent five years earlier to just 62 percent in 2001. Research showed that half of National American's credit card customers had more than one card, sometimes carrying two, three, or even four. The bank closely monitored this share of wallet figure— that is, the percentage of purchases customers put on their National American card as opposed to one of the other cards they carried— as this was believed to be a strong indicator of customer loyalty and future business. At the current interchange rates, the manager calculated that each 1 percent loss in National American's share of wallet was equivalent to a $5 million loss in bank interchange revenue. Therefore, a decline of 7 percentage points at $5 million per percentage point per year over the last five years likely amounted to more than $35 million in lost revenue to the bank.

The issue of declining share of wallet was particularly disconcerting to the new manager. His first step was to determine the amount of revenue that the bank's customers were charging on other cards. He determined that the current share of wallet for National American was 62 percent of its customers' total spending, or $7.8 billion. That, the marcom manager reasoned, left a 38 percent opportunity for the bank, or about $4.8 billion that the bank's customers were charging on other credit cards. By applying the standard interchange rate of 1.1 percent per year, he determined there was approximately $53 million per year in revenue forgone in available but not captured income among National American's existing cardholders.

Additionally, the bank would have been able to earn interest on the $4.8 billion available but not captured income. The manager estimated the lost interest at approximately $46.4 million per year. When combined, the interchange fees and the lost interest revenue totaled a whopping $99.4 million. That is the additional billing that would have been processed on National American credit cards if the bank had captured all the funds in the 38 percent of the available dollars.

Obviously, capturing 100 percent of available funds is not very likely, but it is a good measure of the potential income the bank was leaving on the table for competitors—and just among its own customers. This calculation clearly defines the available potential against which marcom efforts could be directed and a yardstick against which success could be measured.

As the final piece in the puzzle, the marcom manager had to determine why customers were ignoring or not taking advantage of National American Bank's credit card offerings. As previously noted, market research had indicated that 50 percent of the bank's credit card customers held cards from other banks or other card organizations. Additional analysis showed that of the 50 percent who held two or more cards, almost 20 percent had switched their choice of primary card within the last year. Obviously, if this trend was not reversed, National American's share of wallet would continue to decline, as would revenues and profits. The key question was why these customers had ceased using National American as their primary card. Research was again able to provide some insight. The most common response—from half of all customers who had switched from National American as their primary card—stated that the competing bank offered a customer reward program.

At this point, the new manager knew the magnitude of the problem he was facing, what was creating a large portion of that problem, and what he could expect to generate in terms of returns to the bank if he could solve the problem. It is clear to see that everything he had done so far fell within steps 1, 2, and 3 of the IMC process. By going through that process, he began estimating what he might be able to accomplish with a focused marcom solution. Clearly, he felt a well-conceived and well-implemented IMC program could provide a solution to the declining value of the National American credit card portfolio.

The IMC Story Line

To gain approval for a strategic solution to the bank's credit card challenge, the marcom manager had to develop a powerful "story line" for senior management. This presentation had to outline the problem, present the recommended solution, provide the supporting documents, illustrate the assumptions on which the solution was based, and, finally, describe the expected returns. The manager recalled that his predecessor had been unable to provide a solid proposal and, therefore, had been unsuccessful in gaining approval for his recommendations. The new manager was determined this would not happen again. He developed his story line in the following manner, summarizing the current situation and then putting forth his recommended solutions.

Current Situation

The basic premise of the program the manager proposed was to begin treating communication budgets as an investment rather than as an expense. This concept had never been adequately developed nor explained at the bank. In reviewing previously proposed programs, the new manager found that his predecessor had presented his recommendations in a way that avoided any estimate of the return on investment. In fact, the predecessor had argued that it was impossible to measure the return on marketing investments with any precision. He had assumed that, because of the lagged response effect, marketing programs only worked over time and could not be linked to customer behavior. Thus, any measurements that were undertaken were primarily attitudinal and could not be directly linked to overall business objectives, such as increasing cash flows, customer migration, and so on.

The new manager believed if he challenged these assumptions, he might be able to present new approaches that would provide answers to the questions senior management had been asking.

The Solution

The manager proposed that the bank adopt a new set of principles to guide marcom investments. The bank needed not only to measure and justify its marcom investment, but to determine the areas of business in which it should invest and the returns it could expect from those investments.

The manager set two major objectives for a new IMC-driven approach to developing a marcom program for the credit card division:

- To demonstrate how National American Bank could measure the return on its marcom investments
- To determine the appropriate marcom investment level for the National American Bank credit card programs

The net result of this approach, he believed, would enable senior management to compare alternative investments by weighting likely dollar returns to marcom programs versus the alternative uses available to them for the same finite organizational resources.

The marketing manager then went on to present a three-part program that was based on a consistency of efforts approach to attract new customers as well as increase share of wallet among existing cardholders. The three primary efforts were as follows:

- New customer acquisition for the bank's gold, standard, and special-interest credit cards
- An expansion of credit limits for selected, creditworthy current customers
- Usage offers to stimulate demand among existing customers

Detailed ROCI projections were presented for each of these programs showing the returns that could be expected in both the short and long term.

How Return on Customer Investment Was Calculated

The basic premise of the proposal was that only customers could provide returns to National American Bank, and those customers could be influenced through various types of marcom efforts. Thus, the approach the marcom manager proposed was to relate the results of the income generated through marcom programs to the customers influenced, not the delivery systems that took the communication to them. The advertising, marketing, and marcom activities would be considered simply as the tools and techniques by which the bank was able to invest in its credit card customers to influence their behaviors.

This was possible because the bank was in a unique situation with regard to customer knowledge and information; it had a continuing one-to-one relationship with every credit card customer it served. This came about because the bank captured and stored customer-level activity data on each and every credit card customer over time. That quantity and quality of data allowed the credit card marketing team to understand and measure income flows, purchase rates, share of wallet, and product margins. The use of these data contributed substantially to the ROCI model the team developed and in which it had great confidence.

Finally, to meet senior management objectives, the team members needed to calculate the cost-to-income ratios that would result from their programs. Senior management used this evaluation measure to determine what programs met their investment criteria. The guideline was that the cost of any investment by the bank could not exceed 40 percent of the revenue that investment was expected to return. By including this additional calculation on their marcom investment models, the marketers were able to assure management that their programs did not exceed the 40 percent ratio.

The first step in determining the appropriate level of investment in National American Bank's credit card customers was to create an ROCI model, a tailor-made version of the model described earlier in this chapter. The marcom manager assumed that by not investing in current customers, the bank's share of wallet among these customers would continue to fall from the current 62 percent to 60.5 percent in the coming year. On the other hand, by making the recommended investments, he hoped to increase share of wallet by 20 percent among key customer groups, thus giving the bank an average 74 percent overall share of wallet among all its core customers.

Exhibit 10.1 shows a portion of the ROCI analysis he presented to senior management. The analysis was actually conducted over a dozen customer and prospect segments, but only four are shown here. The objective of the model was to account for the additional revenue the credit card team believed could be generated as a result of the proposed investments in marcom programs.

As shown, the goal was to determine the incremental financial return to the bank based on the communication investments made in customer groups, rather than to determine the total sales or profit for the division. The manager also judged that the incremental value approach he was using for new growth through customer acquisition would work just as well for customer retention. He further surmised it could even be used as a methodology to determine how and when the bank should divest certain high-maintenance, low-profit customers. In short, the ROCI analysis process was an excellent basic tool to manage customers—just what the manager was seeking.

The first step in the process was to aggregate the bank's credit card portfolio of customers into four groups, namely gold-card holders, standard-card holders, cardholders who were qualified for an increase in their credit limits, and a special-interest cardholder group. The manager estimated that all groups would, on average, increase their demand for credit card usage at the same rate of 12 percent per year, as shown on line 3. Further, the manager estimated that National American Bank would hold the 62 percent share of wallet it presently enjoyed. Thus, that would be the base case for a calculation of each group's share of wallet (line 5).

The credit card team estimated there would be different noncommunication costs for each group which they determined from previous experience (line 7). Thus, there would be different gross contribution margins (lines 8 and 9) for each group as well. As a result of the "no investment" scenario, it was estimated the change in share of wallet for each group would decline by 2.5 percent (line 10) during the period.

Starting in Scenario B, the manager identified the brand communication programs he was planning and the investments required for each of those activities. We have not shown the detail of the program here; instead, all activities have been aggregated into a total investment figure. This represents the amount that would be invested in communication programs aimed at each group (line 16). Line 17 shows the

Exhibit 10.1 Credit Card ROCI Analysis

Target Segments:	Gold	Standard	Credit Limit	Special Interest
Category Requirement Assumptions				
1 No. of customers in group	1,841	19,676	2,137	6,583
2 Historical category demand	$895,000	$4,307,300	$725,207	$2,175,621
3 Estimated % increase/decrease in demand	12.0%	12.0%	12.0%	12.0%
4 Adjusted category demand	$1,002,400	$4,824,176	$812,232	$2,436,696
Base Income Flow Assumptions				
5 Base share of wallet	62.0%	62.0%	62.0%	62.0%
6 Base income flow to us	$621,488	$2,990,989	$503,584	$1,510,751
7 Noncommunication costs (product, fixed, G&A, etc.)	33.0%	26.0%	28.0%	38.0%
8 Gross contribution margin (%)	67.0%	74.0%	72.0%	62.0%
9 Gross contribution margin ($)	$416,397	$2,213,332	$362,580	$936,666
Scenario A: No Communication Investment				
10 Change in share of wallet	-2.5%	-2.5%	-2.5%	-2.5%
11 Resulting share of wallet	60.5%	60.5%	60.5%	60.5%
12 Resulting customer income flow to us	$605,951	$2,916,214	$490,994	$1,472,982
13 Less noncommunication costs (product, fixed, G&A, etc.)	-$199,964	-$758,216	-$137,478	-$559,733
14 Less brand communication cost	$0	$0	$0	$0
15 Net contribution	$405,987	$2,157,999	$353,516	$913,249

(continued)

Exhibit 10.1 Credit Card ROCI Analysis (continued)

Target Segments:	Gold	Standard	Credit Limit	Special Interest
Scenario B: Brand Communication Investment				
16 Total brand communication investment	$6,200	$59,250	$5,500	$95,000
17 Change in share of wallet	20.0%	20.0%	20.0%	20.0%
18 Resulting share of wallet	74.4%	74.4%	74.4%	74.4%
19 Resulting customer income flow to us	$745,786	$3,589,187	$604,300	$1,812,901
20 *Less* noncommunication cost (product, fixed, G&A, etc.)	–$246,109	–$933,189	–$169,204	–$688,903
21 *Less* brand communication cost	–$6,200	–$59,250	–$5,500	–$95,000
22 Net contribution	$493,476	$2,596,748	$429,596	$1,028,999
ROCI Calculation				
23 Net contribution scenario A	$405,987	$2,157,999	$353,516	$913,249
24 Net contribution scenario B	$493,476	$2,596,748	$429,596	$1,028,999
25 Incremental gain/loss vs. "No investment" scenario	$87,489	$438,750	$76,081	$115,750
26 Incremental ROCI	1,411%	741%	1,383%	122%
27 Cost-to-income ratio	34%	28%	29%	43%

Category requirement assumptions—Gives a total estimate within the category of spending in dollars

Base income flow assumptions—Makes a basic assumption of share of wallet, our share of income, and the share required to cover all fixed and variable costs to run the business other than communication and profit

No communication investment—Establishes a baseline of profitability if we make no further communication investment

Communication investment—Estimates how the value of each customer group would change if we conducted a communication program directed toward them

ROCI calculation—Determines the total incremental gain/loss to the bank as a result of the communication program manager's estimate of returns on the program. He had projected a 20 percent change in share of wallet for each customer group that would receive the marcom programs. From that, he deducted the brand communication costs as shown on line 21. That gave him the net contribution on his marcom investments as shown on line 22.

In the final section (ROCI calculation), the manager and his team determined that an incremental ROCI of over 700 percent would be achieved among all groups except the special-interest cardholders (line 26) if the marcom programs were implemented as planned.

Additionally, the manager calculated the cost-to-income ratio for each of the groups targeted in the program. As shown at the bottom of the chart, the estimate for three of the groups was below the 40 percent guideline senior management had set for the entire firm. The guideline would not be met if the program were implemented among the special-interest cardholders. Based on this analysis, the manager and his team determined that, although the special-interest group could be promoted to profitably, there would be greater returns to the bank by concentrating on the first three segments.

To provide additional support for the proposal he was to make to management, the manager developed more detailed long-term and short-term ROCI estimates for each of the three programs he planned to initiate. (These are presented with limited comments since much of the supporting date is confidential.)

- **Acquisition of new customer activities.** Exhibit 10.2 shows the estimated returns on planned acquisition activities. As shown, the ROCI through the customer acquisition program was estimated to be 54 percent after 12 months and was estimated to rise to 483 percent after 25 months. The cost-to-income ratio starts fairly high in the first few months after the customer acquisition, but after 25 months is well within the management directive of 40 percent or less.
- **Increasing selected customer's credit limits.** The plan to increase the credit limits for selected customers shows the best return of any of the planned programs. As illustrated in Exhibit 10.3, the return after 10 months is over 1,000 percent and is still near that rate at the end of the first year. Also important is that the estimated

Exhibit 10.2 ROCI on New Customer Acquisition Efforts

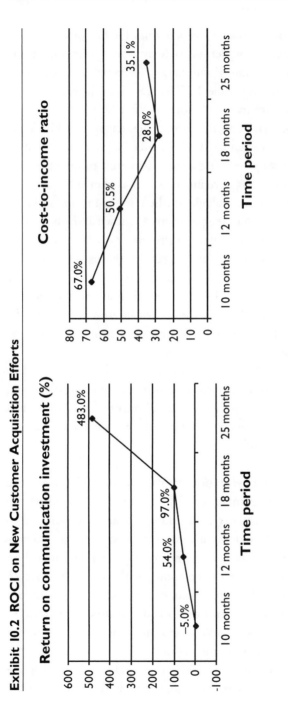

return on the credit limit increase rises to over 2,200 percent after two years. Best of all, the cost-to-income ratio for the program starts below the 40 percent management ceiling and declines to 22.1 percent at the end of nearly two years.

- **Developing customer usage offers.** The third planned marcom program was to develop premiums and merchandising offers for customers who met certain credit card spending or usage requirements. Unfortunately, the manager had little internal data to support his recommendations. Since the decline in communication investment in the credit card division had occurred, data collection programs had been eliminated and thus there were only spotty case histories. As a result, the manager relied on his previous experience with this type of program at other banks, along with some published data from other banks and lending institutions in the country. That provided enough information for him to make some informed estimates.

Based on their review, the team members determined there was considerable evidence from external sources that credit card customers did respond to various merchandising offers. Therefore, that approach appeared to be a good investment for the National American Bank customer base. The marcom manager therefore aggregated the bank's individual credit card customer base into five groups based on the number of merchandising offers they had received during the previous years. These ranged from zero to five offers.

The average outstanding balance was then calculated for each group. (The outstanding balance is the average amount due on the credit card at the end of each month. This is the basis on which interest is charged to customer accounts.) The team then computed the probability that the average balance for any group would exceed that of any other group and by what amount.

Based on two merchandise offers the bank had made to credit card holders in the recent past—a preferred travel service for vacations and excursions and a dining club offer—the team estimated that for every $4.50 the bank invested in usage offers, it would receive $11.50 back in interchange and net interest income. Thus, the team members figured that the proposed merchandise offers and usage programs they planned

Exhibit 10.3 ROCI on Increased Credit Limits

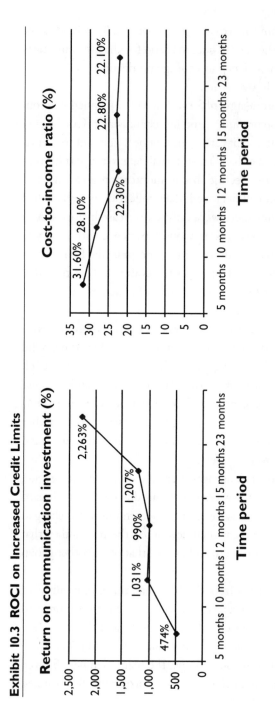

to develop would provide an average 255 percent return on each customer investment made in the first 12 months. Based on these estimates and calculations, the new marcom manager was ready to develop the specifics of the proposed program to rejuvenate the credit card division.

Appropriate Levels of Investment in the Marcom Program

To this point, the estimates and investments requested by the marcom manager had been based on the tactical programs and activities that had been proposed. The next step was to relate these to the customers and prospects against whom the programs would be directed. The manager started by reviewing share of wallet versus outstanding balances. He used this to develop strategies that would reflect the various opportunities that he felt might exist. His approach is illustrated in the six-box matrix shown in Exhibit 10.4.

As shown, the manager allocated all National American Bank credit card customers into one of the six boxes in the matrix. On the x-axis, he plotted outstanding balances. He separated all potential customers into two groups: those with outstanding balances of less than $1,500 and those with balances greater than $1,500.

On the y-axis, he plotted the customer share of wallet that was currently being filled by their National American Bank card. These were then divided into three groups: (a) customers with a credit card from another institution, or those with whom National American Bank presently had no share of wallet; (b) customers who held a National American Bank credit card but allocated less than 64 percent of their credit card requirements to it; and (c) those who held a National American Bank credit card and filled more than 64 percent of their requirements with it.

The development of this matrix allowed the manager to create six customer promotional groups. In each box, the number of customers in that category is given and a general marketing and communication strategy is identified. For example, the strategy for groups A and C would be to try and grow credit card usage since they have high loyalty to National American. The strategy for Group B would be to focus on

Exhibit 10.4 Six-Box Matrix

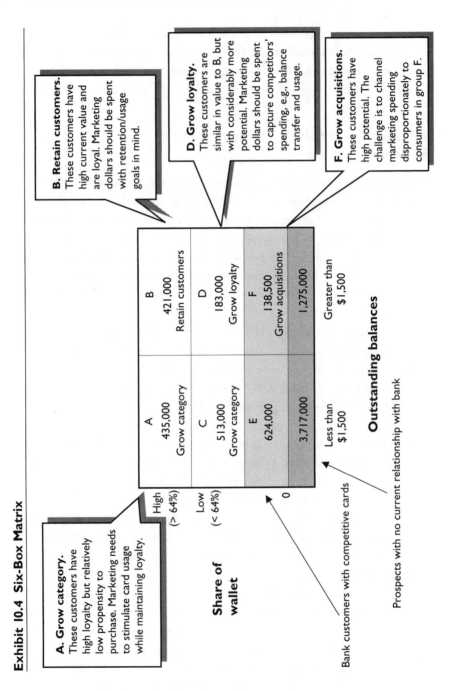

A. Grow category. These customers have high loyalty but relatively low propensity to purchase. Marketing needs to stimulate card usage while maintaining loyalty.

B. Retain customers. These customers have high current value and are loyal. Marketing dollars should be spent with retention/usage goals in mind.

D. Grow loyalty. These customers are similar in value to B, but with considerably more potential. Marketing dollars should be spent to capture competitors' spending, e.g., balance transfer and usage.

F. Grow acquisitions. These customers have high potential. The challenge is to channel marketing spending disproportionately to consumers in group F.

Share of wallet

High (> 64%)

| | A
435,000
Grow category | B
421,000
Retain customers |

Low (< 64%)

| | C
513,000
Grow category | D
183,000
Grow loyalty |

| | E
624,000 | F
138,500
Grow acquisitions |

| | 3,717,000 | 1,275,000 |

0

Less than $1,500

Greater than $1,500

Outstanding balances

Bank customers with competitive cards

Prospects with no current relationship with bank

retention. These customers have high current value and are already loyal, so the bank does not want to lose them. Thus, the goal in this segment would be to retain these customers and keep them happy. Group D appears to have substantial unrealized potential. Therefore the communication efforts would aim to (a) capture or recapture customers' spending on competitive credit cards and shift it to National American, (b) try to get their balance shifted to National American, and (c) generally get them to increase their usage of the National American card.

Groups E and F were felt to represent the greatest challenge. The E segment was split into two groups although both had an outstanding credit card balance of less than $1,500. The top group—approximately 624,000 customers—had a relationship with the bank but also had a competitive credit card. The bottom group—3,717,000 members—had no affiliation with the bank and had no National American credit card. Given the low outstanding balances held among this group, it was felt that the returns would not warrant the investment that would be required to stimulate further penetration into this segment. Thus, no marcom effort was planned against this group.

The F segment was also broken into two groups. The bottom group—1,275,000 prospects—had no current relationship with the bank. The top segment—only about 138,500 customers—represented current bank customers who held and used a competitive credit card. All these prospects, however, appeared to have high potential. Therefore, the manager's plan was to invest marketing resources disproportionately in group F.

Based on the customer valuation scheme shown here, the manager then developed an overall budget and business case for each of the planned marcom investments, which is summarized in Table 10.6. The plan was organized around the key customer segments isolated in Exhibit 10.4. On the left-hand side of the chart the expected ROCI for each effort is listed, with subtotals for each customer segment. The planned activities concentrate on the three efforts the manager isolated as having the greatest ROCI potential—new customer acquisition, credit limit extensions, and offers to stimulate usage of the card. Additionally, the planned program included some efforts especially designed to increase retention among certain key customer groups.

As shown in the exhibit, credit card customers in segment A would receive three marcom programs—a club offer, an in-store retail offer to be organized with a major department store chain, and a travel insurance offer. The marcom investment in these customers would be approximately $40,000. These programs were expected to generate

Table 10.6 Communication Budget by Customer Group

ROCI	Segment	Effort	Proposed Budget (in $000s)	Estimated Revenue Growth (in $000s)
140%	A	Club offer	$ 10	$ 14
250%	A	In-store retail promotion	$ 15	$ 38
450%	A	Travel insurance	$ 15	$ 68
298%		Total group A	$ 40	$ 119
225%	B	Credit limit offer	$ 100	$ 225
375%	B	Best customer retention package	$ 50	$ 188
475%	B	Standard retention	$ 75	$ 356
850%	B	Travel insurance	$ 75	$ 638
469%		Total group B	$ 300	$ 1,406
140%	D	Preferred customer points	$ 75	$ 105
225%	D	Club offer	$ 10	$ 23
250%	D	Credit limit offer	$ 50	$ 125
375%	D	Best customer retention package	$ 20	$ 75
625%	D	Recapture effort	$ 75	$ 469
800%	D	Travel insurance	$ 30	$ 240
399%		Total group D	$ 260	$ 1,036
150%	F	Outside list promotion	$ 750	$ 1,125
150%	F	Web-based promotion	$ 10	$ 15
300%	F	New account promotion	$ 350	$ 1,050
500%	F	In-branch acquisition efforts	$ 500	$ 2,500
306%		Total group F	$1,870	$ 5,726
332%		Totals	$4,680	$15,539

Note: ROCI = return on customer investment.

approximately $119,000 in incremental revenue. That would provide an ROCI of approximately 298 percent for the following year. This was actually the lowest projected ROCI, as groups B, D, and F were estimated to return 469 percent, 399 percent, and 306 percent, respectively. The overall program was budgeted to cost $4.68 million, but was expected to increase revenues by over $15.5 million, with an overall ROCI of 332 percent.

Obviously, there are two final questions: Did senior management approve the new marcom recommendations? And if so, did the program work in the marketplace? The answer is yes to both questions. Senior managers approved the requested budget and the proposed investments against credit card users. Their comment was that this was the first time any marcom manager had presented a real business plan, that is, recommended investments in marcom programs and expected returns. Thus, the manager got off on the right foot with his new employer by using the ROCI approach to support his recommendations and estimates.

In the marketplace, the response to the program was even greater than the credit card communication team had expected. Thus, the proof of the approach was demonstrated in financial returns, the key element in any ROCI program.

Moving On

The ROCI framework illustrated in this chapter works. It does, however, take some time and effort, as well as a new way of thinking—as the National American Bank example shows. The beauty of it, however, is that once the system is in place, the manager can refine and enhance the program quite readily and always be able to prove that the company's investment in customers—via marcom tools—pays off. As we show in the next chapter, those payoffs are not just immediate and short term, but long term as well.

CHAPTER 11

ESTIMATING LONG-TERM RETURN ON CUSTOMER INVESTMENT

W hile the previous chapter provided a framework for calculating return on customer investment (ROCI) from a short-term, business-building perspective, that is only half of step 4 in the IMC process. While most marketers are comfortable talking about communication programs that impact sales in the short term, this chapter leads to less familiar ground. Here, we focus on how to gauge the long-term, brand-building effects of marketing communication on the overall value of the organization (see Chapter 9). This task requires a new set of metrics; a new level of financial acuity; and most of all, a different set of value measures for a different set of customers—the owners or shareholders of the firm. We provide a methodology for measuring long-term communication returns. A case history then helps illustrate the approach in more pragmatic terms.

The Importance of Measuring Long-Term Returns

As we have seen throughout this book, the real value of the organization is in the cash flows it generates currently and the expected continuation of those cash flows into the future. Management sees current returns as being created, to a large extent, by the firm's short-term marcom investments. These incremental returns are the most obvious result of the marcom effort, and they have traditionally received the most attention. Thus, one could argue that long-term returns are of less value to the firm—and, in most accounting and financial valuation systems, they are. The concepts of net present value (NPV) and discounted cash flow (DCF), both defined in Chapter 9, are based on the concept that dollars the organization has today have more value now than having those same dollars sometime in the future. Thus, any NPV calculation discounts future cash flows by some percentage for risk, the time value of money, loss of investment opportunity, lack of flexibility, and so on. While customer loyalty is often paramount in the marketing and communication plans of an organization, it must always be remembered that customer income flows in the future are less valuable than equivalent income flows that can be generated today. But one must also remember that these incremental gains are only a small portion of the firm's total sales and value.

Another important consideration in estimating long-term returns on marcom investments is that maintaining current income flows from present customers is generally less expensive than current time investments made in gaining or attempting to gain additional customers and their income flows. Many marketing experts suggest that it costs a firm anywhere from five to ten times as much to acquire a new customer as it does to maintain an existing one.[1] Obviously, having current customers continue to buy rather than continuously acquiring new ones is a major benefit to any organization simply in terms of current cash flows. In addition, stable customer income flows make the operational and financial management of the firm much easier.

Yet there are some problems with this idea of long-term customer income flows. Under current accounting systems, any marcom investment in a customer during the current period must be taken as a current period expense no matter when the returns occur. So, while long-term returns can and often do occur, the expense of generating those returns occurs and is accounted for in the present fiscal period.

USING DISCOUNTED CASH FLOW ESTIMATES
IN IMC PLANNING

When attempting to estimate the long-term impact of communication activities, marketers invariably try to forecast the long-
term earnings stream that could come from a customer or group
of customers as a result. In doing so, however, they must recognize that these forecasts are subject to risk and that projected
earnings should be discounted to reflect both uncertainty and
the time value of money.

Financial analysts use a method to discount future cash flows
by equating them to today's dollars (net present value, or NPV).
Quite simply, a dollar today is worth more than it will be worth
in one, two, or five years. To illustrate, assume that as chief
executive officer (CEO) of a marketing firm, you are trying to
decide how much investment to make in various activities the
organization wants to carry out. Your choice is fairly simple. You
can either fund a new marcom program or—for guaranteed
income—you can take the same funds and invest them in an
interest-bearing government bond or even a bank savings
account. Since the marcom manager cannot realistically
guarantee a return on a marcom investment, there is some risk
involved in that alternative. And it is this risk, along with other
factors, that provides the basis for any type of NPV or
discounted cash flow (DCF) determination.

As CEO, if you are uncomfortable with risk you will likely
choose the safer alternative. However, if you are willing to risk
the firm's resources, you might choose the marcom investment.
Much depends upon how you are running the business and what
your management style is.

Consider the investment scenario of an organization that
expects to make a 15 percent return on every investment,
whether that investment is a new computer system, a new building, or a new marcom program. The company must also consider

the length of time it will take to generate those expected returns. Thus, an investment that will not achieve a 15 percent return until the end of three years is not worth as much as an investment that will have the same 15 percent return within twelve months. Let's see, for example, how much a $1,000 investment would actually be worth:

Year 1:	$869.56	or	$1,000/1.15
Year 2:	$756.43	or	$1,000/(1.15 × 1.15)
Year 3:	$657.89	or	$1,000/(1.15 × 1.15 × 1.15)
Total:	$2,283.88		

An income stream of $1,000 for three years ($1,000 each in year 1, year 2, and year 3) is not worth $3,000 in today's dollars. Instead, it is worth only $2,283.88 ($869.56 + $756.43 + $657.89). This is the sum that represents the net present value of $1,000 over three years using a discount factor of 15 percent.

Discounted cash flow provides a realistic view of future income flows. It recognizes the net present value of future income from customers, and it accommodates future investments that the firm likely will make in the customer or customer group in the form of marcom programs. This discounted cash flow estimate is important for the marcom manager to be able to justify his or her programs. Remembering that money in hand now is more valuable than money received later is an excellent way to help separate out short-term from long-term returns on marcom investments. The problem, of course, is that all marcom investments are based on future returns, which presents a complicating factor.

Further, having a set of customers who are continually satisfied with the products and services of the firm and their experience with the company also provides substantial future opportunities for that company. These can come in the form of opportunities to cross sell, upsell, and migrate customers through the product or service portfolio, thus adding additional sales and profits that might not have initially been expected. In addition, the advocacy value of satisfied customers is something many organizations are just beginning to recognize, although many find the financial value of advocacy difficult to quantify. Certainly, as the Internet and E-commerce have demonstrated repeatedly, as communities of interest develop, word of mouth about products and services—particularly from those people or firms with firsthand experience of them—becomes a powerful sales development and maintenance tool. So, there are compelling reasons to have an ongoing set of satisfied customers other than just the immediate income flows they may produce now and in the short-term future.

In spite of the challenges that discounted future income flow estimates pose, almost all investments (and marketing communication can be no exception) are assumed to have some ongoing or long-term effect on the business. Otherwise, why would those investments be made? Examples abound. Funds are expended for the construction of plants or factories that are expected to yield value far into the future. The same is true of investments used to create intellectual property, such as research and development, logistical systems, employee training programs, and so on. So, while the common focus of marketing managers is in meeting quarterly or annual sales and profit goals, it is the expected long-term returns that often provide the base for further short-term investments and returns. Indeed, in some cases, organizations often succeed in the future because they have created momentum with products, customers, or channels in the present. That momentum is then carried over to the next time frame or helps them weather difficult situations in the short term. Thus, the momentum developed has provided increased or enhanced returns beyond those that normally might have been expected.

Recall from the early chapters of this book that we suggested that the primary goal of most senior management is to grow the business. The two primary forms of scorekeeping are increases in cash flows and increases in shareholder value. Shareholder value is commonly determined based on expectations of increases in the stock prices of publicly held companies, in larger or more lucrative dividends, or in the long-term value of the firm to the owners. Both cash flows and shareholder value have short- and long-term aspects. Yet both measures are dependent on one basic premise: holding customers and their income flows now and into the future. It is the customer who creates the value for the organization by purchasing and continuing to purchase its products and services over time, in other words, in creating present and future cash flows for the firm.

Challenges of Measuring Long-Term Returns

While there is a strong case for forecasting long-term or ongoing cash flows from customers as a result of investments in marcom programs, these are not as easily identified as are current income flows. The reason? There are a substantial number of variables in long-term measures that confound the marcom planner's ability to predict potential income flows. Four major issues or sets of issues present particular challenges.

Difficulties Inherent in Today's Accounting Systems

The accounting systems in place around the world create difficulties in measuring long-term returns on marcom investments. Much of this has to do with the challenge of valuing intangible assets or income flows in the future. Based on current accounting standards, there is simply no way for an organization to recognize future income flows until they are earned, and the rules for forecasted income are becoming more stringent each day.

The accounting system is clear. Books are opened at the beginning of the fiscal year and are closed 365 days later at the end of the fiscal year. Once the books are closed, the organization repeats the process, starting over with a clean slate. So, if an investment is made in a marcom program in the fourth quarter of the firm's fiscal year and customer income flows start to arrive in the first quarter of the following fiscal year, the current year will show only the expense of the investment and no returns, and the following year will show income but no costs. That is why a customer acquisition program, which commonly costs more to start than it initially returns and whose returns often come back in later accounting periods, creates major accounting difficulties for the organization and the marcom manager as well. In essence, the marketer invests today to get new customers today but must wait until future accounting periods to fully recover the investment and earn a profit through returns that come in the future.

For example, it is not unusual for catalog companies to invest several times more in marketing and communication to initially acquire a new customer than they receive back in profits over the first several purchase transactions. Identifying prospective customers, mailing them free catalogs, setting up billing systems, and the like are all current period expenses. These expenses are not returned until the customer actually purchases something. And that could be several months in the future, if ever.

The same is true for many business-to-business organizations. The firm hires salespeople, equips them with sales materials, and sends them out to identify and develop customers, all at considerable expense. But the sales force may not show any sales results or cash flow returns for a year or more. The toppling of the dot-coms in the late 1990s is another case in point. Building a website, setting up a distribution system, developing awareness for the site, and encouraging customers to visit and (hopefully) buy, all cost current dollars. There was a significant lag between the time the developmental expenses were incurred and when customers could begin to enter transactions. Thus, financial returns did not come for several months or, in some cases, not at all, depending on the business model. Thus, the dot-com firms simply ran out of operating capital and were forced to close.

One of the key elements the marcom manager must understand is the long-term flows of income created by customers and how those income flows are impacted by current period expenses charged against them as a result of current period financial investments in marketing communication. Part of this challenge occurs because marcom managers traditionally have been more focused on managing expenses—that is, the dollar flow out of the organization through the purchase and distribution of various promotional efforts—rather than looking at the income flows coming into the firm as a result of marcom investments.

Difficulties Associated with Lagged Effects of Communication Programs

One of the most common responses to marketing communication is for customers to see or hear the communication but not act on it until a later time. This is what is called a *lagged effect* of the communication program. Lags in response can occur for any number of reasons, ranging from a customer's present lack of need in the category to purchase consideration timing to the need for greater information to make an ultimate purchase decision. Automobiles, replacement windows, overseas vacations, and choices of educational institutions are just a few examples of products that have a fairly long purchase consideration cycle. Some replacement window companies, for instance, have found that the purchase consideration cycle for their products is over a year. Any marcom program for replacement windows will generally come back with returns in the second or sometimes even the third year after its initial placement.

Examples of lagged effects of marketing communication abound in business-to-business marcom programs, too. Product design decisions, ingredient selection, product development, and other activities may take months or even years to develop. Business-to-business firms typically invest communication funds during a fiscal year, knowing that it will take considerable time for returns to occur.

As a result of the lagged effects of communication returns, it is often difficult for an organization to determine exactly when returns will occur, or even if they will occur at all. For the most part, organizations, when faced with this problem of understanding behavioral returns, commonly employ sophisticated statistical modeling techniques, such as *correlation analysis*, or marketing mix modeling. Here, an analysis of historical sales data is correlated to the investments and expenditures on marketing and marcom activities to provide an estimate of their marketplace returns in the past. Models like this, however, are only calculations of what happened historically, not what might occur in the future. They do not, therefore, solve the problem of identifying potential lagged effects.

Difficulties in Predicting Brand Loyalty

Loyal customers have generally been considered profitable customers, creating the best source of future income flows to the organization. Recent research, however, has begun to challenge this long-held assumption. Loyalty alone does not mean a customer will be profitable. For example, a customer who buys one bottle of Windex per year is 100 percent loyal. Yet a customer who buys ten bottles of window cleaner per year, only three of them Windex, has the potential to be three times as profitable as the one-bottle purchaser, even though the ten-bottle customer's share of requirement is only 33 percent.

Research by Frederick Reichheld and others in the early 1990s showed that increases in customer loyalty often provided substantial bottom-line future profits for the marketing firm.[2] For example, Reichheld reported that he found a 5 percent increase in customer loyalty increased bottom-line returns by as much as 75 percent to 100 percent. The reason for this, as discussed earlier, is that the organization does not have to invest as many resources in keeping customers buying as it did to first acquire them. Thus, customer loyalty is commonly a much less expensive investment proposition for the firm than continuous customer acquisition.

By having loyal customers, the organization can also commonly reduce the peaks and valleys of income flows brought about by erratic purchase behavior by their customers. This leads to greater stability in the financial areas of the operation. (Recall from guiding principle 4 that reducing financial volatility is one of the four primary objectives of any marketing or communication investment.) By knowing approximately what type of income flow will occur in the future, for example, over the next two to three years, the company can better manage its finite resources and thus reduce its need for external or even internal funding. The challenge, of course, is to determine which and how many customers will remain loyal to the firm, particularly in the months beyond the current fiscal year.

From this discussion of the first three issues that challenge the long-term measurability of marcom returns, one can see that, in spite of forecasting problems, marcom investments generally meet three of the four requirements that senior management has for any type of investment. These were summarized under guiding principle 4 in Chapter 3:

- Marketing communication should increase cash flows over time. In the case of some types of communication programs, the lagged effects of that communication may play a major role in organizational success.
- Marketing communication should accelerate cash flows by moving them forward, or ahead of the time they might normally be expected. That is, if marketing communication can get customers to buy more, buy earlier, buy more often, or simply purchase at a different time, expected income flows are moved forward from the future to the present.
- Marketing communication should generate returns that stabilize or reduce the volatility of the firm's cash flows, thus providing relief from internal or external financing in the future.

The fourth requirement—that marketing communication should build shareholder value by increasing the equity of the firm or brand—presents the fourth and most difficult forecasting challenge. While there is little question that shareholder value is dependent on stock prices and dividends, these come as a result of profitable income flows from customers over time.

Difficulties in Identifying Increases in Brand Asset Value Over Time

Financial brand asset value—the value investors, as opposed to customers or prospects, place on a brand—presents a key challenge when accounting for the future value marcom programs may generate. While there is little question that marcom has an impact on building the value of a brand both among the investment community and among customers, these two measures are quite different and must be considered separately.

Assessing stability and growth of corporate earnings is a key way in which investors compare the potential value of various stocks. Thus, if investments in marcom can create customer activity, which then translates into ongoing flows of income from customers, those marcom investments have some long-term impact on shareholder value, too. Further, if marcom investments can be made in one period and the returns enjoyed in other, long-term periods, the marketer can truthfully say that there is some contribution to future earnings and some increase in the value of the firm in the marketplace. Yet financial models that directly relate sales levels, customer loyalty, and other effects of marketing communication to stock price and, from there, to shareholder value have not yet been fully developed. (Chapter 13 suggests ways in which such correlations may be made.)

Toward a Solution: A Model for Measuring Long-Term Returns

Two frameworks help marketers overcome the four key sets of difficulties described in forecasting returns on marcom programs in the long term. The first is customer centric, focusing on ongoing income flows that can be derived from a customer or group of customers. The second is brand centric. It examines the financial value of a brand by estimating the brand's contribution to the firm's earnings streams or its asset base, or the value for which the brand could be sold to another organization. We examine the first approach in this chapter, leaving the brand-centric model to a more detailed discussion of brand equity in Chapter 14.

The customer-centric measurement framework is based around the concept of *lifetime customer value* (LTV), developed by direct and catalog marketers to explain potential future customer income flows. It is a method of estimating future returns from customers based on past or current experience with them using probability forecasting models. Once forecasted cash flows are estimated, they are then discounted to account for their NPV and to determine the present-day value of future income.

Lifetime Customer Value

The LTV approach recognizes that some present customers will likely continue to purchase the firm's products or services in the future, thus creating future income flows. At the same time, some customers will be lost through attrition, transfer to competitors, moving, death, or any number of other reasons. It is this combination of retention, attrition, anticipated spending patterns, and estimated costs that defines each customer's LTV.

Lifetime customer value is estimated by calculating the NPV of all future revenues minus all attributable costs associated with the average customer.[3] It is an extension over time of what is done in developing the short-term ROCI measurement described in the previous chapter. For example, to get an estimate of LTV, the short-term estimate of returns (those that will occur in the current fiscal year) is extended to multiple fiscal years, given certain assumptions about the level of customer retention, their anticipated levels of spending, and the ongoing marketing costs to sustain the firm's relationship with them.

While LTV projections are sometimes made in present-day prices or dollar values, such calculations do not take into account the time value of money. Thus, the IMC process takes the concept one step further to reflect *net* LTV, that is, it uses the NPV of all future revenues as the basis of calculation. To do so accurately, two additional assumptions must be established[4]:

- **A return on customer investment goal.** The goal for any marcom investment must be to deliver returns that reflect both the time and risk values of money. Usually, the ROCI goal must be at least as high as the company's traditional return on equity. Thus, if the company is generating a 15 percent return on investment for its owners or shareholders, marcom investments that generate less than a 15 percent rate of return over time are generally not advisable. If the market is volatile, if technology is changing, and if customer loyalty is likely to shift, then a higher rate of return is commonly required to make the marcom investment worthwhile. Obviously, a stable market—one in which, for example, the firm has a patent or is in a protected niche that virtually ensures future income flows—does not require the same level of risk premium for marcom investments.

- **A realistic time frame over which customer value will be estimated.** This must reflect the period for which future purchase behavior can reasonably be predicted and for which the ongoing impact of communication programs can be estimated. That is, some products are relevant to customers only during limited periods in their lives (diapers, school uniforms, magazines directed at teenagers, and so on), so the average time during which a customer remains a customer is relatively short. Other products may span decades of loyal and repeated use (for instance, toothpaste, general-interest magazines, automobiles, various types of music). As a practical matter, however, it is generally difficult to predict with any accuracy for a period of more than three to five years for most products.

How to Calculate Lifetime Customer Value: An Example

Database consultants Jack Schmid and Alan Weber offer the following step-by-step method of calculating LTV.[5] The example is based on a business-to-business organization that sells products through catalogs. The same analytical framework can be adapted for all types of organizations.

1. **Determine the cost of acquiring a new customer.** Let's suppose it costs a company $0.60 to send a catalog to a prospective customer (total cost in the mail, with list rental, postage, printing, and so on). From experience, the firm expects renting an outside list of likely prospects to achieve a response rate of 1.1 percent on the ini-

tial mailing. It will therefore cost $54.55 to acquire a new customer ($0.60/0.11 = $54.55).

2. **Determine how much gross profit is earned on the average sale.** Suppose that the average initial order from a new customer is $70.00, with an average gross margin per customer of 40 percent after the cost of fulfillment (the cost to select, pack, and ship the order). The initial order average profit margin is $28.00 ($70.00 × 40% = $28.00).

3. **Determine net gain or loss of customer acquisition.** Taking the customer acquisition cost from step 1, the marketer subtracts that from the margin on the first sale ($28 − $54.55 = −$26.55).

Thus, the company actually has a net loss on each new customer it acquires, at least on average. Another way to look at it is that the company makes an investment of $26.55 to acquire a new customer with the anticipation that the customer will become profitable over time through subsequent purchases. The question, then, is how long it will take for an average customer to repay the costs of acquisition, and how much profitability new customers represent going into the future.

To determine the likely future profits on newly acquired customers, the marketer must project their future purchases and subtract the cost of recontacting them as well as any service or maintenance costs that will be incurred in this process. The marketer must also consider the time value of money by factoring in the net present value of future earnings streams.

Continuing the same example, Table 11.1 summarizes the net LTV calculation. Assume that new customers will continue to actively purchase from the company for a period of three years after their initial purchase and that they receive four catalogs per year. Once a customer is acquired, any subsequent mailings cost only $0.50 per catalog, since there is no need to rent a prospect mailing list. Additionally, the response rate from established customers is generally much higher than from prospect lists, since a relationship has already been established. Experience has shown that after the initial purchase, a group of customers will typically respond at a rate of 16 percent to each of the four

Table 11.1 Customer Lifetime Value Example

Line			Year 1	Year 2	Year 3
1	No. of mailings per year		4	4	4
2	Average response per mailing		16%	13%	11%
3	Annual response rate	(Line 1 × Line 2)	64%	52%	44%
4	Average repeat order		$75.00	$75.00	$75.00
5	Average gross profit/order @ 40% margin		$30.00	$30.00	$30.00
6	Gross profit per year	(Line 3 × Line 5)	$19.20	$15.60	$13.20
7	Less annual cost for 4 catalog mailings per year @ $.50 each		$(2.00)	$(2.00)	$(2.00)
8	Net earnings per year	(Line 6 − Line 7)	$17.20	$13.60	$11.20
9	Discount factor @ 20%		1.20	1.44	1.73
10	Net present value of earnings	(Line 8/Line 9)	$14.33	$ 9.44	$ 6.48

Total net present value of earnings over 3 years	$30.25
Less original customer acquisition investment	− $26.55
Three-year return on customer investment	$ 3.70

offers within their first year. In the second year, the rate drops to 13 percent and in the third year to 11 percent.

4. **Determine cumulative response rate over time.** Given these response data, it is possible to achieve the following cumulative response rate, depending on the length of time since the customer was acquired. This is done by multiplying the average response rate by the number of mailings per year. That is, in year 1, customers have an average response rate per mailing of 16 percent. Multiplying this by the four mailings per year results in a cumulative response of 64 percent. For year 2, there is a cumulative response rate of 52 percent, and for year 3, customer response rate is 44 percent (shown on line 3).

5. **Determine the margin on repeat sales.** In this case, the marketer uses the same 40 percent gross margin used in the initial mail-

ing. However, the company soon discovers that it has a higher average order from existing customers, with an average of $75.00 on each repeat order. This leaves the company with a $30.00 gross profit margin on each order ($75.00 × 40% = $30.00).

From this, the marketer must subtract the annual cost to market to existing customers. With four mailings to each customer per year, at an average catalog cost of $0.50, the organization would have an annual marketing cost per customer of $2.00 (4 × $0.50). When the annual marketing costs are subtracted from the annual gross profit, the result is a net earnings per customer of $17.20 in year 1, $13.60 in year 2, and $11.20 in year 3.

6. **Discount the expected cash flows to their net present value.** Here, the marketer must factor in the time value of money. The company uses a 20 percent per year discount factor (which is the same as paying interest at 20 percent per year to investors). This time value of money discount factor for year 1 is 1.2 (the principal amount plus 20%). For year 2, it is 1.44 (1 + 20% for two years or 1.2 × 1.2); for year 3, it rises to 1.73 (1.2 × 1.2 × 1.2). The earnings in each year are then divided by the applicable discount factor to arrive at the NPV of the projected earnings for each year. Thus, the NPV of the forecasted earnings is $14.33 in year 1, $9.44 in year 2, and $6.48 in year 3.

From these calculations, it can be stated that the total NPV of earnings over the three-year period will be $30.25 per customer ($14.33 + $9.44 + $6.48). However, to get to the final estimate of profitability, one must subtract the investment made to initially gain the customer. (Recall the company actually lost money at the acquisition stage.) Thus, one must subtract the original $26.55 investment in order to determine if the investment goals will be met.

Acquiring new customers not only provides a 20 percent return on the initial acquisition investment but returns an additional profit of $3.70 as well. It is possible to vary the time value of money discount factor to make the end figure zero and determine the exact projected return on investment. It is also possible to vary the time period to determine how long it takes to recover the investment with interest, based on the initial investment in a customer. Thus, the marcom manager can adapt and adjust the returns to fit the needs of the organization or his or her own analytical requirements.

The figures shown here provide an excellent indication of how much time, effort, and financial investment the marcom manager can allow for attracting new customers. The same type of analysis can be used to determine the level of marketing efforts and investments that can or should be made to influence existing customers.

Comparison of Lifetime Value

Understanding lifetime value is especially useful when one method of marketing to customers is compared with another. Many marketers have discovered to their chagrin that it is very easy to create a consumer loyalty program that maintains customers but loses money in the long run. Alternatively, it is just as easy to "leave money on the table," that is, not generate all possible sales by not marketing to existing customers often enough.

Schmid and Weber provide another example, this time of a consumer catalog organization that is trying to decide whether it should conduct three or four mailings (contacts) per year as a means of providing incentive to encourage larger orders.[6] Three methods are under consideration: method A would entail three mailings per year, method B would raise the number to four, and method C would have four mailings and offer a 10 percent discount on all repeat orders over $60.00. Each method is expected to have a different effect:

- Method A will have the highest response per contact.
- Method B will have the highest annual response.
- Method C will have the highest average order.
- Method A will have lower economies of scale.
- Method B will have the lowest cost per contact.
- Method C will require explanation of the 10 percent offer.

This example compares programs the company is considering for existing customers and does not consider the acquisition costs. Thus,

Table 11.2 Likely Results of Marketing Strategies

	Method A	Method B	Method C
Number of mailings per year	3	4	4
Response rate per contact			
Year 1	12%	10%	10%
Year 2	9%	8%	8%
Year 3	6%	5%	5%
Average order	$75.00	$75.00	$80.00
Profit margin (%)	40%	40%	37%
Cost per contact	$1.00	$0.95	$1.00
Annual marketing cost	$3.00	$3.80	$4.00
Profit per year			
Year 1	$7.80	$8.20	$7.84
Year 2	$5.10	$5.80	$5.47
Year 3	$2.40	$2.20	$1.92
Present value of future profit			
Year 1	$6.50	$6.83	$6.53
Year 2	$3.54	$4.03	$3.80
Year 3	$1.39	$1.27	$1.11
Lifetime return on investment	$11.43	$12.13	$11.44

From John Schmid and Alan Weber, *Desktop Database Marketing*, 1997, NTC Business Books. Reproduced with permission of The McGraw-Hill Companies.

the focus is only on increasing future profits, and the most appropriate method is therefore the one that will produce the greatest value over the next three years. Table 11.2 summarizes the likely results for each method.

As shown, contacting each customer four times per year with no discount produces the most profits over the three-year period. If the discount offer had produced a substantially higher average order or if the response rate had increased, it would have been more profitable. In this case, however, giving margin dollars away simply lowers profits. Notice that reaching customers less often is more profitable when response rates are low (as in year 3). This points out why it is important to segment the customer base and contact some customers more frequently than others.

Moving On

A number of benefits can result from a well-designed program to increase LTV. Clearly, it increases profits from existing customers; improves return on investment; and leads to steady, predictable growth. Just as important, it increases customer loyalty by encouraging more customers to repurchase. Increased loyalty, by enhancing LTV, is a viable investment opportunity for the firm.

With an understanding of customer lifetime value and a framework in hand for determining long-term returns on the communication investment, we are ready to proceed to the final step of the IMC process: budgeting, allocation of funds, and evaluation.

PART VI

STEP 5: POSTPROGRAM ANALYSIS AND FUTURE PLANNING

1. Identify customers and prospects

5. Budgeting, allocation, and evaluation

2. Valuation of customers/ prospects

IMC

4. Estimating return on customer investment

3. Creating and delivering messages and incentives

CHAPTER 12

POSTPROGRAM ANALYSIS

As we stated at the outset of our description of IMC, a problem that has plagued traditional marketers is the inability to close the loop on any communication program by measuring its actual impact in financial terms. The reason for the problem is simple: marcom managers typically have little or no input into the budgeting process for the programs they manage. They work strictly with allocations and/or fixed budget amounts determined by senior management. Since traditional marketing provides no means through which marcom can prove its impact—and therefore its potential returns—marcom managers have been relegated to the role of bystanders in the fast-emerging finance-driven marketplace. All that is about to change. Value-oriented IMC planning finally allows marcom to close the loop by measuring and evaluating its programs in terms that finance-driven firms understand. That is the goal of step 5 of the IMC process.

How IMC Closes the Loop

As we showed in the last chapter, IMC is able to answer the following three questions for senior management:

- How much should we, as a firm, invest in marketing communication programs?

- What type of financial return will we receive?
- Over what time period will our returns occur?

By the time a firm reaches step 5 of the IMC process, these questions have already been answered, since the marcom manager has fairly accurate estimates of both short-term and long-term returns on the marcom investment. In step 5, the manager need only measure actual financial results of the marcom program over time to determine its success. This, of course, requires the cooperation of sales, accounting, finance, customer service, and many other functional groups in the company—all of whom have been involved from the outset through each of the first four steps of the IMC process.

Obviously, once returns have been measured, the next step is to repeat the marketing and communication approaches that have succeeded and revise those that have not. Similarly, evaluations of the customer and prospect groups that were selected for the marcom program must be made. If the groups delivered anticipated returns, it makes sense to continue programs against them. If returns fell short of expectations, some type of change will obviously be needed. Marketers have always known that sometimes customers are just not ready to purchase or are unwilling to change their behavior. But the beauty of the five-step IMC process is that the marketer learns the response from marcom efforts quickly, since short-term results are evaluated within the current fiscal year. Thus, the program can quickly be adapted or adjusted as needed. Identifying successes and failures provides input for future programs, thus closing the marcom loop.

Measurement of Actual Returns

Measuring short-term returns—those business-building returns that are realized within the current fiscal year—is not a complicated process. All the baselines are already in place. The marketer knows the value of certain groups of customers and/or prospects in terms of their current income flows to the organization (steps 1 and 2 of the IMC process). He or she has developed and delivered appropriate messages and incentives through predetermined media vehicles (step 3), and has esti-

BACK-TO-FRONT PLANNING?

Many managers have great difficulty with a key element of IMC planning. They cannot understand why the budgeting part of the process comes last. In traditional marketing, budgeting happens before any marcom program ever gets under way. Management first determines how much can be spent, and marcom managers are charged with building programs within those financial constraints. It is the management style of "command and control," with marcom relegated to a tactical rather than a strategic role.

The IMC process turns this around. Instead of beginning with a budget, one arrives at a budget through the planning process. The reason that budgeting belongs at the end is quite simple: until the marcom manager knows who the best customers and prospects are, has some idea of how and in what way marketing communication can impact their behaviors and change their attitudes and beliefs, and then forecasts what the financial value of those changed behaviors is likely to be, he or she has no idea how to answer the three key questions posed at the beginning of this chapter for senior management. That is, management has no idea how much to invest, what level of returns to expect, or how long it will take to generate those returns.

Viewed in this way, it becomes clear that traditional budgeting and allocation procedures are, for the most part, simply the hopes and dreams of senior management influenced by the marcom managers and their agencies, the media, and others involved in the communication process.

mated potential returns in the form of changes in income flows from these customers or prospects as potential returns (step 4). Because each goal has been thoroughly thought out and investigated in these first four steps, the marketer is in a position to determine easily whether the goals have been achieved and whether forecasted returns have been obtained. All that is necessary is a comparison of actual customer responses and sales data from the current fiscal year.

A key value of postprogram analysis is the opportunity it provides for continuous learning and improvement. It's possible to determine fairly accurately what worked and what didn't by looking at actual outcomes. If a marcom program didn't work or didn't live up to estimates, there is now a basis for evaluation and change. Those programs that did work can be repeated or improved and the others changed, adapted, or abandoned. The marcom group becomes a learning group and, in the process, becomes more relevant to customers, prospects, and management over time.

Long-term returns—those that build a brand's equity over time—are measured using actual sales results in exactly the same way as explained in the previous chapter. Quite simply, the marcom manager determines the financial value of the customers or customer groups over a multiyear time frame—say, three to five years—by looking at their actual income flows during the determined period. As with short-term results, the IMC planner is then able to adapt or adjust the marcom plans—communication programs, investment levels, delivery systems, and the like—to maximize future returns over time.

The planner can also see the relationship between the short- and long-term effects of each program. While it is common to focus on either short-term or long-term financial returns from marketing communication investments, depending on the views of management, there is little question that short-term results have an impact on long-term returns. The challenge is relating the two. In the IMC process, long-term returns that accrue to the organization are an accumulation of short-term returns from investments in the same customers and prospects. The use of customer investments as the basis for all marcom measurement activities is the integrating factor.

Three C Analysis: A New Integrated Model of Long-Term Brand Value

As stated earlier, the IMC evaluation model is based primarily on customer income flows. While the greatest focus is on financial returns, or cash flows, there are other values connected with ongoing customer contributions, customer advocacy being one of the most important.[1] *Customer advocacy*, as we use the term here, goes beyond the traditional view of customer loyalty (that is, willingness and desire to continue a relationship with an organization by repeatedly purchasing or using its brand). Customer advocacy encompasses customer loyalty but also extends to proactive customer behavior to recommend the brand to others, to wear the brand's logo or icon on apparel, or otherwise make a public statement showing his or her enthusiasm and support for the brand.

The ability of the firm to estimate the customer value of the brand results from the development of in-depth and detailed customer data gathering and information created and stored in rich, complex databases such as those described in steps 1 and 2 of the IMC process (see Chapters 4 and 5). Since these databases have only been developed over the past ten to twelve years, it is clear why the approaches to marketing and marcom planning and development are changing so rapidly. The changes are being driven by the new data technology and thus are dynamic and innovative.

To measure the integrated short- and-long-term impact of marketing communication, three items are needed. For convenience, we'll term them the "Three Cs":

1. **Customer contribution.** This is the income flow from the customer or customers over time, measured at the contribution margin line (see Chapter 9). It comprises the net dollars the organization spends on marketing communication; therefore, net dollars must be measured as the return.

2. **Customer commitment.** This is a simplified version of the customer share of requirement or share of wallet concept explained in Chapter 10. The premise here is simple: customers vote with their wallets. They buy products they believe in or prefer. This is a much better measure of customer favor than attitudinal measures that ask how customers feel or relate to the product or service. In the Three Cs approach, customer commitment is determined for each individual segment, because experience shows that various segments show different levels of commitment to the various brand or brands.

3. Customer champions. This refers to how involved with and supportive of the brand the customer is, in other words, how much or how little the customer will advocate the brand to others. The strongest measure here is whether or not the customer actually recommends the brand to a friend, relative, or colleague. Again, it is a measure of behavior, not just attitude. Hopefully, these customer-delivered messages and incentives will then result in an additional sale to a new customer or customers by the firm at relatively low cost.

Exhibit 12.1 illustrates the Three Cs concept. By using basic customer identification, either individually or as part of a group, along with the Three Cs, the planner is able to construct a three-dimensional "customer cube." When these three measures are combined, they create a box within the cube—a number for contribution, a number for commitment, and a number for contribution. This cube not only clearly identifies where the customer currently stands in terms of behavior, it also offers some guidance to marcom managers in terms of what future behaviors would be most beneficial to both the customer and the marketer. Knowing where the customer is on these three key measures is fundamental to measuring the level of investment and return on customers and customer groups. By identifying these numbers, the firm can place a value on the customer. If the customer is low on one attribute, the firm can initiate marketing communication programs to attempt to move them in a specific direction in the cube.

As an example, by knowing where the customer is in the customer cube, the marcom manager can identify certain objectives for the communication program. Some might be as follows:

- To retain the existing behavior of the customer
- To promote new behaviors among the customer group
- To build incentives or rewards to encourage customers to become champions or advocates
- To allow the manager to determine whether or not to invest in the customer based on the current and potential value that might be returned to the firm

Exhibit 12.1 Three Cs Measures of the Brand

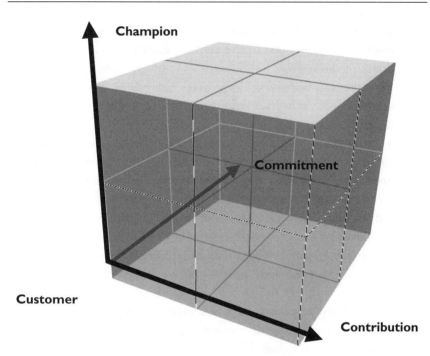

Adapted from Clive Humby, "Customer Measures of the Brand" (presented at the Cranfield School of Management Conference on Leveraging Brand Equity to Create Strategic Value, Cranfield, England, April 19, 2002). Used with permission from dunnhumby associates.

The objectives behind Three C analysis are as follows:

1. **To help the marcom manager understand changes in behavioral activities among individual customers and various customer segments.** For example, Three C analysis helps determine which customers moved from one segment in the cube to another as a result of marcom programs and which did not. Changes by customers over time must be directly related to the various marcom activities that have been implemented, otherwise the credit belongs elsewhere. If, for example, a household starts buying baby food and diapers during a measured fiscal year, this is likely not the result of a marcom program but is more probably due to a change in the structure of the household. Three C analysis provides insight into

what marketing communication has contributed and what has occurred externally, driving behavioral changes.

2. **To help the marcom manager understand how customers migrate from one box in the cube to another.** Analyzing migration provides insights into lifestyles and life patterns. If customer migration can be observed over time, it should be much easier to create relevant, effective, and efficient marcom programs that will influence behavior in the future.

3. **To provide an indicator of how difficult it might be to change customer or prospect behaviors through the use of marcom programs.** Being able to identify customers, communicate with them, and then measure the results of communication quickly helps marcom managers isolate customer groups for whom marcom can be a powerful change agent and those for whom other forms of marketing or corporate activity might be required. Of course, in some cases, customer behaviors simply can't be changed no matter what the organization does. These are the customers and prospects for whom the process provides the most insight. If they cannot be influenced with marketing communication, there is little sense in continuing to invest against them.

Identifying the Benefits of the Three C Approach

There are some obvious benefits to the Three C approach since it combines both short- and long-term measures of the return on marketing communication programs. For example, the approach integrates short-term marcom investment decisions and monitors their impact across each segment. Thus, the analysis provides a measure of both current and future value of each customer or segment.

Perhaps the greatest benefit of the Three C approach is that it provides a direct benchmark of marketing and communication returns, because it measures the critical variable changes in actual customer behaviors. Through that measure, it helps overcome the inherent danger of viewing or measuring "average" customers for the brand. This averaging of customers, marketing activities, and marcom programs creates major problems for the organization. Traditional measures like average purchase cycle, average income, or average usage, for instance, mask critical information on what the individual customer or customer group is actually doing. An example will help illustrate this point.

Comparing Traditional Averaging Measures with Three C Measures

An adventure travel company with a total of one million customers offers vacation trips designed around such activities as whitewater rafting, mountain climbing, bungee jumping, wilderness hiking, and other outdoor activities. Some customers repeat the same vacation each year, while others try a variety of different adventures. Using traditional analysis measures, the marcom manager would see that, on average, each customer generates a contribution margin of $50 each year. The customer base, however, is quite fluid. That is, a certain number of customers each year decide they do not want adventure vacations any longer for various reasons. Thus, there is churn in the customer base of about 20 percent per year on average. (Of course, some customers stay with the company for more than five years and some stay considerably less, but, on average, the defection rate is about 20 percent per year.) As a result of churn, the firm estimates that the average customer stays for about five years. Thus, at the end of the five-year period, the adventure travel company has essentially turned over its entire customer base (20% attrition × 5 years = 100% of customer base).

If the net present value of the total customer base were calculated using the firm's discount rate of 15 percent, it might look something like Table 12.1.

The total projected net present value (at a 15 percent discount rate) of the firm's customer base is approximately $119.5 million. Based on this estimate, the firm could develop some idea of how much it could afford to invest in marcom programs against its total customer base during the coming five years, knowing that on average each customer is responsible for approximately $50 in contribution margin. Further, the firm could likely develop plans that would attempt to acquire new cus-

Table 12.1 Adventure Travel Company
Average Customer Analysis—Old Model

Bases:	1 million customers
	$50 contribution
	20% defection rate
	15% discount rate

	Customer Count	Average Contribution Margin	Total Contribution Margin
Year 1	1,000,000	$50.00	$50,000,000
Year 2	800,000	$50.00	$40,000,000
Year 3	640,000	$50.00	$32,000,000
Year 4	512,000	$50.00	$25,600,000
Year 5	409,600	$50.00	$20,480,000

Net present value over 5 years: $119,583,590

Adapted from Clive Humby, "Customer Measures of the Brand" (presented at the Cranfield School of Management Conference on Leveraging Brand Equity to Create Strategic Value, Cranfield, England, April 19, 2002). Used with permission from dunnhumby associates.

tomers and other plans that would be designed to retain the existing customer base, although this might be somewhat difficult since, in many cases, the firm doesn't know which customers will leave. From this analysis, however, it would appear that the marcom manager would have to develop some very effective acquisition programs to offset the annual departure of approximately 20 percent of the customer base. Additionally, it is likely that some retention programs would be needed as well, since the assumption is that only 20 percent of the customer base presently defects. If that number were to go higher, even less future income could be projected.

The problem with this analysis, however, is that the company almost never has an "average" customer base or an "average" year. Some years, customer income flows are up; some years, they are down. By averaging the years and applying a discount rate across all customers, the management of the adventure travel company has masked the true value of customer groups. This could well mislead the marcom manager in terms of what types of programs are needed. Thus, a careful analysis is needed.

The new Three C model suggests that an analysis be made of each customer group each year to determine and understand the actual value of various customers. If, instead of looking at an average of all customers, the marcom manager estimated the income flow from specific customer groups, dramatic differences in the total value of the adventure travel company customer base would be revealed. As shown in Table 12.2, the customer base is aggregated into loyal customers, core customers, borderline customers, and passive customers. When the net present value of each aggregate group is analyzed, based on customers' contribution rates and their tendency to defect, the income flow to the organization over the next five years comes to $146.2 million not $119.5 million (again using a 15 percent discount rate).

The different estimate of future returns comes from an understanding of the contribution margin income flows from various customer groups, their group defection rate, and their value by year to the firm. For example, 50,000 loyal customers provide the firm with $350 per year in contribution margin, not the $50 from the average of all groups. Further, this "best customer" group has a much lower defection rate, only 2.5 percent, compared to the average for all customers of 20 percent. Thus, different marcom programs are needed for this group than for those customers who provide less contribution margin and have far greater tendency to leave the customer base. The other calculations shown in the table are just as revealing. Thus, an IMC approach places value on customers, in as much detail as possible, for it is this kind of analysis that provides an understanding of the true ongoing value of the brand and the marcom efforts.

Table 12.2 Adventure Travel Company
Segment Customer Analysis—New Model

Customer Count	Contribution Margin	Defection Rate
50,000 loyal	$350 contribution	2.5%
200,000 core	$100 contribution	7.5%
300,000 borderline	$30 contribution	12.5%
450,000 passive	$8 contribution	33.4%
Net present value over 5 years: $146,273,381		

Adapted from Clive Humby, "Customer Measures of the Brand" (presented at the Cranfield School of Management Conference on Leveraging Brand Equity to Create Strategic Value, Cranfield, England, April 19, 2002). Used with permission from dunnhumby associates.

Tracking Customer Migration Through Three C Analysis

To this point, only the existing customer segments have been investigated in different ways, that is, by their differing values. One of the more important challenges facing the marcom manager is to influence the behavior of the existing customer base. Returning to the adventure travel company example, one of the key goals might be to encourage present customers to move from one segment to another. Table 12.3 illustrates this situation and the change in value that occurs if the marcom program is successful.

There are still four basic aggregate groups (loyal, core, borderline, and passive). However, the table shows what happens if only 10 percent of the customers in each of the three bottom groups move up one segment—that is, if 10 percent of passives become borderlines, 10 percent of borderlines become cores, and so on. Further, the table illustrates what happens if another 10 percent of each of the groups moves down one segment. Over the next five years, the total estimated net present value of the adventure travel firm's income flow moves from $146.2 million up to $167.6 million, a gain of over $21 million during the period, or an increase in value of 15 percent during the specified time frame.

Similarly, major benefits occur to the travel organization if different percentages of the customers move from one segment to another. As

Table 12.3 Adventure Travel Company
Impact of 10% Movement Between Segments

Customer Count	Contribution Margin	Defection Rate
50,000 loyal	$350 contribution	2.5%
200,000 core	$100 contribution	7.5%
300,000 borderline	$30 contribution	12.5%
450,000 passive	$8 contribution	33.4%

Plus: 10% of customers promoted up one segment
10% of customers moved down one segment

Net present value over 5 years: $167,646,065

Adapted from Clive Humby, "Customer Measures of the Brand" (presented at the Cranfield School of Management Conference on Leveraging Brand Equity to Create Strategic Value, Cranfield, England, April 19, 2002). Used with permission from dunnhumby associates.

shown in Table 12.4, if 12.5 percent of the customers are promoted up one segment and only 7.5 percent of the customers are demoted down one segment, the value grows to $184.9 million from the $167.6 million, or an increase of roughly 10 percent.

But, income flows and likely profits for the adventure travel company can likely be further improved if the organization is able to reduce customer churn, or the number of customers leaving the company during any one year. Table 12.4 incorporates this scenario. By reducing the overall defection rate for each segment by just 10 percent (among loyals from 2.5 percent to 2.25 percent, and so on), the overall average defection rate decreases from 20 percent to 18 percent. With this reduction in churn, the adventure travel organization would increase its net present value over the next five years to approximately $184.9 million.

From this example, it is clear how important the management of customers, their purchases, and their loyalty to the organization have become. Key, of course, are the analysis and the ability to identify customers and their value and monitor their movement within the organization's portfolio. It becomes very clear as well that having specific behavioral goals for specific customer groups and then developing marcom to influence the behavior of those customers becomes the key challenge for the marcom manager. This ability to segment, measure the value of, and follow the migration of customers through the length of

Table 12.4 Adventure Travel Company
10% Reduction in Churn

Customer Count	Contribution Margin	Defection Rate
50,000 loyal	$350 contribution	2.25%
200,000 core	$100 contribution	6.75%
300,000 borderline	$30 contribution	11.25%
450,000 passive	$8 contribution	30.00%

Plus: 12.5% of customers promoted up one segment
7.5% of customers moved down one segment

Net present value over 5 years: $184,991,712

Adapted from Clive Humby, "Customer Measures of the Brand" (presented at the Cranfield School of Management Conference on Leveraging Brand Equity to Create Strategic Value, Cranfield, England, April 19, 2002). Used with permission from dunnhumby associates.

association with the organization becomes a major factor in the success of the marcom program and ultimately the success of the company.

Moving Forward with the Three C Approach

It should be clear by now that the Three C approach of viewing short-term returns as the foundation for long-term returns makes inherently good sense. Long-term returns are simply a compilation of a series of short-term returns with some allowances for compounding, risk, and the like. The primary value, of course, is that this methodology integrates short-term marketing investment decisions and monitors their impact across each customer segment in terms not just of their current value but of their potential future value as well. In addition, the use of an ongoing method of analysis and evaluation provides a useful benchmark for measuring the value of future marcom programs, since it is directly connected to the behaviors of various customer groups rather than just their attitudinal change.

Most of all, the Three C approach overcomes the danger of looking at data in terms of "average" customers and "average" investments and returns. It shows the value of marcom programs as they relate to actual customer groups and thus refines the traditional measures that are still widely used.

Back to Step 1

As we have discussed, a core activity during step 5 of the IMC process is the evaluation of results, which then become the basis for future marcom programs. In other words, the results of the initial program help define the goals and objectives for the next. The planner quite simply takes everything he or she has learned about customers and prospects and evaluates how well each step of the process worked. He or she can then repeat the same questions asked in the first four steps: Were the correct customers and prospects identified? Were they properly valued?

Was the correct mix between messages and incentives made? What type and level of response was achieved? With answers to these questions in hand, the planner is able to begin again at step 1 of the IMC process, with each new program refining and improving the last. It is this closed-loop approach, where results are used to develop future plans, that distinguishes IMC planning from traditional marketing approaches.

Moving On

Perhaps the greatest value of the Three C approach is that it further confirms that the brand, since it reflects the relationship between the customer and the organization, must be treated as an asset of the firm. While intangible, the brand still contributes great value to the organization as brand equity builds up during relationships with customers. That allows the firm to understand that, for the most part, its success comes from ongoing relationships with customers and prospects and that those returns are commonly generated as a result of customer loyalty. Further, the Three C approach provides a methodology by which investments can be made in various customer groups based on their value and their potential.

This leads back to the four common goals of the marcom manager that have been demonstrated throughout this text: to acquire new customers; to retain existing customers at their present income flow levels; to increase the present and future value of existing customers or prospects by upselling or cross selling; and to change the value of existing customers by migrating them to various products and services in the organization's portfolio. These objectives, in turn, lead right back to the start—the strategic organizational goals set out in guiding principle 4: increase cash flows from customers; accelerate cash flows from customers; stabilize cash flows from customers; and impact shareholder value.

Thus, the circular nature of IMC planning allows marcom managers to close the loop on the marcom process. Step 5 leads back to step 1, as data analyzed during evaluation of the IMC program feeds directly into and acts as a starting point for new and continuing marketing communication programs.

At this point, there is only one additional element of financial measurement to be addressed: finding some way to value the brand or identify the brand equity that has been or could be created as a result of marketing communication. This, of course, directly benefits the shareholders or owners of the firm. That subject is discussed in detail in the next chapter.

PART VII

BUILDING SHARE VALUE INTO THE FUTURE

CHAPTER 13

RELATING IMC PROGRAMS TO BRAND EQUITY AND SHAREHOLDER VALUE

To this point, the value of various forms of marketing communication has been discussed primarily in terms of the income flows they can create or sustain from a group of customers or prospects. Generating income flows, after all, is the only way to build and grow a firm. Yet today's publicly held companies, as well as many under private ownership, have another key objective: building perceived or real value that can be converted for the benefit of owners or shareholders at some point in the future. These not-yet-realized cash flows are known as *brand equity*. This chapter explores the concept of brand equity from a marketing perspective. Chapter 14 offers a methodology for measuring the value of a brand.

Brand Equity and IMC Planning

Webster's dictionary defines *equity* as "the amount or value of a property or properties above the total of liens or charges against it." Just as corporate equity is the value for which a firm can be sold after deducting costs pending against it, so a similar view would consider brand equity as the value of the brand if it were offered for sale in the open marketplace. A brand owner considers brand equity as part of the basic financial value of the firm. While this value is as yet unrealized, it still exists for management and valuation purposes.

The value of the brand to the owner, however, is often different from the value of the brand to the external marketplace. That means the brand value as determined by the organization may or may not be the same amount as an outside investor would be willing to pay to acquire or own the brand. Nor is it the same when brand equity is considered from the customer's perspective. More will be said later on why this value differential commonly exists.

Unfortunately, the dual perspectives of the brand—depending on whether one is buying or selling—has muddied the waters when it comes to determining how much a brand is really worth. For the purposes of IMC planning, however, companies do not need to consider the external—or resale—value of the brand. They look at brand valuation in terms of the inherent value of the brand as a cash-producing corporate asset. With this perspective, managers can approach the valuation of the firm's brands just as they approach valuation of any other corporate asset in which they invest and from which they expect returns.

By placing a financial value on brand equity, the organization is able to do the following:

- Identify or set some level of financial value on the ownership of the brand from the firm's viewpoint
- Understand how the firm is progressing by using brand asset value as a yardstick to determine whether brand equity is increasing or decreasing over time
- Develop some type of financial estimate or expectation of how additional investments in the brand might generate returns, thus optimizing the use of finite corporate resources.

Brand Definition

The term *brand* suffers from overuse among marketing and communication people and is often open to misinterpretation. While to some a brand is a tangible trademark, to others it represents a combination of intangibles. Philip Kotler defines a brand as "a name, term, sign, symbol, or design, or a combination of them which is intended to identify the goods or services of one seller to differentiate them from those of competitors."[1]

Alternatively, John Murphy, founder of the Interbrand organization, has defined the brand as follows: "A trademark which, through careful management, skillful promotion and wide use comes in the minds of consumers to embrace a particular set of values and attributes both tangible and intangible."[2]

In truth, a brand likely embraces both these views and several more. To arrive at a definition that is meaningful for IMC planning, it is necessary to look at brands from three perspectives: as protected legal assets; as relationship-building assets; and, most importantly, as financial assets.

Brands as Legal Assets

In legal terms, the brand consists of a package of separable and transferable legal rights enjoyed by its owner. These include a number of characteristics that can be registered with various governmental agencies or groups and for which legal rights are possible. Names, descriptions, symbols, logos, sounds, colors, smells, packaging, straplines or taglines, advertising, and many other facets of a brand can be protected in a legal sense. Registering these elements allows owners to create legal barriers to use of them by competitors. Registration also enables brand owners to differentiate their products in ways that are protected by the courts. In essence, one might say that the brand creates a legal monopoly for the organization that owns it, because no other firm or individual can use it in quite the same way as the brand owner.

Brands as Relationship-Building Assets

Various types of marketing activities can be used to create relationships with customers or prospects that—like legal characteristics—serve not only to differentiate the firm's products and services but to protect them from competitive inroads. Often, these are functional and emotional attributes that marcom managers attempt to develop through various types of advertising, promotion, packaging, distribution, or other forms of relationship-building communication programs. For example, common types of functional attributes might include the following:

- Ensuring brand identification and recognition through the use of colors, symbols, or icons
- Simplifying customer product or service selection by creating differentiations from other product lines or brands in the category
- Providing a guarantee of origin or evidence of the maker or supplier of the product or service
- Confirming quality based on the trust, reputation, and acceptance that has been built by the brand owner over time

Similarly, a list of emotional attributes might read as follows:

- Reassuring customers that the product or service will perform at the same level of quality or use over time
- Associating ideas or concepts that enhance the brand in the mind of the customer or prospect so he or she prefers it over others
- Meeting customer aspirations by providing a "badge" of expression of what the user believes, accepts, or wishes to be
- Providing a form of self-expression for the customer through the visible use of the brand in the marketplace

While these elements have no specific legal support, they can and often are the strongest ties a brand can build with customers because they represent the relationship or bond that exists between the buyer and seller. It is generally these customer-brand relationships that create and sustain the ongoing income flows that a firm enjoys.

Brands as Financial Assets

While the issues of legal protection and consumer values are important in understanding brands, they do not capture the single most important element of brands from an IMC-planning perspective. Since IMC is primarily concerned with building brand value over time, its definition of brands must include a pragmatic, financial view. Simply put, brands create value for the organization in several ways:

- Brands create a form of security in existing markets. That is, they have the ability to generate ongoing income flows from customers now and in the future.
- Brands often command premium prices; customers are willing to pay more because of the customer value built into a brand. Similarly, brands enable owners to maintain existing prices in times of recession or extreme brand competition.
- Strong brands commonly generate greater sales volume than do unbranded or weakly branded products or services. Thus, brands often provide the additional volume that allows the firm to generate economies of scale.
- Brands allow the firm to expand into new markets by providing an entry point. A recognized brand name in a new segment or category allows easier entry into that market.
- Strong brands provide ease of entry for new product introductions, commonly requiring fewer resources than those needed for entry by unknown products or services.
- Brands enable the firm to enter into new geographies with more initial consumer and marketplace acceptance than that given to unknown or unbranded products.
- Strong brands enable the marketer to enter new sectors of the marketplace with less resistance from new users or the need to make major marketing investments.

From our discussion of these three distinct dimensions of brands—legal, relationship-building, and financial—it's possible to derive a new definition that is meaningful for IMC planning:

> *A brand is a product or service represented by a name, symbol, graphic,*
> *or other visible and recognizable identifying element that (a) can be*
> *legally protected, (b) can be exchanged or sold for consideration, (c) con-*
> *tributes perceptual value to the relationship between buyer and seller,*
> *(d) has some form of financial value, and (e) is managed for ongoing*
> *value creation by the brand owner.*

Existing Definitions of Brand Equity

The reason for any brand valuation is to identify the benefits created by
the brand for the relevant parties. What makes brand valuation difficult
is that a brand generates equity for two different groups: first, the organization, its employees, shareholders, and management; and second, customers, prospects, and end users. There is often a significant difference
between the two groups in terms of how much value each attributes to
the brand.

To compound the problem, there are two forms of measurable brand
equity:

- Attitudinal value among customers and prospects, which is made
  up of the recognition, beliefs, perceptions, and trust that have
  been established and built up over time with various stakeholders,
  differentiating the brand from its competitors
- The financial value that has been built up in the marketplace for
  the brand and can be converted into cash or equivalents by the
  firm, its owners, or its shareholders at some future point in time

Any meaningful definition of brand equity must take these different
perspectives into account. To arrive at a definition that makes sense for
IMC planners, let's first see how others define the term *brand equity*.
The Marketing Science Institute offers a definition that focuses on the
competitive aspects of the brand: "The set of associations and behaviors on the part of the brand's customers, channel members, and parent
corporation that permits the brand to earn greater volume or greater
margin than it could without the brand name and that gives the brand
a strong, sustainable, and differential advantage over competitors."[3]

Management thinker David Aaker offers a managerial rather than a marketing perspective: "Brand equity is a series of assets (and liabilities) linked to a brand name and symbol that adds to (or subtracts from) the value provided by a product or service to a firm and/or that firm's customers."[4] This definition speaks to the dynamic nature of brands, that is, how changing customer experiences or perceptions can enhance (or diminish) their value. Most notably, Aaker defines brand equity from the view of the customer rather than that of the competition.

Leslie de Chernatony and Malcolm McDonald offer yet another view, one that focuses on the financial and accounting aspects of brand equity: "Brand equity consists of the differential attributes underpinning a brand which give increased value to the firm's balance sheet."[5]

Finally, Kevin Lane Keller, one of the leading academicians in the brand arena, offers this attitudinal-based, consumer-oriented view of brand equity: "Customer-based brand equity is the differential effect that brand knowledge has on the customer response to the marketing of that brand. Equity occurs when the consumer is familiar with the brand and holds some strong, favorable and unique brand association in memory."[6]

It's evident that each definition puts a slightly different twist on brand equity, depending on the background and perspective of its author. None of these definitions, however, gets at what we believe are the most meaningful attributes of brand equity for the IMC planner. In their place, we offer our own definition as described in the next section.

The IMC View of Brand Equity

Exhibit 13.1 summarizes five key strategic components of brand equity as we see them. As shown in the four corners, they are brand presence, brand identity and image, brand commitment, and perceived quality. These four cornerstone components combine to give a brand a financial value, as shown in the center of the exhibit. All reflect how customers, prospects, employees, and other constituents—not just the organization—see the brand. Note that brand equity must be viewed in context: first, in terms of how stakeholders perceive it and differentiate it from the competition, and second, in terms of how it is perceived by

Exhibit 13.1 Components of Brand Equity

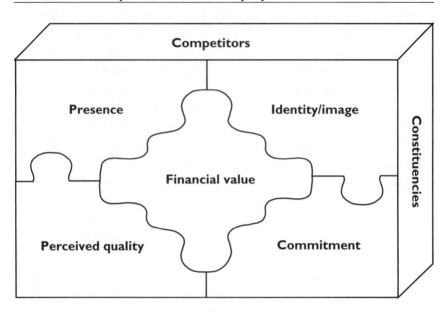

such constituencies as alliance partners, investors, community leaders, and labor unions. Also important is the fact that all four cornerstones of brand equity are measurable and can be monitored over time using a variety of attitudinal, behavioral, and financial metrics.

Let's take a closer look at each of the four cornerstone components that combine to give a brand its financial value.

Brand Presence

Brand presence simply means the degree to which customers, prospects, and other stakeholders know the brand and its meaning. Common measures of brand presence are made through investigations of brand awareness, brand salience, brand preference, and so on. Generally, awareness is classified in two ways:

- **Recognition.** This is the ability of the customer or prospect to recognize the name, logo, product, or other manifestation of the brand when asked or shown it.

- **Recall.** Either aided or unaided, this reflects the ability of the customer or prospect to associate the brand with its product or service category or use, or to make some comparison with competitors.

In either case, awareness is believed to lead, at some point, to stronger *brand salience*, or the degree to which the brand has a prominent position in the customer's mind. From there it is believed it eventually leads to preference and hopefully, at some point, to purchase or continued use of the product or service.

Some marcom managers argue that recall is the primary goal of communication and thus reflects the real value of the brand. If customers and prospects are aware of the brand and have high levels of recall and recognition, it is assumed that marcom has done its job and that purchasing and use are sure to follow. (As explained in Chapter 4, this way of thinking assumes that customer attitude toward a brand leads directly to purchase, an assumption that is questionable at best.)

Brand Identity and Brand Image

Brand identity and *brand image* are the views, impressions, or understandings held about a brand by various groups, such as the brand owners, marketers, customers, and prospects. Both identity and image are based on the values, attributes, traits, and personalities associated with the brand by the various stakeholder groups.

For purposes of discussion, we differentiate between identity and image. Brand identity reflects the view of the marketer or brand owner. That is, identity is what the owner or manager believes or intends that the brand should represent to customers, consumers, prospects, and other relevant stakeholders. Brand image, on the other hand, is what customers, prospects, users, and the like believe or perceive the brand to be or what it represents to them at a given point in time. Separating identity and image in this way underlines the fact that there is often a big difference between what the organization believes or feels about the brand and the experiences customers and consumers have with the brand.

Brand Commitment

Brand commitment reflects the loyalty the brand commands among its customers, consumers, and other relevant stakeholders. Such commitment can be measured behaviorally, for example, through measures of customer retention or repeat purchase. It can also be measured both attitudinally and behaviorally through measures of customer advocacy. Whereas image and identity are perceptual values, retention and advocacy are what customers and prospects actually *do*—that is, purchase, use, or otherwise take a measurable, relevant action concerning the brand over time. Such actions include using the brand on an ongoing basis or advocating its use to others.

Perceived Quality

Perceived quality is a special type of brand association held by customers and other stakeholders that defines the impressions of product performance during use.

There are different types of quality. *Absolute quality* is how the product or service actually performs in the marketplace compared to what is promised, expected, or offered by the organization or competitive products. Quality also relates to the price value expected; a lower price may suggest lower value, but there is still some level of expected quality. Customers may also relate quality to competition and competitive products or services. Further, they can relate quality to their own real or perceived needs. Thus, quality is generally in the eye of the beholder and is not under the control of the marketer.

Because perceived quality is the sum of the overall expectations for the brand from the customer's point of view, it has a direct relationship with the financial value of the brand and ultimately on the stock price and the general marketplace performance of the firm as well.

Converging Elements

Where the four cornerstone components we have discussed converge, adding financial value to the firm, we arrive at our definition of brand equity:

Brand equity is the composite of the brand's presence, identity/image, perceived quality, and commitment among constituents, culminating in long-term financial value to the firm and its shareholders. The dimensions of the brand are affected by the actions of competitors as well as the attitudes and behaviors of customers, prospects, employees, alliance partners, investors, and other key stakeholders.

This definition provides the IMC planner with a means through which to measure the value a brand brings to an organization or its shareholders, both in terms of short-term cash flows and over time. How that measurement is carried out is the topic of the next chapter.

How Brands Add Value for the Organization

If a brand does not add value for the organization or its shareholders, there is little reason to invest scarce resources in it. Yet how does marcom define a brand's value in terms that senior management will understand? The difficulty in valuing brands arises because—unlike such assets as buildings, equipment, or even research and development—they are considered intangible assets in the firm's financial accounting and reporting activities; thus, they are not generally shown on the balance sheet. In the case of a brand acquired from another organization, for instance, the difference between the purchase price and the tangible assets acquired is typically stated as "goodwill" and is subsequently depreciated over a period of time. In the case of homegrown brands (that is, those that have never changed hands), the financial value of the brand is not included anywhere on the firm's balance sheet. Strictly speaking, the asset value of the brand traditionally has not been treated as important to the firm unless it is either being bought or sold or can be separated out for understanding, evaluation, and ultimately some type of financial valuation. While it is true that some firms are beginning to recognize, either formally or informally, the asset value of brands, even to the extent of discussing them in some detail in annual reports and placing them on the balance sheet, this is not a common practice in most companies or countries.

To help overcome this problem of the intangible nature of brands and the more important issue of brand equity, we start with a discussion of intangible assets in general.

Understanding Intangible Assets

For most firms, intangible assets (other than brands) consist of such items as know-how, patents, customer lists, licenses, major contracts and agreements, experienced management, and the like. A new study has attempted to develop a methodology that sets a financial value against assets like these.[7] Brand Finance, plc, a London-based brand valuation firm that operates in Europe, Latin America, Asia, and Australia, recently conducted an analysis of "unexplained values" at 350 companies listed on the London Financial Times Stock Exchange (FTSE).

Exhibit 13.2 shows that 72 percent of the market value of all companies included in the FTSE 350 was not reflected on their balance

Exhibit 13.2 Gap Between Market Capitalization and Net Balance Sheet Assets (December 31, 1998)

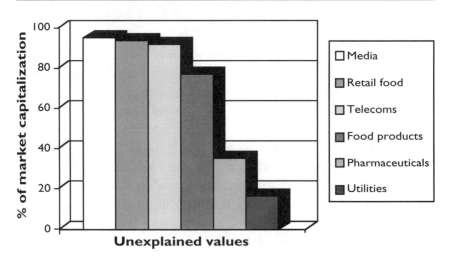

Note: On average, 72 percent of the market value of the 350 companies was not reflected on the balance sheet.

From David Haigh, "Valuing and Managing Brands: Issues in Brand Valuation" (presented at Northwestern University, Evanston, IL, November 21, 2000). Used with permission from Brand Finance.

sheets. The analysis estimated the total market capitalization of each organization (computed by multiplying the number of shares outstanding by the current share price) and then subtracted the value of tangible assets reported on the year-end balance sheet. The data were then consolidated to show the average percentage of unexplained value by industry groupings. This consolidation showed a gap between the total capitalization and the value of the tangible assets that ranged from 95 percent for media organizations to 17 percent for utilities. It is within this broad range, or definition, of intangible assets that brands and their value lie.

Through a similar study among leading U.S. organizations, Brand Finance sought to determine how much of each company's capitalization was tied up in intangible assets. The results imitated the first study and are shown in Exhibit 13.3. For companies like Gap Inc., Exxon, Wal-Mart, and amazon.com, tangible assets account for only about 25 percent of market capitalization, while intangible assets make up the remaining 75 percent. Even such capital-intensive companies as Boeing, Citigroup, and AT&T attribute 20 percent or more of their market value to intangible assets.

From these data, Brand Finance concluded that in the future brands will continue to grow as a proportion of market value. In support of its conclusion, Brand Finance cited data that showed the rise in value of intangible assets at U.K. firms. In the 1950s, tangible assets accounted for almost 80 percent of the value of all firms. By the 1990s, tangible assets had declined to about 30 percent of a firm's value, and by 2010, it is predicted that tangible assets will account for only about 10 percent of a firm's assets as reflected in its market capitalization. This means that brands are expected to increase from about 5 percent of the firm's value in 1950 to 60 percent in 2010. Brand Finance expects to see a similar trend in the United States, the rest of Europe, and emerging markets around the globe.

Seeing the Brand as a Key Value Driver

Exhibit 13.4 illustrates how brands build value for organizations. Brand-building efforts commonly result in four major areas of return to the

Exhibit 13.3 Tangible Versus Intangible Assets

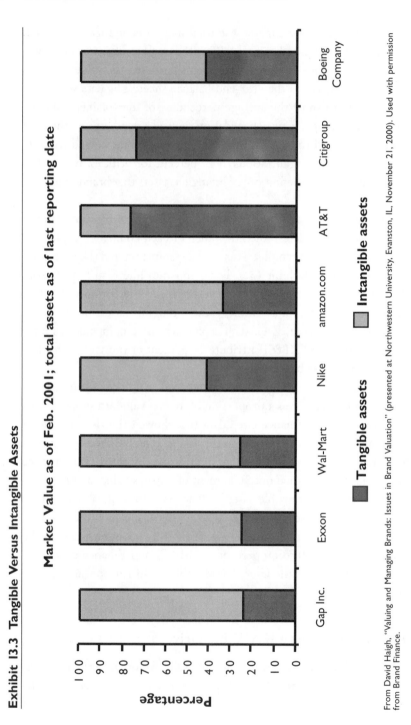

Market Value as of Feb. 2001; total assets as of last reporting date

From David Haigh, "Valuing and Managing Brands: Issues in Brand Valuation" (presented at Northwestern University, Evanston, IL, November 21, 2000). Used with permission from Brand Finance.

Exhibit 13.4 Brand: A Key Value Driver

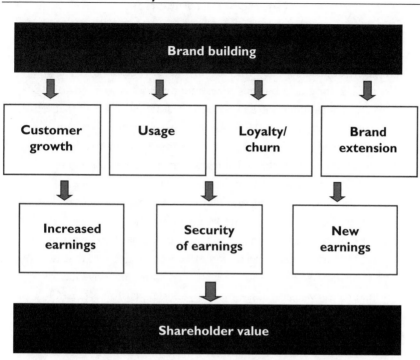

From David Haigh, "Valuing and Managing Brands: Issues in Brand Valuation" (presented at Northwestern University, Evanston, IL, November 21, 2000). Used with permission from Brand Finance.

organization: customer growth, or the sheer number of customers purchasing the brand; usage, or increased purchases by existing customers; increased customer income flows that come from increased loyalty, thereby giving the brand a greater share of requirement or reduced volatility in purchasing; and the ability of the firm to extend the brand into new or as yet unexplored products or categories that would bring in new customers, new sales, or both. (Note how closely these brand returns mirror the four basic goals of marketing communication—acquire customers, retain customers, grow volume and value, and migrate customers through the product portfolio.)

These four income opportunities result in increased earnings for the firm or brand; security or assurance of those earnings, that is, stability of income flows from customers over time; and the opportunity for new

THE MODEL IN PRACTICE

A marketplace example of this simple brand income flow model is shown in Exhibit 13.5. Orange was a telecommunications firm that introduced services within the United Kingdom in 1994. The company's branding-building investment in 1997 amounted to £63 million. These funds were invested in marketing activities that led to the acquisition of 110,000 subscribers who purchased connections from the firm, resulting in income flows to the company. The return on this initial marketing and communication investment was £388 million. That's how much came back in value to the organization, and ultimately to shareholders, as a result of the organization's marketing efforts.

The payback on the marketing and communication investment was made up of £202 million in net subscriber growth, that is, new customers; £31 million in increased subscriber revenue, or additional services or usage made by existing customers; £144 million in increased subscriber lifetime value, that is, the number of customers who were not expected to leave (reductions in the customer churn rate); and £11 million in licensing revenue, meaning the strength of the Orange name allowed the firm to enter new markets and license the brand to other allied companies.

When all these income streams were aggregated into the three income flow categories of earnings growth, earnings and security, and brand diversification, they amounted to £388 million which came as a direct result of Orange's brand-building program. That's a payback to shareholders of over five times the original investment in just one year. Certainly brand building, as developed through brand and marketing communication, appears to have been a worthwhile investment by Orange management on behalf of the entire group of Orange stakeholders.

earnings through new customers brought in by customer advocacy, new geographic areas of service, or other factors. All of these then contribute to shareholder value.

Exhibit 13.5 Brand Income Flow/Payback for Orange (1997)

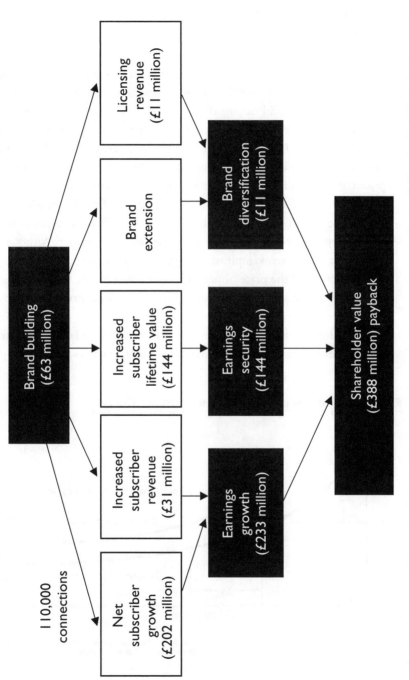

From David Haigh, "Valuing and Managing Brands: Issues in Brand Valuation" (presented at Northwestern University, Evanston, IL, November 21, 2000). Used with permission from Brand Finance.

How Brands Add Value for the Firm and Shareholders

Brands build value for their owners in two ways. First, they generally shift the demand curve for their owners, that is, they drive the product demand curve up and out so that more units are sold, commonly at higher prices. (Recall the Marketing Science Institute definition of brand equity cited earlier in this chapter.) So, a strong brand helps the marketer either sell at a higher price or sell a greater volume at a given price compared with a generic or weakly branded competitor.

As shown in Exhibit 13.6, the volume and profits of a product or service are driven by the demand curve, that is, how many units or the quantity customers are willing to purchase and at what price. Although the exhibit is only an example, it shows the demand for a branded product is greater and the price obtained is commonly higher for a branded product than for an unbranded one. This is the basic premise of why organizations develop and maintain brands—it moves the product from a commodity status that competes primarily on price and availability to a higher level that generates greater value for the owners.

Exhibit 13.6 Branding Shifts in the Demand Curve

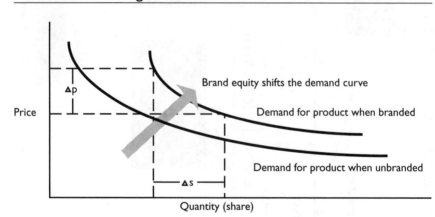

From David Haigh, "Valuing and Managing Brands: Issues in Brand Valuation" (presented at Northwestern University, Evanston, IL, November 21, 2000). Used with permission of Brand Finance.

The shift in the customer demand curve can occur for a number of reasons, including the following:

- The brand and its perceived value grows the total market category, for example, the introduction of the Sony Walkman grew the entire category of portable music.
- The brand can acquire new customers for the firm by encouraging consumers to switch from a competitor's brand.
- The brand can gain new customers from those who are just entering the category, that is, they have not purchased in the category in the past but have now become users simply because of the availability of the marketer's brand.
- The brand can retain a larger percentage of customers than expected. By reducing defection or churn, the brand influences the demand curve positively in the organization's favor.
- Existing customers can cross buy or upbuy to the marketer's brand simply because they are satisfied with the current brand.
- The brand can simply allow the firm to charge a premium price for its products or services as a result of the increased perceptual value created by the brand, or it can allow the firm to maintain an existing price in the face of falling overall pricing simply because of the value of the brand.

As an example of this ability of the brand to shift the demand curve, Toyota used the brand name Corolla for an automobile it manufactured and marketed in the United Kingdom. The firm was able to sell more automobiles and obtain a higher price for cars sold as Corollas than for those sold in a joint venture with General Motors as Geo Prizms. This volume and price differential was important, since both automobiles were almost exactly alike in terms of features and performance, the only exception being the brand. Indeed, the automobiles were made in the same factory by the same employees using the same equipment and the same chassis and framework for both cars, so there was no actual product difference. It was clearly the value of the brand that made the difference to buyers.

The second way a brand builds value for an organization is by shift-ing the supply curve. As shown in Exhibit 13.7, strong brand equity can help reduce costs for the organization as a result of greater volume demand for the brand than for a generic product. The increased demand for the brand and resulting increased sales provide the firm with greater economies of scale in manufacturing and distribution.

In general, this shift of the supply curve comes about in six ways:

- Selling a brand generally requires lower sales conversion costs because prospects have a better understanding and perception of the value being provided.
- Commonly, there is a lower average trade discount required by channels and others, that is, the brand marketer can generally sell products or services at closer to full margin than can the generic or weakly branded marketer.

Exhibit 13.7 Strong Brand Equity Shifts in the Supply Curve

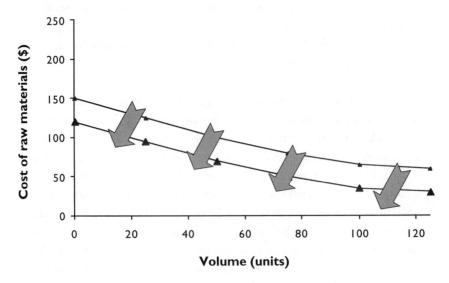

From David Haigh, "Valuing and Managing Brands: Issues in Brand Valuation" (presented at Northwestern University, Evanston, IL, November 21, 2000). Used with permission from Brand Finance.

- Generally, firms with strong brand equities have lower staff costs, lower costs to acquire those staff, and higher retention rates among those they employ.
- Firms with strong brand equities are usually able to obtain more favorable supplier terms, that is, they have better negotiating power with the companies from whom they buy raw materials and business services.
- A firm with strong brands can often obtain lower costs of capital since creditors tend to place more confidence in the firm's ability to sell products or services and generate profits than a firm with generic products.
- As a result of the first five points above, branded firms generally are able to achieve overall production economies of scale.

Thus, one is able to see how strong brands translate into larger brand equities that result in greater value for the firm's stakeholders.

Moving On

In this chapter, we have discussed how brands build value for the organizations that own them. Although brands are generally intangible assets, they do have financial value and provide financial levers for the firm and its managers.

With this understanding of brands, it is now possible to begin our discussion of how various aspects of brand equity might be measured. That follows in the next chapter.

METHODS OF MEASURING BRAND EQUITY

N ow that we have identified the components of brand equity—
brand presence, brand identity and image, brand commitment,
and perceived quality—and seen how they converge to provide financial value to organizations, the next challenge is to measure the value of
brand equity over time. In general, two approaches have evolved. The
first measures levels of consumer or customer attitudes, emotional
attachments, and other perceptual relationships of the customer to the
brand. The second, which is ultimately of greatest importance to the
IMC planner, measures brand equity in financial terms. This chapter
explores both of them.

Measurement of Brand Equity Using Customer Attitudes

For the most part, historical measures of brand value or brand equity
have relied primarily on attempts to measure the attitudinal value of the
brand among customers or prospects. That is, research techniques have
focused on the customer's or prospect's knowledge and understanding

of the brand, its qualities, its attributes, communication messages, and the like. Indeed, one of the simplest measures of brand knowledge is found in the well-known hierarchy of effects model discussed in Chapter 4.

In spite of the difficulty in linking them to financial outcomes, attitudinal measures nevertheless play an important role in helping the manager understand how customer choice and preference help drive the value of the brand for customers. The market research industry has developed dozens (if not scores) of tools and techniques to measure and monitor various aspects of consumer's, customer's, and prospect's views of brand health, strength, and value. Thus, for the sake of completeness, a brief discussion of four of the most prominent attitude-based brand equity models follows.

Before we begin, it is important to understand that all attitudinal measures share much of the common ground and terminology established by the hierarchy of effects model. In one way or another, they generally seek to measure such factors as brand awareness, as well as associations, beliefs, and perceptions about the category or brand, how it is used, by whom, and under what circumstances.

Each of these areas can be captured, analyzed, and interpreted to reveal the various aspects of a brand's strength. For example, one could say a brand is strong because many people have heard of it or spontaneously think of it when its category is mentioned. It could certainly be said that the brand is strong if many people express great loyalty or affection for it, either in their words or in their actions. In addition, a brand might be called strong if it is closely associated with imagery or functional, emotional, or self-expressive benefits that can be interpreted as desirable for customers or prospects.

Ultimately the bottom-line relevance of all this perceptual material is that it somehow translates into consumer behavior. In other words, attitudinal measures assume that attitudes and perceptions precede behavior and lead people to buy the brand, stay with the brand, pay more for the brand, and/or recommend the brand to friends and family.

Based on this assumption, researchers have offered various models for measuring brand strength and performance, four of which are discussed here. All of them tend to rely on some form of research that relates the brand to competitors in the same category and often in other categories as well. All have broad-scale geographic capability and are in use by a number of leading organizations around the world. They are known as BrandDynamics, the Conversion Model, EquiTrend, and Brand Asset Valuator.

BrandDynamics

BrandDynamics, developed by Millward Brown, tracks brand equity along five stages of a brand relationship.[1] Of the four models discussed here, it has the most in common with the hierarchy of effects, because it views customer attitudes and preference moving along a continuum from establishing brand presence to creating a bonded connection with customers. The purpose of the BrandDynamics analysis is to help companies understand the size and shape of their franchise across the five stages. This is depicted graphically as the BrandDynamics Pyramid, shown in Exhibit 14.1. At any one stage, the width of the bar is determined by the percentage of customers and prospects who can be counted at that level.

Exhibit 14.1 BrandDynamics Pyramid

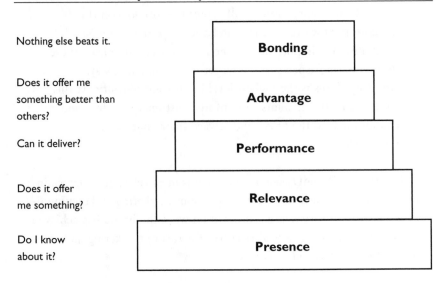

Nothing else beats it. — **Bonding**

Does it offer me something better than others? — **Advantage**

Can it deliver? — **Performance**

Does it offer me something? — **Relevance**

Do I know about it? — **Presence**

Each level in the pyramid represents a stage in the customer-brand relationship. It also provides a distinct communication challenge, showing what needs to be accomplished to move the customer to the next level. The various stages in the model are as follows:

1. **Presence.** A measure of brand awareness among the target group. If customers are not aware of the brand name or cannot recall its usages, the marketer should reevaluate spending levels, messages, or media placement.
2. **Relevance.** A measure of whether customers and prospects believe the brand offers them something that is relevant to their lives. If the relevance score is low, the marketer may need to demonstrate all the uses of the product or depict users to whom the customer can relate.
3. **Performance.** This relates to the perceived quality, durability, and functionality of the product. If customers and prospects do not believe the brand delivers on its promises, the marketer may need to validate the product's delivery capabilities via action tests, demonstrations, trial offers, and so forth.
4. **Advantage.** This metric determines whether the target audience perceives or understands the unique features or attributes of the brand. Commodity brands will typically score low on this dimension. However, if the brand does have truly unique attributes, it is important that the marketer communicate these differentiating aspects to the target in a compelling way.
5. **Bonding.** This is the highest level of customer loyalty. At this level, the marketer wants to reinforce customers' faith in and commitment to the brand and reward their continued relationship.

Clearly, the BrandDynamics approach is most relevant to determining the success or lack of success of previous marketing and communication efforts. It serves as a scorecard on what the brand has achieved in the market and suggests alternatives for future marketing and communication actions and activities.

The strength of the BrandDynamics methodology is that it can be used to monitor the movement of a brand (as well as that of its competitors) by tracking the percentage of participants who fall into each level. From this, the marketer can develop a detailed view of the characteristics of customers comprising each level for the firm's brand as well as for competitors. However, since it is an attitude-based methodology, the model looks at only one side of the brand equity question— how customers and prospects feel about the brand now. Thus, it cannot be linked to any financial measures of brand equity.

The Conversion Model

The Conversion Model was developed by Research Surveys of South Africa. It is currently being offered globally through a licensing agreement with Taylor Nelson Sofres. The model is designed to measure the depth of what is called the "consumer commitment" to the brand. This simply means it tries to identify the level of relationship the customer has to the brand. Commitment is measured continuously alongside traditional tracking measures such as advertising awareness and brand image.

The hypothesis of the Conversion Model is that customer commitment is a performance measure that is different from, and far more effective than, traditional advertising and marketing attitudinal measures. The commitment measure uses a small battery of questions to measure four factors believed to be involved in the decision-making process:

• Involvement in the category
• Satisfaction with the brands used
• Disposition toward competitors
• Ambivalence toward the brand

Based on the data gathered on these four factors, the Conversion Model plots customers and prospects on a continuum of eight different relationship categories as depicted in Exhibit 14.2.

Exhibit 14.2 The Conversion Model

Current customers			
Secure users		Vulnerable users	
Entrenched	Average	Shallow	Convertible

Available	Ambivalent	Weakly unavailable	Strongly unavailable
Open nonusers		Unavailable nonusers	
Noncustomers			

The first four relationships reflect the brand's current customers and represent the strength of commitment they exhibit toward the brand:

1. **Entrenched.** Customers who are strongly committed to the brand they currently use. They are highly unlikely to switch brands in the foreseeable future.
2. **Average.** Customers who are committed to the brand they are currently using but not as strongly as entrenched users. They are not likely to switch brands in the foreseeable future.
3. **Shallow.** Customers who are uncommitted to the brand and could switch to another brand quickly and easily. Some customers in this category are actively considering alternatives.
4. **Convertible.** Current users of the brand who are unhappy, dissatisfied, or simply looking for something new. They are highly likely to defect in the near future.

The remaining four relationships on the continuum comprise nonusers of the brand. The research tools attempt to gauge their availability as well as the likelihood they would switch from the competing brand they currently use.

5. **Available.** Nonusers of the brand who are most likely to be acquired in the short term.
6. **Ambivalent.** Nonusers who are as attracted to the marketer's brand as they are to their current brand.
7. **Weakly unavailable.** Nonusers who are not available to the brand but could be swayed.
8. **Strongly unavailable.** Nonusers who are highly unlikely to switch to the marketer's brand. Their preference lies strongly with their current brand of choice.

The value of the Conversion Model is that it allows the marketer to see the impact of marketing activities on latent consumer behavior. The model measures the lagged effects of marketing activity and helps to predict when sales will flow from such activity. Some critics have claimed that it is not a brand equity measurement at all, but rather an advertising/communication observation, focusing on effective versus efficient marketing communication tracking and measurement.

EquiTrend

The EquiTrend approach, offered by Harris Interactive, is an online study conducted twice a year that tracks over one thousand leading brands across a range of categories.[2] Respondents to the study are each asked to rate one hundred brands, twenty of which are core brands (given to everyone) and eighty of which are randomly selected and rotated from the remaining brands being studied. The EquiTrend methodology is based on three measurements:

- **Quality.** Rated on a scale of 0 to 10, with 0 meaning "unacceptable/poor quality" and 10 meaning "outstanding/extraordinary quality"

- **Salience.** The percentage of people who feel aware and informed enough about a brand in order to rate it
- **Equity.** Quality score multiplied by salience score

EquiTrend interprets a quality rating of 8 or more as indicating the brand is "world class." Among the brands rated world class in the spring 2002 study, Discovery Channel was the leader, as shown in Table 14.1.

Brand Asset Valuator

The Brand Asset Valuator, first used by Young & Rubicam (Y&R) in 1993, is a proprietary global brand-tracking database and is perhaps the best known of the four services discussed so far.[3] Since the initial fielding, more than 121 studies have been conducted in forty countries and involving over 180,000 consumers, all using the same methodology. Thus, the database is eminently reliable and likely the best overall study on brands conducted on a global basis. The methodology uses fifty-six underlying metrics that are then aggregated, or rolled up, into four key "pillars" (dimensions) of brand performance. According to Y&R, these

Table 14.1 EquiTrend Spring 2002 Study

Rank	Brand	Quality	Salience	Equity (quality × salience)
1	Discovery Channel	8.38	92	77.1
2	Craftsman tools	8.37	89	74.5
3	Hershey's Kisses	8.16	99	80.8
4	Bose stereo and speakers	8.15	70	57.1
5	WD-40 spray lubricant	8.15	91	74.2
6	Crayola crayons and markers	8.15	92	75.0
7	Reynolds Wrap aluminum foil	8.12	84	68.2
8	TLC (The Learning Channel)	8.12	84	68.2
9	Neosporin ointment	8.11	86	69.7
10	M&M's chocolate candies	8.09	98	79.3

Note: The brands rated all are primarily U.S.-based brands. Thus, they are rated "World Class" although they may not be marketed globally.

four dimensions were selected because movement in them, more than in any other combination of dimensions, appears to explain why brands grow, how they can get sick, and how they can be managed back to health once they have begun to decline. The four pillars used in the study are as follows:

- **Differentiation.** The degree to which brand distinguishes itself from others in category
- **Relevance.** The degree to which the brand is personally meaningful to customers
- **Esteem.** The degree to which customers like the brand and hold it in high regard
- **Knowledge.** The degree to which customers are aware of the brand and understand what it stands for

When combined, the first two measurements—differentiation and relevance—are considered to be indicative of brand strength. The second two—esteem and knowledge—are combined to give a measure of brand stature. The overall framework used to diagnose the brand and the relationship between the different measures is depicted in Exhibit 14.3.

The underlying premise on which the Brand Asset Valuator is built is the assumption that brands are built sequentially, that is, they begin by differentiating themselves from other brands and then culminate the branding process by developing strong brand knowledge among consumers. In this approach, differentiation is the key element in the process and drives all the other elements. The model starts with differentiation, then leads to relevance to give the brand its initial strength. This is followed by esteem and ultimately by knowledge, at which point the brand has achieved stature. However, the measures in each pillar are dynamic, and a brand can lose value in both strength and stature, although they may not necessarily decline at the same rate.

To understand and compare different brands based on their underlying scores, a brand power grid has been developed and is shown in

Exhibit 14.3 Brand Asset Valuator Framework for Diagnosing Brands

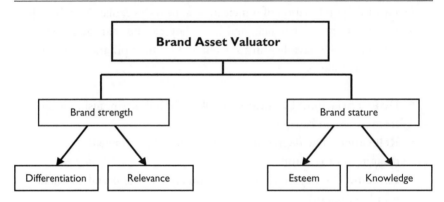

From "White Paper on the Brand Asset Valuation," 2000, yr.com. Used with permission from Young & Rubicam Inc.

Exhibit 14.4. The grid crosses the scores on brand strength with those on brand stature.

A brand with both low brand strength and low brand stature—in the lower left quadrant—is likely to be a new brand or one that is so unfocused that few people are aware of it or what it stands for. On the other hand, brands with high brand strength scores but low brand stature scores—in the upper left quadrant—have begun to establish themselves, although they still have significant room for growth. This is typical of emerging brands or ones with unrealized potential.

In the upper right-hand corner are the solid leadership brands, such as Disney, Sony, and the like. They score high on both dimensions and enjoy strong loyalty and market performance. Unfortunately, strong brands do not remain so forever. If not properly managed, a brand can begin to lose its differentiation and relevance in the marketplace power grid. This is the unhappy fate of brands that, while well known, have lost their uniqueness and importance among customers. In recent years, Brand Asset Valuator has reported that such formerly strong brands as TWA, Greyhound, Holiday Inn, and others have dropped to the "eroding potential" quadrant, which presents a challenging assignment for the owners of those brands.

Exhibit 14.4 Brand Power Grid

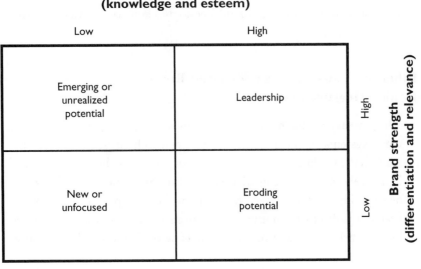

From "White Paper on the Brand Asset Valuation," 2000, yr.com. Used with permission from Young & Rubicam Inc.

The Brand Asset Valuator is essentially a diagnostic tool that can be used to spot market opportunities, stem brand erosion, and help marketers understand the value of their brand relative to similar products and brands. Of particular interest is the fact that, historically, the Brand Asset Valuator placed no financial value on the brand nor did it indicate what returns an organization might enjoy if the managers were able to increase the two key measures of differentiation and relevance. However, it should be noted that Y&R recently entered into an agreement with Stern Stewart to establish what is now being called Brand Economics. The organization will link data gathered under the Brand Asset Valuator with financial data and the Stern Stewart Economic Value Added (EVA) financial valuation approach. The two companies believe that this combination could provide the best of all brand valuation worlds. The Brand Asset Valuator portion could identify where the brand stands and how it might be improved, and the EVA approach could identify the economic value of the brand, which could be quite valuable to managers in terms of investments and returns. It will be interesting to see how the Brand Economics approach develops in the next several years.

Inherent Flaws in Attitude-Based Brand Equity Measurement

The primary problem with all attitude-based brand equity measurement systems is the inability of the research organization or the marketer to relate attitudinal measures to actual buying behavior. Intuitively, it would seem that such a link exists but it is still to be proven. Thus, while marketers may know how people "feel" about the brand, it is difficult if not impossible to relate that to how they behave in the marketplace and to attach any type of financial value to those feelings.

To be sure, knowing the brand's presence, salience, quality perceptions, or strength of consumer commitment are important for the brand manager. However, measured alone, they give the marketer little guidance in how much to invest in the brand, what financial returns might accrue, and over what period of time those returns might occur. Attitudinal measures do provide the marketer with some comparison of his or her brand with that of competitors, but again, there are few if any ways to connect those competitive measures to any type of financial value. Thus, it becomes clear that to meet senior management's requests for measurement of *outcomes* and not just *outputs*, some type of financial measure of brand value or brand equity is needed.

Financial Measures of Brand Equity

Several methodologies have been developed over the years to determine the financial value of brands or brand equity. We start with a look at the five major approaches: historic cost method, replacement cost method, market value method, royalty relief method, and economic use method. For reasons that will become clear, the economic use model is most closely aligned with value-oriented IMC. Let's look at each in turn.

Historic Cost Method

Historic cost is exactly what it says—what has the brand owner invested in the development of the brand over the years to build the brand to the level it is at today? This figure generally includes investments in marketing communication, packaging, logo and icon development, signage, and the like. By adding up all the investments made by the brand owner during the relevant development period, the actual investments made can be determined.

There are, of course, several problems with this approach. These range from the difficulty of collecting accurate investment figures over what often is a long period of time to the near impossibility of restating costs in current market value to the lack of similar brands for comparison. The major difficulty with this type of valuation, though, is that costs, or investments made in the brand, commonly have little or nothing to do with the current marketplace value of the brand in terms of customer income flows or what purchase price it might bring in the market.

Replacement Cost Method

Similar to the historic cost approach, this valuation method relies on development of an estimate of what it might cost in marketing, communication, design, and other brand-building investments to replace the brand in the current marketplace. Thus, it seeks to calculate what would be required to build a similar brand in the same marketplace using existing tools and activities. Given the multiplicative nature of brand development, it is generally difficult to determine what levels of investment might be required for restoration or replacement of the brand in the current marketplace or for building a new brand from scratch to take the place of the existing brand. Likewise, it is difficult to determine the relevant costs that might be required to create the same brand value in the current or future marketplace. This approach has been borrowed from traditional accounting where the value of tangible assets (machinery, rolling stock, computers, and so on) can be estimated based on some determination of replacement costs of the materials or equipment. Generally, this approach is inappropriate for the measurement of the intangible and dynamic nature of a brand, although there are research organizations that attempt to estimate those costs and resulting values.

Market Value Method

We touched on the market value approach to brand valuation earlier; it is simply finding the marketplace value of the brand or what it might bring if it were put up for sale to interested parties. While this approach does determine the true marketplace value among buyers, it is of little use to organizations that do not wish to sell the brand but only want to value it for purposes of better management of their assets and resources or as a basis for future investments. Therefore, the market value method, while accurate in terms of its ability to identify the true marketplace value of the brand, usually is not very helpful to the brand owner in terms of ongoing management costs or investment levels.

Royalty Relief Method

This approach gets closer to the actual ongoing market value of the brand. The basic premise is that if the organization doing the brand valuation did not currently own the brand, it would have to pay a fee or royalty to get the value and benefits of the brand in the marketplace. Thus, the royalty relief approach attempts to determine what amount of franchise fee or royalty the firm would have to pay the brand owner for use of the name and its various attributes in the marketplace. In other words, from a brand valuation standpoint, how much does the organization save by owning the brand rather than renting it by paying royalties for its use?

To determine the royalty rate, the company could use available licensing rate comparisons for similar products or could obtain an estimate of the appropriate rate from an outside expert. Today, large databases contain the current royalty rates for large numbers of organizations. In spite of these data resources, the primary problem with the royalty relief method is finding a relevant brand with which to compare, along with the difficulty of developing complex rate structures and gaining a transparency of terms to set the royalty rate.

Table 14.2 provides an example of how the royalty relief method of brand valuation can be determined. The estimated net sales of the brand being valued are projected out for a period of five years with the base year being taken as year 0. The royalty rate, shown here as 10 percent, is taken against those sales. This calculation creates a royalty income of $50.00 in year 0, $52.00 in year 1, and so on. From that, the estimated taxes must be deducted. A rate of 33 percent is used in the calculation, resulting in taxes of $16.50 in year 0, $17.16 in year 1, and so on. This provides the net royalty (line e). From this net royalty, a discounted cash flow calculation must be taken to determine the net present value of the royalty income, which is shown as 15 percent. By deducting the discount factor (line f) from the net royalty, one arrives at a discounted cash flow for each of the five years (line g). The value to year 5 (the sum of each of the five years in line g) is $129.11, as shown as line h in the example. In addition, an annuity amount must be added to the royalty rate total to account for the future income beyond year 5; that amounts to $144.35. When this is combined with the discounted cash flow value of $129.11, it gives a total brand value of $273.46. This is the current value of the brand based on this methodology. Accordingly, if the marketer were to franchise the brand or pay a royalty for its use, this is the amount that would be paid, or the value of the brand to its owner.

Economic Use Method

Since this is the preferred method of estimating or calculating the value of a brand or brand equity, it is explained in detail in the next section. The approach is based on the theory that incremental earnings are

Table 14.2 Royalty Relief Method
Simplified Example

		Year 0	Year 1	Year 2	Year 3	Year 4	Year 5
Net sales	a	$500.00	$520.00	$550.00	$580.00	$620.00	$650.00
Royalty rate	b	10%	10%	10%	10%	10%	10%
Royalty income	c	$50.00	$52.00	$55.00	$58.00	$62.00	$65.00
Tax rate		33%	33%	33%	33%	33%	33%
Tax	d	$16.50	$17.16	$18.15	$19.14	$20.46	$21.45
Net royalty	e	$33.50	$34.84	$36.85	$38.86	$41.54	$43.55
Discount rate		15%					
Discount factor	f	1.00	1.15	1.32	1.52	1.75	2.01
Discounted cash flow	g		$30.30	$27.86	$25.55	$23.75	$21.65
Value to year 5	h	$129.11					
Annuity	i	$144.35					
Growth	0%						
Brand value		$273.46					

Used with permission from Brand Finance.

derived from the ownership of the brand and that the value of the brand is the future income flows that will accrue to the brand owner. The significance of the economic use method is that there is strong evidence to show that if the brand valuation is well constructed, it can provide managerial insights into the brand's impact on the overall business model.

The example that follows explains how the economic use model works. It was developed by Brand Finance, plc, a London-based consultancy specializing in brand valuation.

How Economic Use Methodology Works: The Brand Finance Model

This model of brand valuation starts by determining present and projected future earnings that the brand will likely generate. These income flows are then discounted to bring them back to some type of net present value. The discounted cash flow (DCF) approach, explained and illustrated in the following sections, is the most common and accepted method of accounting for future income streams.

The Brand Finance model is shown in Exhibit 14.5. The model consists of three basic parts:

- A determination of the brand segmentation and current business forecasts
- A brand value-added (BVA) index that is used to determine the branded value of income streams
- A Brand Beta analysis that is used to determine the discount rate to account for risk and the present value of money

Brand Segmentation and Business Forecasting

First, the value of the brand is determined by using financial data (historical sales and profit information that management uses to operate the

Exhibit 14.5 Brand Valuation Model

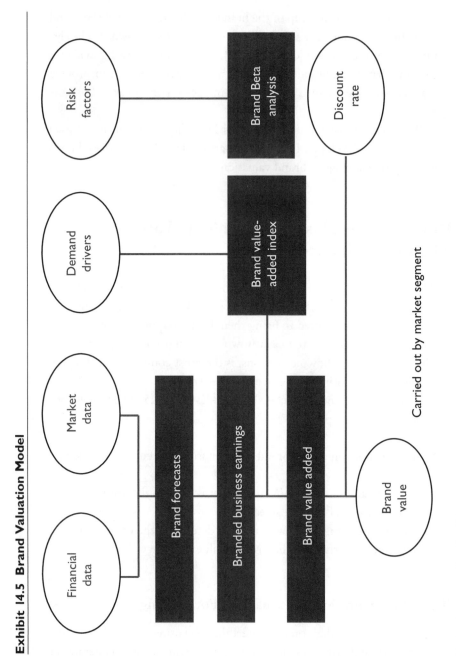

Used with permission from Brand Finance.

business) and combining it with market data factors such as growth rates, share of market, distribution patterns, and the like. From this, brand forecasts are determined through internal and external firm and market data analysis.

These brand forecasts are then separated into branded and non-branded business earnings. This is accomplished by determining what portion of earnings is attributable to the firm's tangible assets (plant, machinery, inventory, and so on) using a notional rate of return on the capital invested. Earnings above this level are considered attributable to the firm's intangible assets, primarily the brand. This figure may also include factors for such items as patents, customer lists, and so on that create specific value for the owner of the brand. The determination of branded versus nonbranded earnings varies substantially from one industry or category to the next and may even vary from one company to another within a given category. For example, in a highly capital-intensive industry such as airlines, utilities, or paper manufacturing, one would expect the overall contribution of the brand earnings to be a lower percentage than those in categories such as fashion apparel, cosmetics, or packaged goods, where tangible resources and capital investments are not nearly so critical.

Critical to the brand valuation process is finding the right level of segmentation for the brand and the business. Segmentation can use existing company approaches, or in some cases, new segmentation approaches must be developed by the analysts. The segments must be homogeneous and can be developed by geography, product, channel, demographics, or other identifiers. In many cases, the segmentation approach is defined by the availability of data. The critical ingredients of any segmentation approach are driven by market and market research information, financial data, and competitor brand information. Understanding the value of the brand to each of the market segments is key to the approach, since it is how the customer values the brand that is the critical variable in the process.

Once the branded business earnings have been isolated, the next step is to determine the key drivers of the brand in order to determine the brand value added and ultimately the financial valuation of the brand.

Demand Drivers and BVA Index

The second step in the brand valuation process is to understand the demand drivers, that is, what elements are responsible for the acceptance and value of the brand in the marketplace. Brand Finance calls the sum and averaging of these drivers the BVA index. As depicted in Exhibit 14.6, the drivers of demand vary by customer type, channel, and so on. Thus, a complete and detailed examination of the drivers for the specific brand in the specific market is required. The critical ingredient is an understanding of how brand preferences are developed and how they are impacted or influenced by switching barriers and switching inducements, all of which result in purchase behavior that is ultimately illustrated through sales volume and financial value. When the BVA index is applied to the branded business earnings, the actual brand value added is determined.

Risk Factors and Brand Beta Analysis

Through the first two steps, the development of the model allows the analyst to determine an estimate of the brand's contribution to earnings at a given point in time. However, since the true purpose of the model is to estimate the ongoing value of the brand into the future, an assessment must be made of the likelihood that brand earnings will continue, grow, or perhaps even decline. Thus, the final element in the brand valuation model is an assessment of risk to the organization that the forecasts are accurate and predictive; this drives the determination of an appropriate discount factor to be applied to brand earnings.

Risk can be defined in a number of ways, the most common of which is the risk that historical experience will not continue into the future, that is, that the future will not be like the past. To assess the various factors that could shape the brand's future potential, Brand Finance uses a proprietary Brand Beta analysis template to score the brand on a series of ten factors, namely time in market, distribution, market share, market position, sales growth rate, price premium, elasticity of price, marketing spend/support, advertising awareness, and brand awareness. The

Exhibit 14.6 Understanding the Drivers of Demand

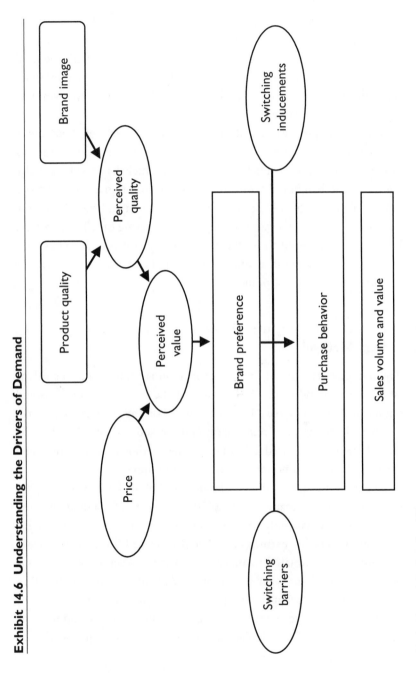

brand is scored from 0 to 10 on each factor, using both behavioral and attitudinal measures to arrive at a total score. The brand is rated on the basis of a maximum ten points for each of the attributes, with the total providing the rating of the brand. It should be noted that the total score is not the actual value but is used instead to develop a comparison rating scheme, as illustrated in Exhibit 14.7.

In this example, two brands are compared in terms of their scores on the various attributes. The scores are then converted into ratings ranging from AAA to D. Here, brand X, which has a substantially higher rating than brand Y on almost every factor, is given a total score of 83 and a rating of AA. Brand Y, which outperforms brand X on only two factors, has a total score of only 58 and a rating of BB. Therefore, Brand Y is considered to be the riskier of the two brands. Thus, one would expect a higher discount rate to be applied to its future earnings estimate than to that of brand X.

Brand Valuation Output: Discounted Future Earnings Method

The output of the Brand Finance evaluation is summed up in a calculation called brand value. An example of the various calculations and outputs is shown in Table 14.3. This is based on the same earnings forecast used in the royalty relief method discussed earlier. Although the same discount rate is used in both cases, this method evaluates the brand at a slightly higher amount, at least in this example.

As before, we start with net sales in year 0 of $500.00. Sales are projected to grow at a steady pace to $650.00 by year 5. (It should be noted that net sales exclude unbranded and own-label production by the organization.) Operating earnings are then determined. In the earlier case, earnings were estimated to increase 15 percent each year on a compounded basis. Thus, year 0 earnings of $75.00 increase to $97.70 in year 5 with the relevant figures presented for the intervening years.

The next step is to segment earnings into their tangible and intangible components. This calculation is to determine what proportion of

Exhibit 14.7 Brand Beta Index Scoring Profile

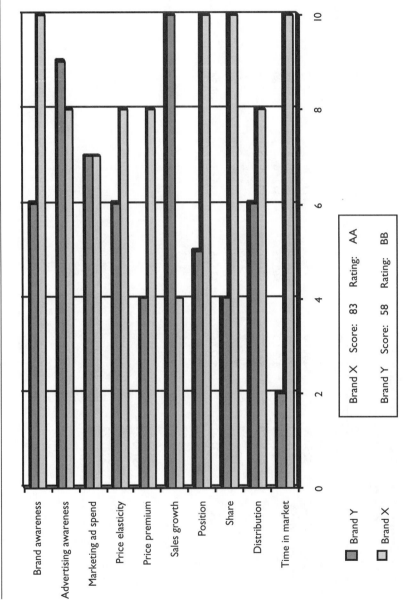

Brand X   Score: 83   Rating: AA

Brand Y   Score: 58   Rating: BB

Brand Y

Brand X

Used with permission from Brand Finance.

Table 14.3 Simple Brand Valuation Example
DISCOUNTED FUTURE EARNINGS METHOD

		Year 0	Year 1	Year 2	Year 3	Year 4	Year 5
Net sales		$500.00	$520.00	$550.00	$580.00	$620.00	$650.00
Operating earnings	a	$75.00	$78.00	$82.50	$87.00	$93.00	$97.50
Tangible capital employed		$250.00	$260.00	$275.00	$290.00	$310.00	$325.00
Charge for capital @ 5%	b	$12.50	$13.00	$13.75	$14.50	$15.50	$16.25
Intangible earnings	c	$62.50	$65.00	$68.75	$72.50	$77.50	$81.25
Brand earnings @ 75%	d	$46.88	$48.75	$51.56	$54.38	$58.13	$60.94
Tax rate		33%	33%	33%	33%	33%	33%
Tax		$15.47	$16.09	$17.02	$17.94	$19.18	$20.11
Posttax brand earnings	e	$31.41	$32.66	$34.55	$36.43	$38.94	$40.83
Discount rate		15%					
Discount factor	f	1.00	1.15	1.32	1.52	1.75	2.01
Discounted cash flow	g	$31.41	$28.40	$26.12	$23.95	$22.27	$20.30
Value to year 5	h	$152.45					
Annuity	i	$135.33					
Growth 0%							
Brand value		$287.78					

Used with permission from Brand Finance.

earnings can be attributed to the firm's hard, tangible assets (plant, equipment, materials, and so forth) and how much to its intangible assets (such as its brand or brands). In order to make this distinction, it is necessary to estimate the tangible capital employed in the development and production of the product for which the calculation is being developed. Tangible capital employed includes fixed and working capital at the current market value. In this example of a manufacturing company, the capital employed consists of the plants, factories, conversion equipment, and the like employed in the process of manufacturing the company's products and services. This amounts to $250.00 in year 0, increasing to $325.00 in year 5. This illustrates the increasing tangible capital employed of 50 percent of net sales that is being compounded annually. To understand the brand value, some notional rate or remuneration must be paid the firm for the use of this tangible capital and the facilities provided. The rate used in this example is a charge for capital of 5 percent of the tangible capital employed each year. (Note that this charge for capital is the "real" rate, excluding inflation.) In essence, the first 5 percent of earnings will be allocated to the tangible capital employed for any given year. As shown, that amounts to $12.50 in year 0 ($250.00 × 5%), increasing to $16.25 in year 5 ($325 × 5%). The balance of earnings in each year is therefore attributed to the firm's intangible assets.

The intangible earnings amount (line c) is obtained by deducting the charge for capital (line b) from operating earnings (line a). In year 0, operating earnings are $75.00 less the charge for capital ($12.50), leaving the intangible earnings at $62.50.

The next step is to calculate or estimate the amount of intangible earnings directly generated or contributed by the brand. In this example, the brand was calculated or estimated to contribute 75 percent of the value of all intangible earnings, meaning that most of this particular firm's intangible earnings come from its brands, with a small portion (25 percent) attributed to its patents, human capital, and other factors. As shown in line d, when calculated at 75 percent of intangible earnings, the brand earnings for this firm amount to $46.88 in year 0 and are estimated to rise to $60.94 in year 5.

Taxes, either current or future, must be deducted from the brand earnings to arrive at posttax brand earnings (line e). The tax rate used in this example is 33 percent, a fairly standard figure for most types of companies in most developed economies. Taxes in year 0 amount to $15.47 (33 percent of the brand earnings in line d) and rise to $20.11 in year 5. Subtracting these taxes from the branded earnings results in the brand having an after-tax earning of $31.41 in year 0, which rises to $40.83 by year 5. This after-tax earnings estimate is the actual value the brand is expected to contribute to the firm over the next five years.

There is, however, more to the process. Cash today is generally more valuable than cash tomorrow, according to the rules of discounted cash flow. As already noted, estimated earnings must be discounted to accommodate the time value of money and the potential risks that brand earnings will not continue at the predicted pace. In this example, a discount rate of 15 percent has been established. (Note that the appropriate discount rate is based on a market, sector, and Brand Beta analysis.) This creates the discount factor (line f), which must be subtracted from the posttax brand earnings (line e). Line g gives the discounted cash flow for the brand starting with year 0 at 1.0 and rising to 2.01 in year 5. This amounts to 1.15 in year 1, resulting in a discounted brand earnings cash flow of $28.40 ($32.66/1.15). Periods that are further into the future are discounted more heavily; for example, a factor of 2.01 applied to year 5 results in a discounted cash flow estimate of $20.30 ($40.80/2.01).

The next step is to determine the brand value through year 5. This is simply a matter of adding up the brand's discounted cash flow for years 0 through 5. As shown on line h, the value to year 5 for this example is $152.45.

There is one last step in determining the true value of the brand. So far we have only valued the brand through the end of year 5. Obviously, if the owner continues to market the brand beyond year 5, there must be some ongoing value from owning the brand into the future. This amount is determined by the calculation of the annuity shown on line i. In most cases, this is determined at a 0 percent growth rate. The annuity is simply the ongoing value of the brand into the future. This is estimated through the use of an annuity table, which is a common tool used in accounting and other financial activities. The annuity in this case has been calculated at $135.33 (line i). When the brand value to year 5 of $152.45 (line h) is combined with the annuity (line i), the total brand valuation in this example is $287.78.

What the Brand Valuation Really Means

Knowing the financial value of the brand is interesting and sometimes uplifting for management. But what does this knowledge actually mean to the marcom manager?

First, an understanding of the brand's estimated value can be a major aid to management, because it gives them a comparison of the value of the brand as a corporate asset so that it can be compared with the other, more tangible assets being managed. For example, using the calculations from the preceding example, if management knew that the value of a tangible asset—say, a plant or factory—was $25.00 and the value of the brand was $287.78, it would put the importance of managing the brand in a much better perspective. Simply knowing that brands are some of the most valuable assets the firm controls would provide excellent proof of the need for management and attention by the board of directors and senior operating managers.

Second, knowing the value of the brand provides a basic rule of thumb by which investments in the brand can be made and measured. If there is evidence that brand value is increasing or can be increased by 5 percent or so on a compounded basis each year, then an investment in marketing and brand communication of perhaps 1 or 2 percent might be a logical method of determining a brand investment budget. In the previous example, if only 1 percent of the current brand valuation were allocated for marketing and communication investments, that would amount to approximately $2.87 per year, a hefty and totally justifiable investment based on the asset value being protected or enhanced.

Third, determining brand value provides some basis for measuring returns on marketing and communication investments over the long term. If the firm knew that the brand value was $287.78, as in the example, this would then provide a base for measuring future returns on brand investments. For example, say an investment of $1.00 was made in the brand through a marcom program. That would have to be deducted from the discounted cash flow in year 0 and further discounted in years 1 through 5. Yet if posttax brand earnings were to increase by $2.00—in other words, if marcom could cover its costs and provide an additional $1.00 at the brand earnings line (line d in Table 14.3)—that would require only a 2 percent increase in posttax brand earnings to break even. Certainly, this would not seem an impossible task.

Thus, if the current value of the brand is known, managers can then rerun the valuation model each year, or more often if desired, taking into account investments in marketing and communication programs. The value those investments are creating for shareholders on an ongoing basis can be determined with a fair amount of accuracy. So, while such concepts as being able to charge premium prices, creating barriers to entry, reducing marketing costs, and the like are interesting methods of valuing the brand, they are not nearly as persuasive or rational as actually determining the increased shareholder value that can be generated by proper management of the brand. And, based on the Brand Finance model, it would seem that this would be possible for almost all organizations.

Moving On

With this discussion of brand value and brand valuation, we have completed the discussion of the five-step IMC process. There are, however, other topics that are relevant to developing and implementing a strategic IMC program. Those are organizational structure and barriers to implementation of an IMC approach, which are discussed in the next chapter.

CHAPTER 15

ORGANIZING FOR INTEGRATION

Clearly, a process-driven, systematic approach to marketing and marketing communication is the wave of the future. As the business environment becomes increasingly more complex and moves at an ever-faster pace, integrated marketing communication can spell the difference between success and failure. However, there is little question that the entire field suffers from a lack of formalized, structured approaches to help marcom managers develop and implement long- and short-term strategies and marcom programs. It is our belief that this book answers that demand by offering a strategic process for the implementation and financial measurement of marketing activities.

The question now becomes, why aren't the processes we describe—which make eminent good sense in today's finance-driven business environment—adopted and implemented by companies on a more consistent basis? The answer is organizational structure. This chapter examines how today's companies are organized and suggests changes that will help make integration a reality.

Organizational Issues That Impede Integration

Firms, companies, partnerships, and corporations—in fact, almost every type of organization imaginable—are hampered by a common problem that stifles attempts toward integration: ineffective organizational designs and obsolete organizational structures. In our experience, it is the structure of the organization that usually inhibits integration, alignment, and the efficient use of people and resources to achieve maximum returns from organizational investments. Only by developing processes and systems that coordinate and align all the functional elements of the organization can the output of the planned marketing and communication programs optimize cash flows and generate optimal shareholder value.

Unfortunately, most organizational structures today inhibit the company from serving customers effectively, efficiently, usefully, and consistently. As a result, they often fail in management's overall goal of generating cash flows and building shareholder value. Yet this need not be so. There are better means and methods. But to develop the types of processes and approaches outlined in this text, some organizational changes are generally required.

To understand how to develop an integrated organization, one must understand how to organize and align the firm's material resources, people, activities, and actions. In our more than a dozen years of consulting on IMC and helping organizations move toward an integrated marketing/brand/communication approach, we have found four major challenges that managers must address to develop effective, aligned organizations that can deliver integrated programs. The four specific areas that organizations must address are as follows:

- Moving from an internal to an external focus
- Developing horizontal communication systems
- Installing effective reward systems
- Building long-term customer and organizational value

Issue 1: Moving from an Internal to an External Focus

As we discussed in Chapter 1, the industrial-age organization was built on the concept of manufacturing, that is, specialization, assembly lines, processing, and efficiency. Thus, the organizational goal of most companies was to develop management approaches that were simple, direct, easy to set up, and—most of all—easy to direct and control. It was the age of "command and control," with a focus on time clocks, efficiency experts, and slavish operating systems. The human elements in the organization, either employees or customers, were not considered very relevant. The goal was economy of scale: the bigger, the better; the faster, the more efficient; the fewer changes, the more efficient the process and the greater the speed. In short, organizations were structured and designed to produce *outputs*, not to achieve relevant *outcomes*. And that is clearly reflected in the manner in which they were organized and how human resources were used.

Taking raw materials and turning them into finished products required specialization. In order to specialize, firms developed functional activities to handle such areas as accounting, finance, pricing, manufacturing, purchasing, and even sales and marketing. All the functional activities were designed to assist in the corporate goal of organizing, processing, manufacturing, and distributing products. Services, when there were any, were primarily designed to move the products through the system more easily or to inform or explain product benefits to buyers.

Marketing and marketing communication activities were developed over the years using much the same model. Because the organization made "stuff," the job of sales—for marketing was merely a hazy notion to a limited number of managers—was to get rid of, or sell, the stuff that the organization produced. Thus, the entire focus was on product movement. Find buyers. Find distributors. Find markets. It was the age of acquire, make, deliver, and (if necessary) inventory.

The result of all this internal product and delivery focus was the development of siloed and hierarchical organizations. As we explained in Chapter 3, the various functions—accounting, production, marketing, research and development, logistics, operations—in traditionally structured firms were designed to report upward through the ranks to top management. And the functional units controlled all the organization's activities. Thus, the functional manager became a mini-king in the organization. Build the function. Build the resources. Build the power of the function in comparison to other functional managers and activities. For senior management, the structure was simple, easy to control, and easy to manage—by controlling the functional heads, leaders could control the entire organization.

Since the functional managers reported up through the chain of command, their input eventually reached senior management. It was there, at the top of the pyramid, that everything was finally supposed to come together. From that lofty perch, senior management was supposed to be able to see how all the pieces and parts fit together and to be able to "manage" the organization for maximum shareholder or owner benefit.

Notice that there is no mention of customers. The entire focus of senior management was, and had to be, on managing internal activities, resources, people, and elements. The manufacturer was an internally focused, output-driven organization with little interest in customers.

Even the so-called new marketing approach introduced by Procter & Gamble in the 1930s, which was based around the brand or product manager, still focused on the product rather than on customers, users, or prospects. The product manager still interacted with various other functions, including manufacturing and distribution, research and development, legal, market research, sales, purchasing, packaging, media, and advertising. But there was not a customer in sight. All contacts were internal. All activities were focused on building a better product or finding a better way to operate or a more efficient use of finite corporate resources. In short, the goal was to find the best and most efficient way to get rid of the stuff the organization made.

While one might argue that there is an inherent focus on the customer, consumer, or end user in any type of manufacturing organization, even in the brand or product manager system, most experience shows that functional managers focus on what they perceive to be important or what they are rewarded for doing. The entire structure rests on what senior managers use as their criteria to judge success— commonly increased sales and profits. Again, there isn't a customer in sight.

It is to put the customer squarely in the picture that IMC recommends an organizational structure that, rather than looking inward, looks outward and focuses on customers and prospects rather than product. Achieving this external perspective requires a revamp of the organizational structure and that can generally only be done by senior management. That is why so many attempts at organizational change by midlevel managers commonly fail. The midlevel manager, no matter how dedicated, does not have the power, prestige, or influence to enact substantial organizational changes. And worst of all, many midlevel managers do not have the influence to attract the attention of top management to get the required assistance in making those changes. Thus, to truly integrate the firm, the first step is to find a senior management champion to help drive the revamping process.

As we showed in Chapter 3, achieving an external perspective means putting the customer at the center of the organization. Look again at Exhibit 3.3 on page 52. It is not until the customer becomes the nexus of the organization that any meaningful integration of management, product development and delivery, and certainly marketing and communication become possible. Thus, the structure of the organization becomes the critical element for success in the development of an effective IMC program.

In an integrated and customer-centric organization, the managerial focus shifts from managing products or even brands to managing customers and customer groups. This means the primary interest of the firm must be in determining what customers or prospects want or need, not on what the organization can make or do. That is why steps 1 and 2 of the IMC process are important. Knowing, understanding, and aggregating customers and prospects is how the firm can become customer focused. But again, while the marcom manager can lead the charge, he or she will need the support of senior management to make any IMC process work.

Unfortunately, customer focus is not something even top management can dictate. It requires support at all levels of the organization. Customer focus is not just born from a series of organizational charts, management memos, or employee pep rallies. It comes from a real commitment by everyone in the organization, both internally and externally, to putting customers first.

All this means that integration is not something that can be entered into lightly, nor is it something that can be done by one or two of the functional groups no matter how well they work together. It is a totally new way of operating the firm. And while integration may be difficult, it is not impossible, as dozens of organizations like Dow Chemical,

USAA, Nordstrom, Starbucks, IBM, FedEx, CIGNA Insurance, Ben & Jerry's, Hyatt International, and others have demonstrated over the past few years.

In spite of what some managers believe or have been told, customer focus and customer relationships also are not created as the result of the installation of the latest technology or software. Customer focus is built on a base of directing the attention of the firm toward acquiring, building, and maintaining customers over time. In other words, the goal must be to build ongoing customer relationships, not to find less expensive forms of contact management or identifying cross selling or upselling opportunities for the firm. And that takes time and effort on the part of all areas of the organization. USAA, one of the most successful of all customer-oriented firms, does not attribute its success to having the most sophisticated software or computer systems in place. Indeed, because the company has been built over a period of time, many of its systems and processes are legacy-based and some of its software is several years old. Instead, it is the vision and values and mission of the organization to which every employee subscribes that really drives the company toward a customer focus. Employees and management are totally devoted to serving customers, not just to selling insurance or financial products. USAA is customer focused from top to bottom, and its 98 percent customer retention rate is proof that the system works.

Several successful companies have achieved customer focus by moving from a strictly functional organizational structure to one based on processes and outcomes. Marketing moves from being a separate functional group to acting as a supplier and supporter of the cross-functional teams and groups that fit and furnish the capabilities, resources, and processes needed by the entire organization to serve customers properly. In this type of firm, marketing and marcom commonly work with and through the various cross-disciplinary teams, whether they have been designed to obtain new customers, manage present customers, or help migrate customers through the product portfolio.

This does not mean that there is one clear way to restructure. There are any number of methods. The key ingredients, however, are the same: a focus on outcomes, not outputs; the development of cross-functional teams to achieve specific goals and results; and an emphasis on customer satisfaction rather than market share or product volume. Those are the things that really drive customer-centric organizations.

Exhibit 15.1 illustrates the various customer management activities required in a customer-focused organization. It shows how customer and prospect acquisition and retention might best be set up. Here, the organization is structured around the four primary customer tasks of customer acquisition, customer retention, current customer growth, and migration of customers through the firm's product or service portfolio.

New customer acquisition is shown on the left side of the chart. These activities and people are focused on designing, identifying, valuing, and acquiring desirable new customers. At the opposite end of the management system are the retention specialists. These people and their activities are focused on maintaining customers and their income flows over time. This might be done by keeping present customers satisfied; making sure they are served quickly and efficiently; and most of all, providing whatever is needed to ensure that they will continue doing business with the company in the future.

In the center of the organization are customer/product managers. These are the people who match products to customers and customers

Exhibit 15.1 Structure to Manage Customers

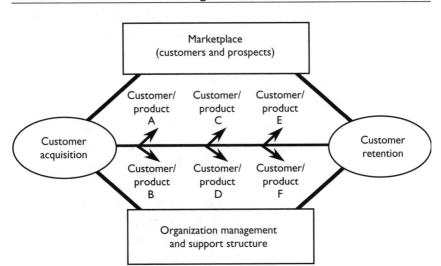

to products during the time customers do business with the firm. The managers' job is to find the "fits" between customer needs and what the company can provide in terms of products and services. As shown, these managers are responsible for managing a group of customers. They do that by identifying the group's needs, by understanding its requirements, and by helping its members find the products and services they need or want either within or outside the organization. While many companies view these activities and the management of customers as "cross selling" or "add-on selling," they only work when customer needs are satisfied with other products or services, not just by selling products the organization wants to sell or believes the customer should buy.

Exhibit 15.1 also shows that, in some cases, customers will move beyond the areas of expertise of their particular customer/product manager. In those situations, the internal manager may shift the customer to another group or another manager who is better able to serve that customer's needs or wants. In some cases, those products or services may be inside the organization as shown in the chart. In others, customer needs and wants may require the manager to go outside the firm to find the required products or services. That's why affiliations and associations with other companies are so important in managing customers effectively.

Once an organizational customer focus has been achieved, the next natural step is to find ways to develop horizontal internal communication systems. That subject is the topic of the next section.

Issue 2: Developing Horizontal Communication Systems

The second issue related to the development of an integrated organizational structure is the need to develop processes that encourage and enable horizontal communication systems. That need becomes apparent when one looks at the traditional structure of marketing organizations. For example, in a large, complex organization with multiple lines of business such as a petroleum company, the marketing department would generally be specialized by function and by product (that is, product supply and transportation, asphalt sales, pricing, construction, wholesale marketing, retail marketing, and marketing operations). Further, each manager typically would have a number of specialists reporting to or through him or her, always in a vertical mode. Each manager, in turn, would report upward to the marketing vice president at the top of the structure. Generally, none of the functional units have any responsibility for customers, only for products or tasks. Furthermore, all organizational communication is typically driven from the top down or from the bottom up, with limited cross-functional exchange. That's the major challenge of vertical communication systems: trying to find ways to communicate internally.

The problem is compounded, of course, if managers in different units have the same customer with similar questions, concerns, and relationships with the firm. The organizational structure is the primary obstacle preventing these managers from having a common customer view, as there is no efficient or effective way for them to know about the common needs of the customer and no way for them to provide a common company solution or communication approach to solve that problem. In short, the traditional hierarchical organizational structure is set up to encourage vertical and discourage horizontal communication within and among the various functions of the firm. Clearly, if integration is to occur, there is a need for some type of horizontal process to enable the units to work across these structural barriers to achieve some type of activity and communication integration.

Management theorist Adrian Payne maintains that this challenge is one of the primary factors preventing organizations from becoming customer focused. Exhibit 15.2 illustrates both the problem and his solution.

According to Payne, most organizations develop their internal operating systems and processes around siloed functions. The vertical triangles under marketing, finance, human resources, information technology, and operations demonstrate this. The managers of each of these functional groups report upward to the chief executive officer (CEO). Without an integrated approach to planning, each functional group develops its own individual system or operational process.

Payne argues that what is really needed today is a horizontal approach to planning that can unite and integrate the functional ele-

Exhibit 15.2 Integration of Planning Processes

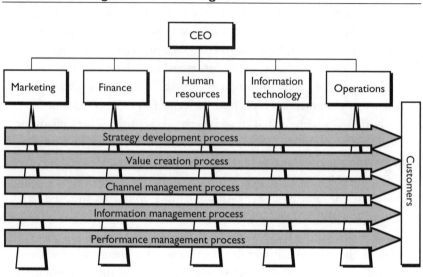

Adapted from Adrian Payne, "Customer Relation Management" (presented at Northwestern University, Evanston, IL, November 11, 2001). Used with permission from Adrian Payne.

ments across the vertical silos. This alternative, cross-functional planning system is represented by the horizontal arrows in the exhibit. The functional experts within each vertical area are now united by common processes for strategy development, value creation, channel management, information management, and performance management. These five processes are all focused on aligning the activities of the organization toward serving the customer or customers the firm has identified.

The most important value of Payne's approach is that by developing these processes on a horizontal, rather than the typical vertical basis, the organization can cut across the various functional groups and align and integrate all of its resources to meet the needs and requirements of customers and prospects. That's what is meant by customer focus and customer orientation.

Obviously, when horizontal processes are developed, they enable all units to be connected and coordinated to serve customers and prospects rather than just attend to the various internal activities of the firm. Furthermore, these processes provide natural horizontal communication systems so that customers and functions are connected through various ongoing communication dialogues. It is through these types of horizontal processes and approaches that real integration of marketing and marketing communication can occur.

Issue 3: Installing Effective Reward Systems

The third requirement for integration and customer focus is that the managers and employees need to be rewarded for what is most important to the organization: obtaining and maintaining customers. This simply means that managers and employees must be rewarded based on how well they serve customers and prospects, not on how many products or units or services they have sold for the company. Recall the four basic customer tasks we've described. When the organization moves to a customer focus, it becomes natural for it to begin to deliver on new organizational objectives: the development and maintenance of customers and their income flows. This customer income flow approach to management is a direct result of steps 1 and 2 in the IMC process (customer identification and valuation) and step 4 (calculation of return on customer investment). In short, managers and employees should be rewarded on the basis of how well they have managed to acquire, maintain, grow, and migrate customers and their income flows through the organization.

A reward system based on customer income flows makes a dramatic change for many organizations. When the firm starts to consider customer income flows as a method of management and employee reward, the focus shifts from functional activities to customer understanding and customer relationships. Further, this new system encourages employees to become responsible for the financial management of customers, not just the mastery of tactical activities. The big change, of course, is that the organization must begin to make what were formerly its innermost secrets—product margins, profits, costs, and the like—available to managers and line employees. How can an employee determine how to allocate his or her time, skills, efforts, and resources without knowing who the most important and valuable customers are; what general return is being gained from each customer or customer group; and how the acquisition, maintenance, and growth of a customer or customer group impacts the overall success of the organization? Indeed, moving to a customer focus means making such substantial changes in the organization. Without it, there is little hope for integration or the development of an integrated marketing and communication process.

Since the identification, valuation, and estimation of customer income flows and their returns was covered in some detail in previous chapters, we need not belabor the point that employee rewards should be based on customer income flows. But it is clear that the management of income flows, generally meaning cash flows and customer profits, is and will continue to be a critical element in the success of firms and the development of shareholder value.

Issue 4: Building Long-Term Customer and Organizational Value

One of the most difficult tasks in developing an integrated organization is moving the financial focus from the typical quarterly report—every ninety days—to one in which long-term values become equally important. While most marketing and communication managers rail against the current organizational scorecard of quarterly financial reports to shareholders, many do not realize that it is not the market that is creating this short-term reporting pressure. Instead, it is the accounting system the organization employs that is at the root of this orientation.

For the most part, accounting has not changed much in the past five hundred years since the Venetians invented double-entry bookkeeping. At that time and ever since, the focus has been on accounting for the tangible assets an organization owns or controls. Accounting has meant just that: accounting for changes in the value of those tangible assets, which have commonly included cash, land, buildings, inventories, equipment, and the like. Thus, accounting has focused on regular evaluations of tangible assets, usually once a year, to determine any difference in value. As accounting became more important to investors over the years, it took the shape of more frequent reports, now the quarterly reports that are so common for publicly held companies.

The problem with accounting is, of course, that everything accounted for traditionally has some tangible, physical form. That tangible form must be accounted for in terms of what the asset is worth now compared to what it was worth in some earlier period. Thus, traditional accounting is always looking back over its shoulder to compare present situations or values with previous examples. The problem, of course, is that today tangible assets make up only a small portion of the market value of many organizations, as we discussed in Chapter 13.

Fortunately, new accounting approaches are being developed to help firms account for these intangible values, one of the most critical of which is the treatment of the organization's brand or brands (see Chapter 14). Several financial and accounting firms have created ways of approaching this topic; these methods range from Stern Stewart's Economic Value Added methodology to PricewaterhouseCooper's Value Reporting procedures.[1] All, however, are focused on moving the view of the value of the organization from what historical worth has been to what future worth might be. And when one starts to consider future value, that quickly elevates customers, customer income flows, customer retention, and all the other activities necessary and required in an IMC approach to a higher level of importance.

It is clear the new financial, accounting, and valuation approaches will revolve around future value rather than historical worth, which means the organization will likely start to focus on the future in terms of how it measures itself. To us, that means future organizational value will depend on all the things discussed so far in this text. It also means the view of the organization and its value will move from a retroactive one of what it earned or the value it created over ninety days to a proactive view of what value it might or could achieve in the next two, five, or even ninety years.

This move to future value is a major one that every publicly held firm must face. From the view of the IMC manager, this can only be a move for the better, for it will require that the organization take a customer focus and organize around customers and their value, not products and services and their movement or distribution.

Useful Organizational Designs for the Integrated Organization

As we have shown, marketing and communication have historically been managed as functional activities within the firm. Depending on how important marcom was thought to be, the organizational structure of the company varied. In his seminal marketing text, *Marketing Management*, Philip Kotler chronicled the evolution of the marketing department in modern organizational design.[2] According to Kotler, marketing has moved from being subservient to sales to existing on a more equal footing. For example, in a sales-driven company, the sales force is the primary form of customer contact, and marketing (if there is such a function) is often thought to be simply an activity that supports the firm's selling efforts. In such cases, marketing communication activities are often delegated to a relatively junior employee or outsourced to a marketing services firm.

In a more modern and market-oriented organization, the marketing function moves up in stature and is considered of equal importance to the sales function. However, sales and marketing are often still separated as functionally distinct activities, reporting up to a vice president of sales and marketing. In these cases, sales is commonly responsible for contact with channel customers, while marketing generally acts as the research and planning function, possibly developing sales collateral material as well as communication to end users.

Of more importance, however, is how the marketing function should be structured in an organization that is or is in the process of moving to a customer focus. While many organizational designs are still oriented toward a series of functional groups, the marketing and communication areas are generally much more developed. The Conference Board has compiled numerous examples of how leading marketing-oriented companies have structured their marcom functions. An example of one contemporary and sophisticated structure is shown in Exhibit 15.3.

While the marketing group is highly specialized in this design, note that the communication activities are spread across and through the various marketing functions. For example, the senior director of marketing management is responsible for promotions, competitive analysis, and

Exhibit 15.3 Marketing Chart from The Conference Board

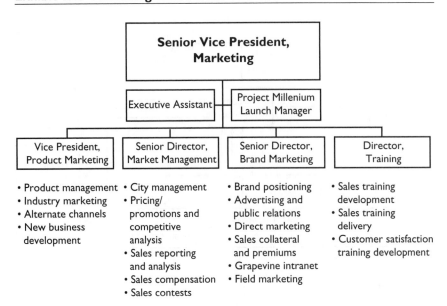

sales contests, whereas the senior director of brand marketing is responsible for advertising and public relations, and the director of training is responsible for sales training. Thus, the various ways in which the organization touches customers and prospects are spread throughout the marketing group with no real consistent customer focus or control.

A much better design, or at least one that combines all forms of marketing and communication into a coordinated and consolidated approach, was first developed in *Integrated Marketing Communications*[3] and is shown in Exhibit 15.4. Here, the marketing manager and communication manager are on equal levels. Marketing is primarily responsible for the identification and valuation of customers (steps 1 and 2 in the IMC process), while marketing communication is responsible for step 3, the development and delivery of communication programs. Of particular importance is the fact that marcom develops and implements both internal and external communication programs, in addition to being involved with senior management communication activities. In this design, marcom is responsible for all major types of communica-

Exhibit 15.4 Marcom Management Structure

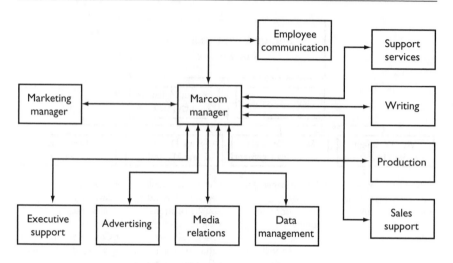

tion. That's a key ingredient in the development of an effective and integrated IMC program.

While this is an effective way to handle communication activities, it is still based on a functional approach, that is, the managers are responsible for activities and not customers. One of the best ways to manage customer communication is to focus the organization on customer markets. An example of this type of structure is illustrated in Exhibit 15.5. All activities related to the customer are organized under a customer or market team. The team consists of all the functional groups and corporate activities that are necessary to identify customers and their needs, determine their value, identify how products and services might be needed or wanted, decide how those products or services might be distributed to them, and so on. Thus, the organizational structure of a firm might consist of a number of customer or market segment teams all focused on specific and identifiable customer groups. When this type of structure is combined with the acquisition/retention approach illustrated in Exhibit 15.1, the organization becomes totally customer focused and customer driven, particularly in the areas of marketing and communication. Indeed, a process structure as advocated by Payne can often be developed. This approach seems to work for almost any type of organization, no matter what its products or services.

Exhibit 15.5 Market Segment Management

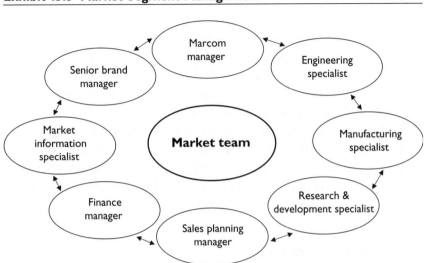

In this section, we have assumed that firms will plan, develop, and implement most of the marketing communication activities internally. Such is not usually the case. Thus, a view of how firms can develop effective structures to make use of external resources such as advertising or public relations agencies, direct marketing, database groups, and the like should be helpful.

How to Work with External Communication Groups

Not all the planning, development, and implementation of most marketing communication activities occurs internally. More often, companies must depend on outside resources to contribute many of the components of their communication programs. Such external resources include ad agencies, public relations firms, direct marketing, and database groups that provide an array of skills and level of expertise not usually found within the organization.

As we have recommended throughout this book, marketing and marcom groups should put their efforts into the development of communication strategy rather than into tactical communication activities. This is not to say that tactics and implementation are unimportant, but the increasingly vital role for the organization is the development of communication strategies to lead and support its overall objectives and goals. Thus, in the strategic IMC approach, the marcom manager becomes the strategist, relying on a cadre of implementation specialists to develop the actual communication programs.

This change in role requires an organizational structure that allows the manager to operate at the strategic level and supervise the development of the specific programs. Several organizational structures can provide this type of relationship with external vendors. Several of the most relevant of these are discussed here.[4]

Client-Centered Integration

Client-centered integration allows the marcom manager to become a "communication czar" responsible for the relationship with all external communication vendors. Within this structure, there is one central contact with whom all external suppliers work. This can be one person or perhaps a team responsible for the various areas of marketing communication. This person or team serves as the central hub of all internal communication activities and acts as the conduit between the client organization and the various external resources and suppliers.

Federal Integration Structure

In the client-centered structure, external vendors are managed as separate units—that is, any integration is done internally by the client organization. An alternative approach—known as federal integration structure—allows the client organization and its various external suppliers to share responsibility for the integration of communication programs. Inherent in this structure is the need for the external vendors to work together to help deliver an IMC program for the client.

Commonly, this type of structure is used when there is a client organization that needs a wide variety of communication skills and abilities that might only be available from separate, distinct business groups such as are often found in the major communication holding groups. Examples might be such groups as Interpublic, WPP, Havas, and Omnicom. Although it is assumed that "sister agencies" operating under a global umbrella can work together, this is not always the case. As a result, while this structure looks good on paper, it is often difficult to implement in practice. It becomes even more complex and difficult when communication vendors come from competing organizations and agency groups where there is often pressure on each to obtain more of the overall communication budget or investment for that functional area.

Lead Agency Structure

One method of achieving the objective of having external vendors work together to develop an integrated marketing communication program is to have one vendor, often an agency of some type, serve as the lead for the entire communication effort. In this way, a single vendor serves as the leader for all the others. The lead agency works directly with the client organization to not only help develop the communication strategy, but to provide some of the implementation or activities as well. One of the primary roles of the lead agency is to coordinate the activities of other external vendors, which might include an events group, a promotional agency, a direct marketing and fulfillment group, and so on. Here, the lead agency takes on the sole responsibility for developing a truly integrated program. This gives the client organization one contact point even though the lead agency may be working with several market or customer segment groups within that client organization or may even be working with separate client functional groups.

The Global Structure

Increasingly, as organizations find it necessary to develop integrated global marketing and communication programs, the need for integration both inside and outside the firm becomes apparent. Exhibit 15.6 illustrates one example of how a global integration structure might be developed.

Here, the client organization has centralized its communication activities in some type of communication group. That group works

Exhibit 15.6 Global Integration Structure

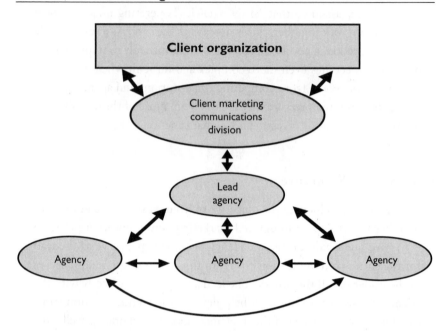

From David Pickton and Amanda Broderick, *Integrated Marketing Communications*, © Pearson Education Limited, 2001, reprinted by permission of Pearson Education Limited.

directly with the other groups in the organization to bring together all the communication activities to a central point. The same is done on the agency or vendor side. A single lead agency or group coordinates all the external vendors and suppliers and serves as a central point of contact for the client.

This type of organization is particularly effective for firms that are managing a global brand or brands. As shown, there is central, global control over all marketing communication activities from the client side. Likewise, there is central control among the various agencies. Thus, global programs can be executed across many geographies through agencies or through local marcom groups. Where local or country-by-country agencies are used, this structure is particularly effective, since it provides the central control necessary for brand focus yet enables the individual markets or marketing groups to develop local or regional versions of a central theme. This structure epitomizes the concept of "think global and act local."

Moving On

This chapter has highlighted the problems associated with organizational structure that act as barriers to integration. It has also looked at alternative structures that may point the way forward for the development of IMC programs in the twenty-first century. We continue to look ahead to see what the future may hold in the next and concluding chapter.

CHAPTER 16

FUTURE DIRECTIONS FOR IMC

In our enthusiasm to extol the virtues of IMC as an evolving business theory and successful business practice, we have so far neglected to share insights into where this new approach to marketing communications is likely to take the marketing practitioner. In this final chapter, we attempt to provide that future direction and address new issues that are likely to emerge that both help and hinder the integration process. We have divided the chapter into two parts. First, we look at likely barriers, both internal and external, to the further development of IMC and how marcom managers can meet the challenges those barriers represent. Second, we set forth what we believe to be the natural next steps in integrated marketing communication in the future.

Barriers to Advances in IMC

When the concept of IMC developed more than ten years ago, we identified four barriers to its successful implementation:

- Resistance to change
- Organizational structures
- Capabilities and control
- Marketing planning systems

In spite of progress since then, all four barriers still exist to varying degrees. In spite of technological advances that have revolutionized the workplace, there is still tremendous resistance to any type of change in marketing and communication, both within and outside organizations. While data gathering and analysis have grown exponentially, there are still many firms that do not know who their customers are and have no way to determine their present value or potential. Mass marketing thinking is still with us. It is safe, comfortable, and what many current managers understand. The lessons of the "dot-bombs," which were here and gone in the blink of an eye, make people wary of putting too much faith in technology. So, while the industry has made giant steps toward an interactive and networked system of marketing and communication, there are still many skills to be developed in most organizations.

Organizations still struggle with how to become more customer focused or develop a customer-centric structure. The old "command and control" systems still persist, despite efforts to develop cross-functional teams and outsourced skills.

Though the flaws in traditional marketing planning systems have become more and more apparent over the years, too many organizations still hang on to the tired concept of the Four Ps of marketing: product, price, place, and promotion. Regardless of evidence to the contrary, marketers still believe that if they can manage those four functional activities, they can dominate the market. The problem? Customers are nowhere in sight in a Four Ps planning model.

The same is true of communication planning. The industry's reliance on the hierarchy of effects communication model with its singular, outbound approach to message distribution totally ignores the multitasking, multimedia-using customers and prospects of the early twenty-first century. It also assumes that the only contacts a customer has with a brand are those that the organization initiates and pays for.

Yes, old systems are hard to change. In our view, that is the major barrier to the rapid development and full implementation of IMC. Yet while they are slow to come about, there are signs that much-needed changes are occurring. Slow but sure, many organizations are transforming the way they develop their marketing and communication programs as the demand for accountability grows. Almost all marketing directors agree that integration is needed, and that need is increasingly driving their organizations. In truth, it is hard to find a marketing firm, a marketing director, or even a functionally focused agency that suggests a nonintegrated approach is the way of the future. It simply takes time. And it clearly takes more time in some organizations than others.

A Review of Mandatory Factors for Integration

In the early days of IMC, we identified four mandatory factors or prerequisites that would enable the integrated communication model to become a business reality:

- Integrated marketing communication must start at the top.
- The organization must be customer focused and practice customer-oriented marketing.
- Communication must become a sustainable competitive advantage for the firm.
- Communication must be centralized.

While some progress has been made in each of those areas, there is still a lot of room for improvement.

Starting at the Top

Over the last decade, senior managers have focused a great deal more attention on the overall impact of marketing on the success of the firms. Recognition of the importance of brands as intangible assets has grown, as has the need to understand and predict income flows from customers. Chief executive officers and chief financial officers are much more involved in the entire process of marketing, branding, and communication than they were a decade ago. The shift to a financial base to determine the success of the firm, using such concepts as increased cash flows and the development of shareholder value, has done much to raise the level of interest in how marketing and communication can contribute to those areas, both internally and externally. And the increasing pressure on top management to verify and justify its investments and allocations and to be responsible for the future financial success of the firm has certainly moved marketing and communication investments and returns to the top of senior managers' list of priorities.

Unfortunately, in some cases, marketing and communication management has not kept pace with the increasing attention and demands being made by company leaders. Most marketing managers, regardless of their background or experience, still have difficulty answering the three senior management questions we posed earlier:

• How much should we spend or invest in marketing and marketing communication?
• How much return will we receive from those investments?
• Over what period of time will those returns occur?

The value-based IMC approach described in this book provides the answers. This means that getting top management's attention and responding meaningfully to questions about investments and returns are eminently doable. To us, it is more a matter of making use of and implementing the approaches and concepts that have already been developed rather than continuously trying to create new concepts and approaches.

Being Customer Focused

There is little question that, for many companies, developing a customer-focused organization is still a "work in progress." The difference today is that for the first time marketers have the necessary tools to tackle the job. When IMC concepts first evolved, key technologies like databases, data analytics, and data modeling were just starting to emerge. Similarly, the ability to generate dialogues with customers—that is, true interactive discussions, not just outbound messages with bounce-back coupons attached—was in its infancy. All these developments mean that organizations increasingly have both the opportunities and the capabilities to listen to their customers wherever or however those contacts occur. For the first time, companies really have the ability to become customer focused.

Unfortunately, organizational structures still get in the way. Functional departments and turf wars continue to create internal challenges. Even so, customer-focused and customer-oriented organizations are becoming much more of a reality than they were ten years ago. And it is these outward-looking firms that are likely to grow faster, because they recognize that the real value of the firm is its customers—not its plants, factories, and inventories—and invest their resources accordingly.

Providing a Sustainable Competitive Advantage

Most forward-looking companies generally accept that communication, in its myriad forms, is a strategic resource and competitive tool. No longer do they think of a brand as simply the logo that appears on packages. Product and corporate brands are now legal tender in mergers and acquisitions. Senior management lives and dies based on the way it manages its brand responsibilities, as the CEOs of Ford, Arthur Andersen, and WorldCom learned to their chagrin. But there is still too great a disconnect between the brand and the organization. Too few managers understand that the brand represents all the organization is, does, and relates to customers. It is not some quixotic thing that is manufactured and delivered through a series of slick, clever television commercials.

One area we did not foresee in the early days of IMC was the huge increase in the importance of the brand. Nor did we foresee that by the mid-1990s the brand would become one of the firm's major corporate assets. As a result, many organizations still struggle with the whole concept of valuing intangible assets like brands and measuring returns on brand communication programs. These areas will still require much work in the future. One thing that has become evident, however, is that organizations increasingly recognize that they can use their communication resources as sustainable competitive advantages in support of brands in the hypercompetitive marketplaces of the twenty-first century.

Centralizing Communication

The last mandatory factor we identified when developing the IMC concept was that communication needed to be centralized as much as possible. That, we believe, is still a relevant point and probably will be even more important in the future. As we have moved further and further toward the brand as the centralizing element of the organization, clear direction and senior management control becomes even more important. With the value of some brands—such as Coca-Cola, Microsoft, Dell, and Boeing—running into the hundreds of millions of dollars, it is clear that brand management cannot be left to just anyone and everyone.

Further, we recognize that brands have to be adapted to the markets they are intended to serve. In other words, there is likely no single, monolithic brand image for most products or services. In fact, there may well be multiple brand images built around some central core of meaning. That is clearly not something that can be left to the local marcom director or the on-the-road manager. Thus, there must be a consolidated and articulated agreement within the organization of what the brand is, what it means, and how it should be represented to the world. This means an organization can't have three hundred local managers running off in all directions and interpreting the brand for their individual markets or needs, no matter how empowered they would like to be. So, there needs to be central control of the brand, particularly the corporate brand.

This does not mean, however, that the brand should be treated as a "corporate symbol" that is placed on a pedestal, never to be questioned or challenged. The brand is the organization and, as such, it is dynamic and ever-changing, just like the firm, product, or service it represents. But there must be central direction. There must be broad guidelines. There must be boundaries, such as where the brand can and cannot go. And these boundaries must come from the core of the organization— the senior managers and the employees who live and breathe the brand every day. So, communication must be centralized because the brand and brand communication must be clear, concise, and well orchestrated. And such a goal can only be reached by charging a small group with the responsibility and having it translate the brand to employees, share-holders, business affiliates, channel partners, suppliers, communities, and consumers.

Seven Future Challenges for IMC

The future of integrated marketing communication is bright. The foundation is well laid and the guiding principles we explored in Chapter 3 have been proven and continue to develop in the marketplace. Still, full implementation of IMC presents some remaining challenges which we identify here, along with their solutions. Overcoming these challenges enables IMC to perform to its fullest capacity, but these are not tasks that can be accomplished overnight. Instead, they are likely to evolve as principles that guide IMC to become the norm for all types of organizations. There are seven major challenges:

Challenge 1: Aligning Internal and External Marketing and Communication

Initially, IMC focused primarily on the outbound communication programs the firm developed and delivered to customers, consumers, and prospects outside the organization. Commonly, these consisted of activities such as advertising, public relations, direct marketing, sales promotion, events, sponsorships, and the like. All were developed internally and distributed externally. They typically consisted of messages and/or incentives the organization thought were important to customers and prospects and ones that appeared to have the greatest potential for financial return. Thus, IMC evolved as a method for coordinating and aligning the various external marketing communication activities. In some cases, IMC is still defined that way.

The rise of the importance of brands brought the importance of integrating communication touch points to the fore. These touch points—or brand contacts—were not limited to initiatives the marketer managed and controlled but included all the ways the customer or prospect came in contact with the product, service, organization, or brand.

Today, marketers are beginning to understand that internal communication is just as important as external communication or, in some cases, even more important. Getting customer-facing employees and associates to understand and deliver the firm's brand messages and support the customer's brand experiences is and absolutely will remain critical. In other words, it is as important for the organization's people to perform well as it is for the products or services. One cannot exist without the other.

Yet internal communication, or internal marketing, is often not within the purview of the marketing or communication manager. It typically falls to human resources, operations, or manufacturing—or to no one. So, one of the key ingredients in successful IMC in the future will be to align both internal and external communication programs so that customers have a consistent experience with the brand whenever, wherever, and however they touch the brand or the brand touches them. The firm must deliver what the marketing and communication promises. That's why internal marketing is the next major step in IMC development.

Nowhere is the need for integration and alignment more necessary than in bringing together sales and marketing activities. Unfortunately, in too many cases, sales and marketing are separated or siloed within the organization. Sales goes in one direction, focusing primarily on the retailers or resellers or on direct sales to end users. Marketing, while still involved with those same groups, goes in another direction, with the end result that customers at all levels are confused. Too often, it seems the actions and activities of the sales force are unrelated to what marketing is doing and vice versa. This is a prime area for the development of internal programs that will help align and integrate the entire organization.

Challenge 2: Moving to a Behavioral Base for Marcom Outcomes

As we have stated throughout this book, most marketing and communication evaluation is still based on some type of attitudinal measure or communication effect. That is, we evaluate the supposed effectiveness of marketing communication programs through measures of awareness, recall, recognition, and the like. While these are useful tools, they simply cannot be related to financial returns, which are the key to making any type of marketing or communication investment. So, one of the key elements that will drive the future of IMC will be the ability to identify financial returns from financial investments in marketing communication. That will require moving to a behavioral approach to measurement and evaluation. Instead of looking at how people feel, marketers will look at what they do. Behaviors result in actions, and actions result in sales. And the better the relationship between dollars out of and dollars back to the firm, the more solid the support for investments in marketing and communication.

Nowhere is this need for a move to behavioral measures more apparent than in the field of outbound media. Currently, all media models are based on delivery and hoped-for exposures as a result of broadcasting, print delivery, or even ambient media such as outdoor or place-based outlets. All the marketer currently knows is that the message was sent out. He or she doesn't know if anyone received it. Thus, for IMC to grow and prosper in the years ahead, behavioral measures of media planning and buying must be developed and made available to the marcom manager. The old days of evaluating the results of the campaign on the basis of how many messages were sent out or how many press mentions were received are—and should be—over. Marketers must find ways to connect broadscale forms of media to the behavior of those exposed to the message or incentive.

Challenge 3: Reversing the Flow of Marketing Communication Programs

For the most part, marcom programs have always been financed by the organization. That simply means the company has invested scarce resources to send communication to prospects and customers in the hope of generating an immediate or long-term sale. Since the marketer didn't really know who was buying the products or even who might be interested, the best approach was to cast a broad net and hope that through creative messages or substantial incentives, nonbuyers could be lured to make a purchase or commitment. When there were large numbers of nonusers, this approach worked, although there was still huge waste in terms of sending messages or incentives to people or organizations who would likely never buy or were not even prospects. It is this waste factor that now haunts many marketers, particularly since media alternatives have expanded almost geometrically and audiences have been driven down to almost noneconomic levels when compared to the cost of message and incentive distribution.

Over the past few years, however, it has become evident that the success of the organization depends as much on maintaining present customers as it does on acquiring new ones. Thus, the organization has been or should be able to reduce its overall marketing communication investments by focusing on existing customers or by directing its marketing and communication efforts toward those suspects, prospects, and customers who are the most likely to respond. The problem, however, is that even though marketers are becoming very sophisticated in terms of customer identification and the ability to predict customer responses, they still waste substantial amounts of money in developing and delivering messages and incentives to customers or prospects who, for any number of reasons, are either not ready to buy or not even ready to look or listen. Thus, it is incumbent on marketers to find ways to reduce their outbound marketing communication costs.

One way is to further develop interactive systems that allow customers and prospects to access information from the organization on demand. Whether that means Internet websites, automated telephone and fax lines, or the development of interactive and networked systems, it is clear that organizations must create two-way communication alternatives that allow customers to interact at their convenience and within their own time frames through the medium of their choice. In short, marketing communication can no longer be outbound and delivered according to its cost to the marketer. In the future, the goal must be to provide interactive systems that allow the buyer and seller to share the cost of communication. For example, presently, when a customer accesses an organization's website, it typically incurs a cost to the customer, not the marketer. While the marketer has invested in making the website available and has kept it refreshed and current, the customer accesses the information using his or her own resources—computer, telephone, or broadband connection—using his or her own time and efforts. In other words, the marketer has shifted some of the cost of communication to the customer. In many cases, customers not only accept that cost, they welcome it, because the convenience of the communication makes their life and their acquisition of needed and wanted information, products, and services much easier.

In many of today's organizations, there is a lack of integration in selling systems. That is, the sales force is disconnected from marketing, marketing efforts are disconnected from customer service, and manufacturing and operations are disconnected from delivery systems. For IMC to succeed, all communication systems must be interconnected and interactive so the customer is served and not impeded.

Challenge 4: Making the Brand the Key Element in the Marketing Effort

As technology has reduced the ability of the organization to make innovations in products or services, marketers must rely more and more heavily on brands and brand communication to sustain competitive advantages. This will be a major change for organizations that have viewed the brand as simply a product name and marketing communication as something that can be turned on and off like a spigot, depending on the whims of senior management.

Brand communication must move from being a simple tactical activity to becoming the primary strategic tool of the organization. As we explained in the opening chapters, the skill of firms to develop communication programs that build relationships with customers and prospects is probably the most important capability organizations will have in the twenty-first-century marketplace. For those skills to develop, senior management must be actively engaged in brands, in marketing, and in marketing communication. The people at the top must support the development of new marketing, communication, and branding concepts as aggressively as they presently support research and development of products and services.

It is this ongoing commitment to build relationships with customers through brands that will truly differentiate forward-moving organizations. And this will require investments on the part of the firm in marketing and communication programs; in research; and, most of all, in people. The skill levels of marketing managers must be improved on an ongoing basis, which will mean investments in research, training, and recruitment. But without skilled managers for the IMC programs, there will be slow and likely not very noticeable change.

Challenge 5: Developing a Global Perspective

When IMC concepts were first developed, the global marketplace was just emerging, with worldwide systems of communication, transportation, finance, and management still in their infancy. Today, all those capabilities are givens. What happens in any place in the world impacts almost every other part of the world. Yet leaders continue to manage organizations as if nothing had changed. They still look out the window expecting to see their customers and competitors.

We live in a global marketplace, and whether or not the IMC manager subscribes to a global view of communication and branding, the truth is the marketplace is global, interconnected, and interactive. Thus, marketing and marketing communication must move from the historically restricted view of markets and marketing systems to one that accommodates international, multinational, and global views that cross physical and political boundaries and at the same time deal with the many cultural differences as well. Thus, there will likely be a need to develop a new breed of IMC managers that moves as freely across boundaries and cultures as today present-day managers move across and around media systems. Only by taking a global view of the entire area of communication can the twenty-first-century organization develop the skills and talents it will need in the months and years ahead.

Challenge 6: Developing Forward-Looking Systems of Forecasting, Measurement, and Evaluation

Today, most marketing measurement systems simply calculate returns on money spent. That is, there is no forecasting of potential returns from marketing investments. In order to tell senior management exactly what will come back if money is invested in certain ways, marketers must move from measuring what happened in the past to what might happen in the future. That requires forecasting future returns by estimating what would likely occur if various alternatives were developed or used.

This forecasting system is likely to be less difficult than it may seem. Once the organization learns who its customers are, their values and their past behaviors, the use of probability models of their future actions can be developed and implemented. So, while it has taken literally years to develop and verify various types of return on investment systems, the forecasting systems based on customer knowledge, information, and tracking can become a corporate skill. Having once opened the door to measurement and financial analysis, marketing and marcom managers have the opportunity to make forecasts of future returns that are as accurate and reliable as those generated by any other area of the organization. Thus, while measurement may seem to be an insurmountable problem today, it is likely it will be one of the challenges that will be met most quickly and easily.

Challenge 7: Developing New Organizational Structures and Compensation Methods

We have left for last the most difficult challenge to the future development of IMC. That is the organizational design of the firm and the compensation of employees. We believe this will be the most difficult challenge not just for marketing and communication managers, but for all types of senior management as well.

We have already explored in detail what the organizational problem is, namely, that most organizations are built around a structure that enables them to make and sell "stuff" or provide services. Few are organized to serve customers. Our present organizational designs are a carryover from the Industrial Age, where command and control structures put people and processes into functional silos. Thus, firms were organized vertically and oriented internally, and they still are. The movement to a horizontal structure will be the most difficult change for any organization to make in the twenty-first century.

Inherent in this functional structure is the compensation system that rewards employees and other people for the stuff they make. As long as the people inside, or even outside, the organization are rewarded for doing measurable tasks and not serving customers, the compensation system will reinforce the present design systems and little progress can be made.

To achieve true customer focus, the organization must be designed around customers or customer groups. And until the design of the organization is based on customers, compensation systems cannot motivate employees to service or focus on customers. It is the organizational design and compensation systems that will be the biggest challenges to marketing communication managers in the future. Unless and until senior management is able to build a structure that is outward looking and focused on customers and in which employees are rewarded for maintaining and serving customers, IMC's challenges will continue to be more internal than external.

Moving On

Value-based integrated marketing communication not only provides us with insights into what the future is likely to bring, but it gives us the tools to meet those challenges. In the turmoil of today's business environment, competition for customers is fierce, costly, and global and increasingly takes place on an interactive playing field. Given this environment, our experience tells us that the entire field of marketing needs a new way to deal with and communicate with customers on their own terms. Integrated marketing communication offers just such a process, and it is our hope that it will rise to the challenges the future presents.

NOTES

Chapter 1

1. W. Edwards Deming, *Out of Crisis* (Boston: MIT Center for Advanced Engineering Study Press, 1982); Joseph M. Juran, *Juran on Quality by Design* (New York: The Free Press, 1992).

2. Michael Hammer and James Champy, *Reengineering the Corporation* (New York: Harper Business Press, 1993); Gary Hamel and C. K. Prahalad, *Competing for the Future* (Boston: Harvard Business School Press, 1994).

3. Deming, *Out of Crisis*; Juran, *Quality by Design*.

4. Robert D. Buzzell and Bradley T. Gale, *The PIMS Principles: Linking Strategy to Performance* (New York: Free Press, 1987).

5. Robert J. Coen, *Insider's Report: Robert Coen Presentation on Advertising Expenditures* (New York: Universal McCann, Erickson Worldwide, December 1999).

6. Clark Caywood, Don Schultz, and Paul Wang, *Integrated Marketing Communications: A Survey of National Consumer Goods Advertisers* (Chicago: Northwestern University Report, June 1991).

7. Report from Lynn Gray, "The U.S. Generic Prescription Drug Industry," Business Communications Company Inc., August 2002, buscom.com/biotech/C058U.html.

8. Report from Private Label Manufacturers Association, "Store Brands on Course for Another Record Year: First and Second

Quarter Market Shares Are Historic Highs for U.S. Supermarkets," New York, January 2003, plma.com.

9. "The Year of the Brand," *The Economist* III, no. 12 (24 December 1988): 95; Roger Baird, "Assets Tests," *Marketing Week* 21, no. 40 (1 October 1998): 28–31; David A. Aaker, *Building Strong Brands* 111, no. 12 (New York: Free Press, 1995).

Chapter 2

1. Clark Caywood, Don Schultz, and Paul Wang, *Integrated Marketing Communications: A Survey of National Consumer Goods Advertisers* (Northwestern University Report, Chicago, June 1991); Thomas R. Duncan and Stephen E. Everett, "Client Perceptions of Integrated Marketing Communications," *Journal of Advertising Research* 33, no. 3 (May–June 1993): 30–40; Michael Kiely, "Integrated Marketing Starting Out," *Marketing* (April 1993): 44–46; Glen J. Nowak and Joseph Phelps, "Direct Marketing and the Use of Individual-Level Consumer Information: Does 'Privacy' Matter," *Journal of Direct Marketing* 11, no. 4 (Fall 1997): 94–109; Lou Wolter, "Superficiality, Ambiguity Threaten IMC's Implementation and Future," *Marketing News* 27, no. 19 (13 September 1993): 12–14.

2. Thomas Hunter, "Integrated Communications" (Ph.D. dissertation, University of Salzburg, June 1999); Jerry Kliatchko, "Integrated Marketing Communication Theory and Practice: The Case of the Philippines" (Ph.D. dissertation, University of Navarre, Pamplona, Spain, 2001); Kirsti Lindberg-Repo, "Customer Relationship Communication—Analyzing Communicating from a Value Generating Perspective," publication of the Swedish School of Economics and Business Administration, No. 99, Helsinki, Finland, 2001; Duncan and Everett, "Client Perceptions of Integrated Marketing Communications."

3. "Integrated Marketing Communication: Best Practices Report," American Productivity and Quality Center (Houston: APQC, 1998).

4. Don E. Schultz and Philip J. Kitchen, *Communicating Globally: An Integrated Marketing Approach* (Lincolnwood, IL: NTC Business Books, 2000).

5. Don E. Schultz and Philip J. Kitchen, "Integrated Marketing Communications in U.S. Advertising Agencies: An Exploratory Study," *Journal of Advertising Research* 37, no. 5 (September–October 1997): 7–19.

6. Much of the data gathering was done using a series of contingent statements on a ten-point Likert-type scale (1 = strongly disagree; 10 = strongly agree). Most responses came from U.S. agencies (126), followed by British agencies (65), and then agencies in New Zealand (20), Australia (19), and India (13).

7. "Leveraging Customer Information," American Productivity and Quality Center (Houston: APQC, 2000).

Chapter 3

1. "Intel Annual Report," 2002, intel.com.

2. "The Best Global Brands," *Business Week*, August 5, 2002: 92–95.

3. "Success One Account at a Time," *Business 2.0*, April 9, 2001.

4. Rajendra K. Srivastava, Tasadduq A. Shervani, and Liam Fahey, "Market-based Assets and Shareholder Value: A Framework for Analysis," *Journal of Marketing* 62 (January 1998): 2–18.

5. John Wannamaker, cited in Rajeev Batra, John G. Myers, and David A. Aaker, *Advertising Management*, 5th ed. (Englewood Cliffs, NJ: Prentice Hall, 1996).

6. William Bolen, *Advertising* (New York: John Wiley & Sons, 1981).

Chapter 4

1. Don Peppers and Martha Rogers, *The One to One Fieldbook* (New York: Doubleday, 1999): vii.

2. Andrea Ovans, "Market Research: The Customer Doesn't Always Know Best," *Harvard Business Review* 76, no. 3 (May–June 1998): 12–13.

3. "Case Study: BMW," dunnhumby.com.

4. Robert J. Lavidge and Gary A. Steiner, "A Model for Predictive Measurements of Advertising Effectiveness," *Journal of Marketing* 25, no. 6 (October 1961): 61.

5. Clive Humby, personal conversation with author, London, September 14, 2000.

6. Don Peppers and Martha Rogers, "Smart Marketing: Remove the Burden of Choice," altagerencia.com/freestuff;articulos ;peppers_burdenchoice.htm.

7. Kelly Mayer, resident at Time Inc., personal conversation, September 2002.

8. The balanced scorecard is a set of financial and nonfinancial measures by which organizations track performance over time. The use of such a scorecard expands the focus of the organization beyond summary financial measures and focuses attention on the "people, systems, and procedures necessary to improve future performance." Robert S. Kaplan and David P. Norton, *The Balanced Scorecard* (Boston, MA: Harvard Business School Press, 1996).

Chapter 5

1. "Case Study: Tesco," dunnhumby.com.

2. Garth Halberg, *Not All Customers Are Created Equal* (New York: John Wiley and Sons, 1995): 39–40.

3. Much of the customer valuation methodology described in this chapter first appeared in *Measuring Brand Communication ROI* by Don E. Schultz and Jeffrey Walters (New York: Association of National Advertisers, 1998). Used with permission of the publisher.

4. Michael E. Porter, *Competitive Advantage: Creating and Sustaining Superior Performance* (New York: Free Press, 1985).

Chapter 6

1. J. Barnes, ed., *Complete Works of Aristotle*, Revised Oxford Translation (Princeton, NJ: Princeton University Press, 1983).

2. Ibid.

3. J. S. Adams, "Inequality in Social Exchange," in *Advances in Experimental Social Psychology*, ed. L. Berkowitz (New York: Academic Press, 1963), 2:267–88.
4. Ibid.
5. Ibid.
6. Materials and illustrations in this section were first presented by Don E. Schultz and Dana Hayman at the National Center for Database Marketing Conference, "Fully Understand Consumer Behavior Using Your Database," Chicago, July 30, 1999.
7. Materials and illustrations in this section were first presented by Don E. Schultz and Scott Bailey at the ARF Week of Workshops, "Building a Viable Model for Customer/Brand Loyalty," New York, NY, October 7, 1999.

Chapter 7
1. Stephen Yastrow, "Fully Integrated Marketing," *Journal of Integrated Marketing Communications*, (1999–2000): 5–12.
2. Adapted from Lisa Fortini-Campbell, "Communications Strategy: Managing Communications for the Changing Marketplace" (presented at Northwestern University, Evanston, IL, October 19, 1999).
3. Adapted from Ed Faruolo, "Building the CIGNA Brand" (classroom presentation at Northwestern University, Evanston, IL, Fall 1998).
4. Fortini-Campbell.
5. Frank Wilberding, interview by author, Chicago, IL, October 2002.
6. R. Chase and S. Dasu, "Want to Perfect Your Company's Service? Use Behavioral Science," *Harvard Business Review* (June 2001).
7. Tom Duncan, *IMC: Using Advertising and Promotion to Build Brands* (New York: McGraw-Hill, 2002): 126.
8. Ibid.

9. Christian Gronroos, "Que Vadis, Marketing? Toward a Relationship Marketing Paradigm," *Journal of Marketing Management* 10, no. 5 (July 1994): 347–60.

10. Juliet Williams, "Internal Marketing" (presented at Northwestern University, Evanston, IL, November 12, 1998).

11. Giep Franzen and Margot Bouwman, *The Mental World of Brand: Mind, Memory, and Brand Success* (Henley-on-Thames, England: World Advertising Research Center, 2001): 178.

12. Scott Davis, "Mending the Broken Brand Contract: What McDonald's Could Learn from Others," *Prophet* (2001), prophet.com.

Chapter 8

1. This section adapted from Lisa Fortini-Campbell, "Building Brand Relationships" (presented at the Communications Strategy Conference, Northwestern University, Evanston, IL, April 1998).

2. Ibid.

3. This case was originally developed by Stanley Tannenbaum and published in our first book on IMC, *Integrated Marketing Communications* (Lincolnwood, IL: NTC Business Books, 1994). While we have adapted the example slightly, by and large it reflects the same process we recommend and use with clients and students today.

Chapter 9

1. Russell H. Colley, *Defining Advertising Goals for Measured Advertising Results* (New York: Association of National Advertisers, 1961).

2. J. P. Jones, *When Ads Work* (New York: Lexington Books, 1994).

3. Simon S. Broadbent and T. Frye, "Ad Stock Modeling for the Longer Term," *Journal of the Market Research Society* 37 (1995): 385–403.

4. Rajendra K. Srivastava, Tasadduq A. Shervani, and Liam Fahey, "Market-Based Assets and Shareholder Value: A Framework for Analysis," *Journal of Marketing* 62 (January 1998): 2–18.

Chapter 10

1. This material is derived from *Measuring Brand Communication ROI*, Don E. Schultz and Jeffery S. Waters (New York: Association of National Advertisers, Inc., 1997).

Chapter 11

1. Frederick Reichheld, *The Loyalty Effect* (Princeton, NJ: Harvard Business Press, 1996).
2. Ibid.
3. Bob Stone and Ron Jacobs, *Successful Direct Marketing Methods* (New York: McGraw-Hill, 2001).
4. Jack Schmid and Alan Weber, *Desktop Database Marketing* (Lincolnwood, IL: NTC Business Books, 1997).
5. Ibid.
6. Ibid.

Chapter 12

1. Adapted from Clive Humby, "Customer Measures of the Brand," (presented at the Cranfield School of Management Conference on Leveraging Brand Equity to Create Strategic Value, Cranfield, England, April 19, 2002). The material here on consumer advocacy is based on a methodology developed by consulting group dunnhumby associates, plc, London.

Chapter 13

1. Philip Kotler, *Marketing Management*, 10th ed. (Upper Saddle River, NJ: Prentice Hall, 2000): 404.
2. John M. Murphy, ed., *Brand Variation* (London: Business Books, Ltd., 1989): 173.
3. Marketing Science Institute, quoted in Kevin Lane Keller, *Strategic Brand Management*, 2nd ed. (Upper Saddle River, NJ: Prentice Education, 2003): 43.
4. David A. Aaker, *Building Strong Brands* (New York: The Free Press, 1996): 7–8.

5. Leslie de Chernatony and Malcolm McDonald, *Creating Powerful Brands in Consumer, Service and Industrial Markets,* (Boston: Butterworth-Heinemann, 1998): 397.

6. Kevin Lane Keller, *Strategic Brand Management: Building, Measuring, and Managing Brand Equity,* (Saddle River, NJ: Prentice-Hall, 1998): 45.

7. The section that follows is adapted from David Haigh, "Valuing and Managing Brands: Issues in Brand Valuation" (presented at Northwestern University, Evanston, IL, November 21, 2000).

Chapter 14

1. "Brand Dynamics Online Information," millwardbrown.com.

2. "Discovery Channel Rated #1 for Overall Quality According to Latest EquiTrend Best Brand Study," June 19, 2002 (Rochester, NY: harrisinteractive.com).

3. Young & Rubicam, "White Paper on the Brand Asset Valuation," 2000, yr.com.

Chapter 15

1. G. Bennett Stewart III, *The Quest for Value* (New York: HarperCollins, 1990); Robert G. Eccles, Robert H. Herz, E. Mary Keegan, and David M. H. Phillips, *The Value Reporting Revolution: Moving Beyond the Earnings Game* (New York: John Wiley & Sons, 2001).

2. Philip Kotler, *Marketing Management,* 11th ed. (Englewood Cliffs, NJ: Prentice Hall, 2003).

3. Don E. Schultz, Stanley I. Tannenbaum, and Robert F. Lauterborn, *Integrated Marketing Communications: Putting It Together and Making It Work* (Lincolnwood, IL: NTC Business Books, 1994).

4. D. Pickton and A. Broderick, *Integrated Marketing Communications* (Harlow, England: Prentice Hall [UK], 2001).

LITERARY CREDITS

Chapter 2, Pages 20–33: Material from "Integrated Marketing Communication: Best Practices Report," American Productivity and Quality Center (Houston: APQC, 1998). Used with permission from American Productivity and Quality Center.

Chapter 6, Pages 131–142: Material from Don E. Schultz and Dana Hayman, "Fully Understand Consumer Behavior Using Your Database" (presented at National Center for Database Marketing Conference, Chicago, July 30, 1999); Don E. Schultz and Scott Bailey, "Building a Viable Model for Customer/Brand Loyalty" (presented at ARF Week of Workshops, New York, NY, October 7, 1999). Used with permission from Targetbase Inc.

Chapter 7, Pages 145–153: Material from Lisa Fortini-Campbell, "Communications Strategy: Managing Communications for the Changing Marketplace" (presented at Northwestern University, Evanston, IL, October 19, 1999). Used with permission from Lisa Fortini-Campbell.

Chapter 7, Page 149: Material used with permission from CIGNA Insurance.

Chapter 7, Pages 153–154: Material used with permission from Brand Imprinting Inc.

Chapter 8, Pages 171–175: Material from Lisa Fortini-Campbell, "Communications Strategy: Managing Communications for the Changing Marketplace" (presented at Northwestern University, Evanston, IL, October 19, 1999). Used with permission from Lisa Fortini-Campbell.

Chapter 10, Pages 217–238: Material from Don E. Schultz and Jeffrey Walters, *Measuring Brand Communication ROI* (New York: Association for National Advertisers, 1997). Used with permission from the Association for National Advertisers.

Chapter 12, Pages 284–294: Material from Clive Humby, "Customer Measures of the Brand" (presented at the Cranfield School of Management Conference on Leveraging Brand Equity to Create Strategic Value, Cranfield, England, April 19, 2002). Used with permission from dunnhumby associates.

Chapter 13, Pages 310–319: Material from David Haigh, "Valuing and Managing Brands: Issues in Brand Valuation" (presented at Northwestern University, Evanston, IL, November 21, 2000). Used with permission from Brand Finance.

Chapter 14, Pages 323–325: Material used with permission from Millward Brown North America.

Chapter 14, Pages 327–331: Material from "White Paper on the Brand Asset Valuation," 2000, yr.com. Used with permission from Young & Rubicam Inc.

Chapter 14, pages 336–347: Material used with permission from Brand Finance.

Chapter 15, Page 358: Material adapted from Adrian Payne, "Customer Relation Management" (presented at Northwestern University, Evanston, IL, November 11, 2001). Used with permission from Adrian Payne.

INDEX